Charles Ray
Figure Ground

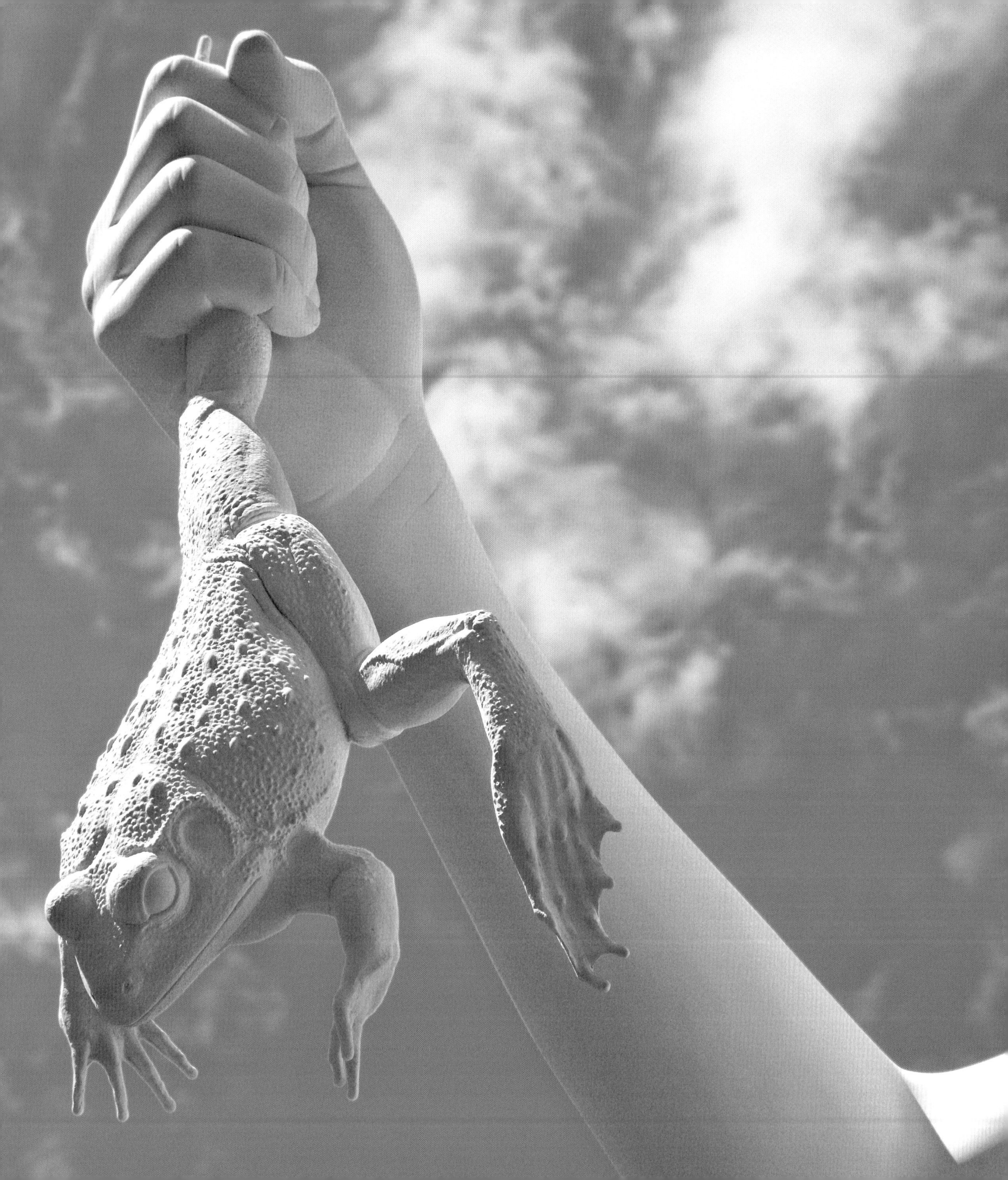

Charles Ray
Figure Ground

Kelly Baum and Brinda Kumar
With contributions by
Charles Ray and Hal Foster

The Metropolitan Museum of Art,
New York
Distributed by Yale University Press,
New Haven and London

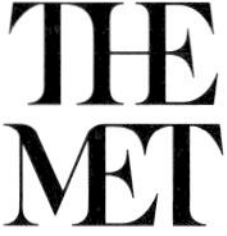

Contents

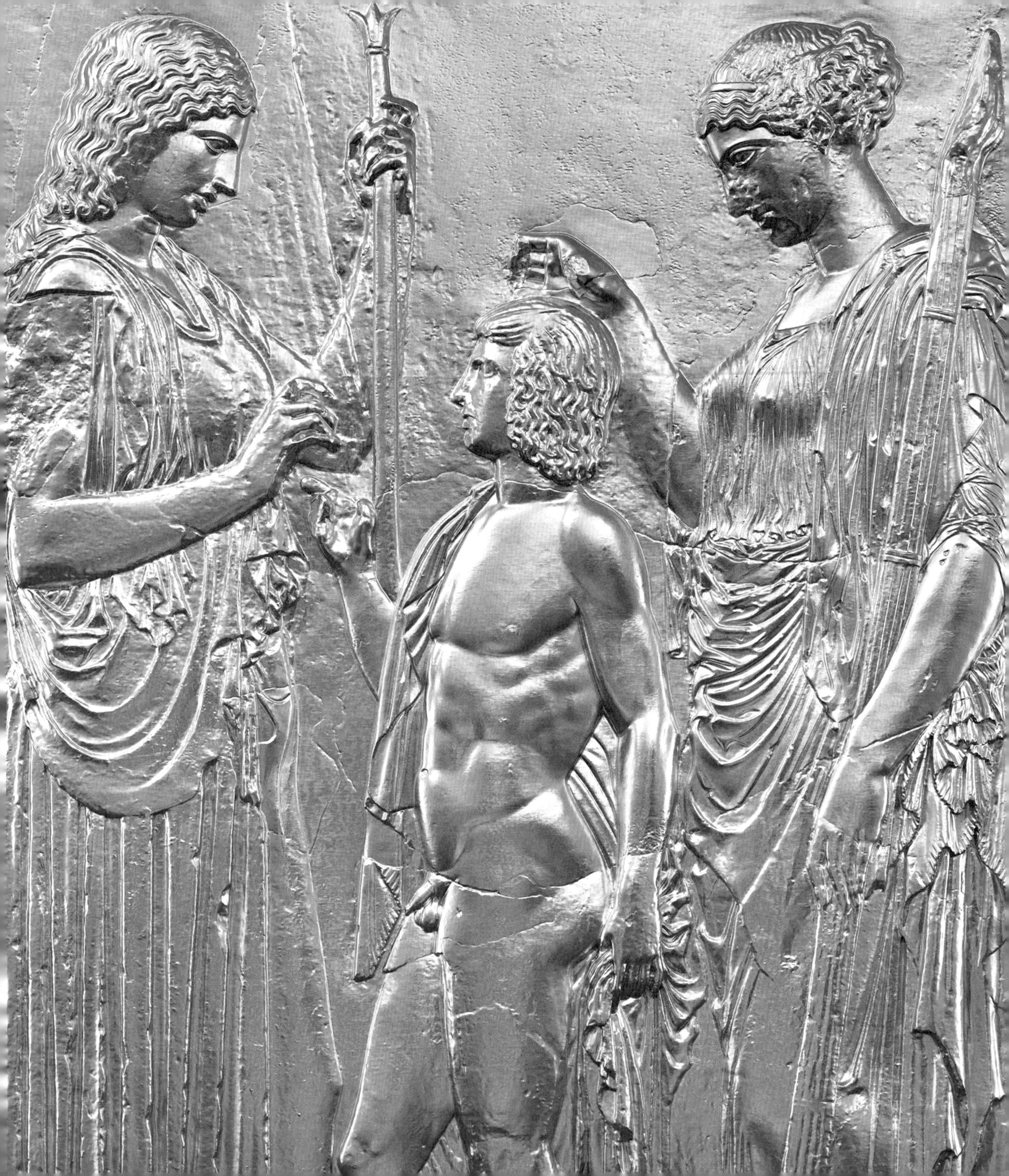

Director's Foreword

Since the beginning of his career in the 1970s, Charles Ray has challenged and provoked, confounded and amazed. Besides encompassing a range of media, including performance, photography, and sculpture, Ray's work has also responded in deeply critical, sometimes irreverent ways to art history, popular culture, and mass media while addressing some of the era's most urgent subjects, from identity and mortality to race, gender, and sexuality. As such, it is invariably demanding, requiring viewers' commitment, engagement, and patience. Furthermore, Ray has pioneered major advances in sculptural production and has expanded the fundamental terms of sculptural language. He is one of the most consequential artists working today, and The Met is delighted to present a timely and illuminating assessment of his oeuvre in *Charles Ray: Figure Ground*.

I am grateful to Sheena Wagstaff, Leonard A. Lauder Chair of the Department of Modern and Contemporary Art, who initially conceived of an exhibition on the work of Charles Ray in exploratory conversations with the artist. Kelly Baum, Cynthia Hazen Polsky and Leon Polsky Curator of Contemporary Art, assumed the role of curator and, working closely with Brinda Kumar, Associate Curator, evolved the exhibition into what it is today. I thank them both. The exhibition and its accompanying catalogue were produced in direct collaboration with the artist, to whom I extend my deepest gratitude for his time, energy, and resources. Engaging with living artists is one of the most rewarding privileges at The Met; just as our collections provide fascinating perspectives on contemporary art, so too does contemporary art offer an intriguing lens through which to consider five thousand years of art history. Ray does so openly and strategically, making him an ideal partner.

Additionally, I am grateful to all of our institutional and private lenders, without whom this exhibition would be inconceivable. Special thanks are also due to the organizations and individuals who supported the project financially. For making the exhibition possible, the Barrie A. and Deedee Wigmore Foundation has my tremendous gratitude. The generosity of the Jane and Robert Carroll Fund, the Diane W. and James E. Burke Fund, the Gail and Parker Gilbert Fund, Lisa and Steven Tananbaum, The Andy Warhol Foundation for the Visual Arts, Amanda and Glenn Fuhrman, Glenstone, and Linda Macklowe helped to bring the project to fruition. I extend my thanks to Christie's for its sponsorship of the exhibition's opening celebrations. Lannan Foundation and The Sachs Charitable Foundation have my sincere appreciation for their support of the exhibition catalogue. We are honored to have the endorsement of all of these valued partners.

Max Hollein
Marina Kellen French Director
The Metropolitan Museum of Art

Acknowledgments

Charles Ray: Figure Ground is the artist's first institutional solo exhibition in New York in almost twenty-five years. It is also the first to include sculptures from every period of his career and to unite them with important photographs from the 1970s, resulting in a comprehensive investigation of his oeuvre. Featuring nineteen objects, the show introduces Charles Ray to a new generation of viewers while making his work fresh for those already familiar with it. It does so, moreover, from within The Metropolitan Museum of Art, whose collections have served as a long-standing source of inspiration for the artist. Housed in the spacious Iris and B. Gerald Cantor Exhibition Hall, the presentation takes the form of a kind of indoor sculpture garden. Each work has room to breathe, facilitating focused contemplation, while carefully choreographed sight lines forge subtle connections between objects, opening up multiple avenues of interpretation. This sense of expansiveness and possibility is re-created in the accompanying catalogue, which will persist long after the show closes.

The project benefited from the wisdom, generosity, and encouragement of numerous individuals. First and foremost, enormous thanks are due to Charles himself, who worked in close collaboration with us and many other colleagues. He accommodated multiple studio visits and weekly phone calls, and after the advent of the COVID-19 pandemic attended regular meetings over Zoom in preparation for the opening of the show. The partnership with Charles was a journey in the truest sense of the word, and we are grateful to have learned alongside him over the last several years. We also owe a special debt of gratitude to Silvia Gaspardo-Moro and to the members of Charles Ray's studio, especially Morgan Canavan, Rachel Arena, and Eric Torborg. Mark Rossi, from Handmade, was indispensable as well.

Sheena Wagstaff, Leonard A. Lauder Chair of the Department of Modern and Contemporary Art, initiated an exhibition on and with Charles, and thanks are due to her for inviting us at different moments to shape its curatorial contours. We are also grateful to Daniel H. Weiss, President and Chief Executive Officer, and Max Hollein, Marina Kellen French Director, for their endorsement of this project. Quincy Houghton and Katy Uravitch provided important counsel from the Exhibitions Office, with Katy expertly managing the organizational details of the exhibition.

We sincerely appreciate the tremendous work of all the colleagues who helped bring this exhibition to fruition. Elsie Alonso as registrar shepherded all logistical arrangements and ensured the safe movement of art. The installation plan and graphic identity benefited from the extraordinary creativity of designers Fabiana Weinberg, Frank Mondragon, Anna Rieger, Maanik Chauhan, and Daniel Koppich. Taylor Miller and Matthew Lytle from Buildings brought their considerable engineering expertise to the project. The works were conscientiously cared for by conservators Kendra Roth and Nora W. Kennedy, Sherman Fairchild Conservator in Charge of the Department of Photograph Conservation. In External Affairs, Kenneth Weine and Alexandra Kozlakowski played a vital role in honing the exhibition's message. Amy Desmond Lamberti provided essential assistance from the Counsel's Office, as did Marci King from Exhibitions. For the crucial role they played in fundraising and cultivation, we thank Clyde B. Jones III, Daphne Butler Birdsey, Jennifer M. Brown, Elizabeth A. Burke, Evie Chabot, Julie Hamon,

Jason Herrick, Kimberly McCarthy, Julia Schloss, Jessica M. Sewell, and John L. Wielk.

Much gratitude is owed to our colleagues in Publications and Editorial, led by Mark Polizzotti, Peter Antony, and Michael Sittenfeld. Briana Parker's consummate editorial skills helped shape the book's content as well as the show's didactic program. Paul Booth oversaw the book's production and printing, and Jenn Sherman secured images. Jon Key of Morcos Key brought his singular vision to the catalogue's design. The volume is enriched by the involvement of Hal Foster, the Townsend Martin, Class of 1917, Professor of Art and Archaeology at Princeton University, whose conversation with Charles is featured herein.

In the Department of Modern and Contemporary Art, Pari Stave offered support and guidance all along the way. Clare Davies and Shanay Jhaveri shared key insight at a crucial moment in the project's evolution. Padget Sutherland and Cynthia Iavarone were tremendously helpful, as were Lizzie Doorly, Lionel Carre, Jeff Elliott, Brooks Shaver, and Jasmine Kuylenstierna Wrede. For providing a work from the Department of Photographs, we thank Jeff L. Rosenheim, Joyce Frank Menschel Curator in Charge, and Meredith Reiss.

Matthew Marks and Stephanie Dorsey of Matthew Marks Gallery provided aid and advice over a long period of time—we thank them.

We are especially grateful to the institutions and private collectors that lent work to this exhibition, and to the directors, curators, registrars, conservators, collection managers, technicians, and shippers who either endorsed these loans or facilitated them.

We are exceptionally grateful to the Barrie A. and Deedee Wigmore Foundation for making this exhibition possible. The contributions of the Jane and Robert Carroll Fund, the Diane W. and James E. Burke Fund, the Gail and Parker Gilbert Fund, Lisa and Steven Tananbaum, The Andy Warhol Foundation for the Visual Arts, Amanda and Glenn Fuhrman, Glenstone, and Linda Macklowe benefited the final presentation immeasurably. We also appreciate Christie's generous support of the exhibition's opening celebrations. Finally, we offer our heartfelt thanks to Lannan Foundation and The Sachs Charitable Foundation, who have brought the present publication to life. Their support is deeply meaningful.

Kelly Baum
Cynthia Hazen Polsky and Leon Polsky Curator of Contemporary Art

Brinda Kumar
Associate Curator, Modern and Contemporary Art

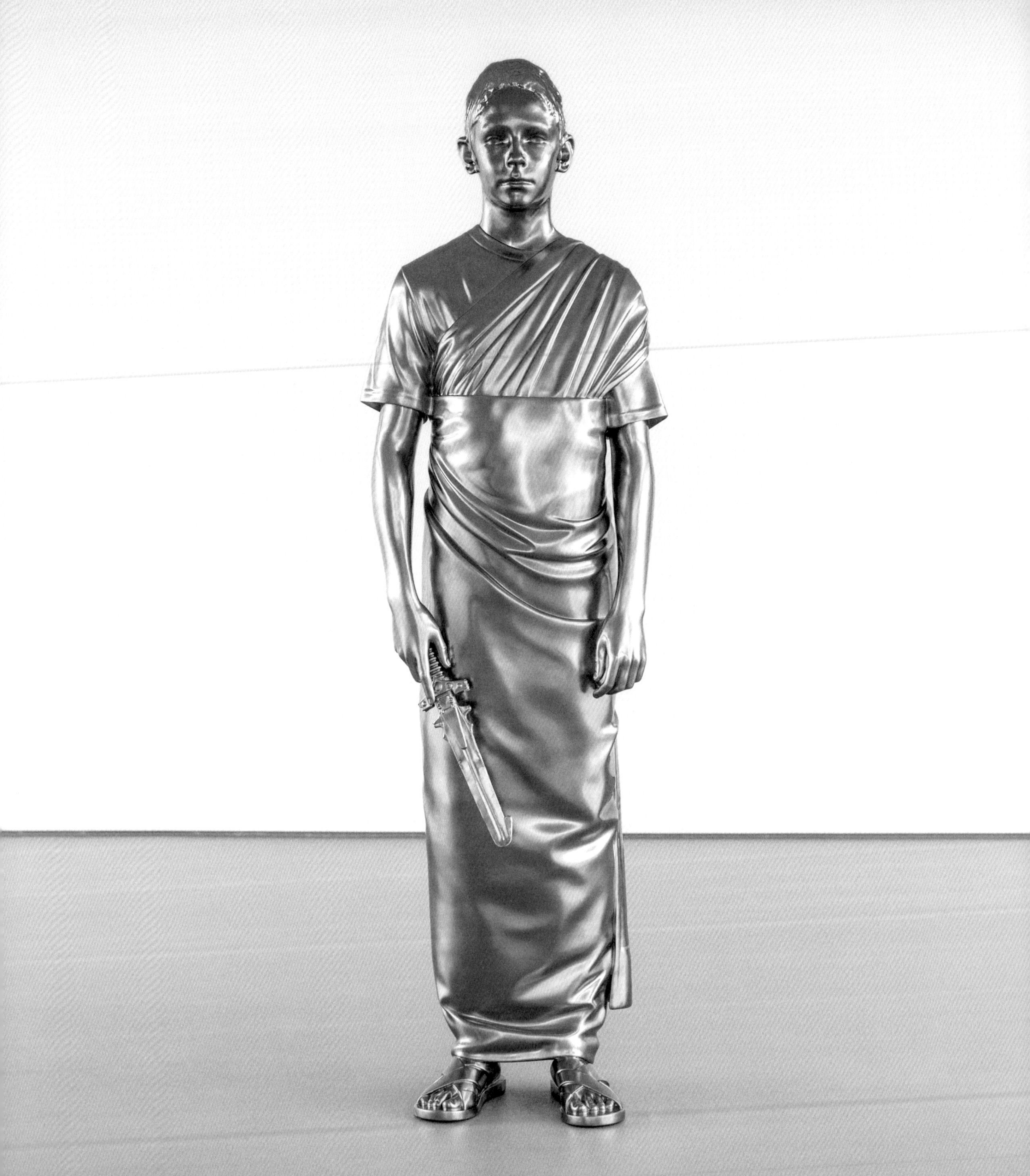

Patterns

Kelly Baum

It's impossible to tell the story of American sculpture after 1970 without including Charles Ray, so important is his output over the last fifty years. In many ways, his sculpture narrates the history of sculpture itself, self-consciously referencing traditions associated with the past, from classicism (*School play*, 2014; fig. 1) to minimalism (*Ink box*, 1986).[1] If works such as these appear to "tumble through time," to occupy many historical registers simultaneously, it is precisely because Ray attends so carefully to earlier artistic movements.[2] For the artist, these function as prototypes or patterns that he appropriates, reiterates, and recontextualizes, making them contemporary in the process.

The noun "pattern" and the verb "patterning" offer an intriguing lens through which to consider Ray's work in its entirety at the levels of content and production. Indeed, "pattern" is a word the artist himself uses frequently, referring to the clay, plaster, and fiberglass models that serve as the foundation for sculptures later cast, carved, and machined out of materials such as wood, steel, and aluminum.[3] A long-standing term in sculpture, "pattern" also has currency in the world of sewing, manufacture, and industrial production. In those contexts, it is the name given to the two- or three-dimensional templates from which a wide variety of products are assembled. Repetition is fundamental to patterns: first and foremost, they exist to be copied. Additionally, most of Ray's sculptures are patterned, at least in part, on preexisting models, some concrete, others abstract, from novels and mannequins to discursive formations like childhood and masculinity. At least a few works include actual found objects, such as the bathtub in *Tub with black dye* (1986; fig. 2). When it comes to his source material, Ray looks for patterns, whether objects or

Fig. 1. Charles Ray (American, born 1953). *School play*, 2014. Stainless steel, 76 × 23 × 15½ in. (193 × 59 × 40 cm). Courtesy of Collection of Marguerite Steed Hoffman, the artist, and Matthew Marks Gallery

ideas, that embody the irreducible, "absolute manifestations of a culture,"[4] Western and Euro-American culture especially. The latter has long preoccupied the artist. He is a student of its many incarnations—from the popular to the vernacular to the high-brow—likewise the many fantasies, stereotypes, and contradictions of which it is comprised and to which it has given rise. His relationship to Euro-American culture is complex: he does not romanticize or idealize it, but nor does he critique or disavow it. Instead, Ray speaks from its very center, from the point of view of a sculptor.

Although the patterns on which Ray draws are of great import, they should not be mistaken for the origin or the source of his work, either conceptually or logistically. For the artist, patterning always involves invention—sculptural invention, to be more exact—with the readymades on which he relies subject to both intellectual and physical remaking. None of his works constitute a literal interpretation of a pattern. Moreover, Ray's patterns very often lead to other patterns; behind every prototype is another prototype to which it is related via a chain of signification. The genealogy of *Boy* (1992; pl. 16), for instance, can be traced from department store mannequins as well as figurative sculpture in the West and the discourse of White American boyhood. That some of these traditions deliberately parade their artificiality—their own status as copies—makes the search for originality even more futile.[5] Additionally, Ray's patterns never come to him in their pure, unadulterated form. Before work on a sculpture has even begun, whatever myths, stories, and conventions to which it might refer have already been filtered through layers of memory and experience and subjected to recombination and alteration. For example, Ray has referred to the "tangled heap of personal and cultural structure" that underlies *Archangel* (2021; pl. 11), elaborating further: "Middle class education, Catholic upbringing, illustrations from primary school catechism textbooks, while not the limit of what made the sculpture, they do hold the armature for my inspiration."[6]

Ray's conceptual patterns are further detached from their original incarnations during fabrication, over the course of which they endure multiple rounds of editing and pass through a great many detours. The same holds true for his physical patterns, or prototypes, which are part of a drawn-out production process involving several iterations. The creation of *Mime* (2014; pl. 17), for example, involves a circuitous path that begins with three-dimensional digital scans of the human model; proceeds to foam carvings, clay layups, silicone molds, and Forton or fiberglass casts; and ends with the machining of commercial-grade billet aluminum, along with dozens of other intermittent steps, some involving multiple pairs of human hands, others tools and computers.[7] The sculpting of the cot on which the figure lies is an object lesson unto itself: instead of making a direct mold from the original, Ray modeled each component part in clay and then cast those pieces in various materials, forming a disaggregated

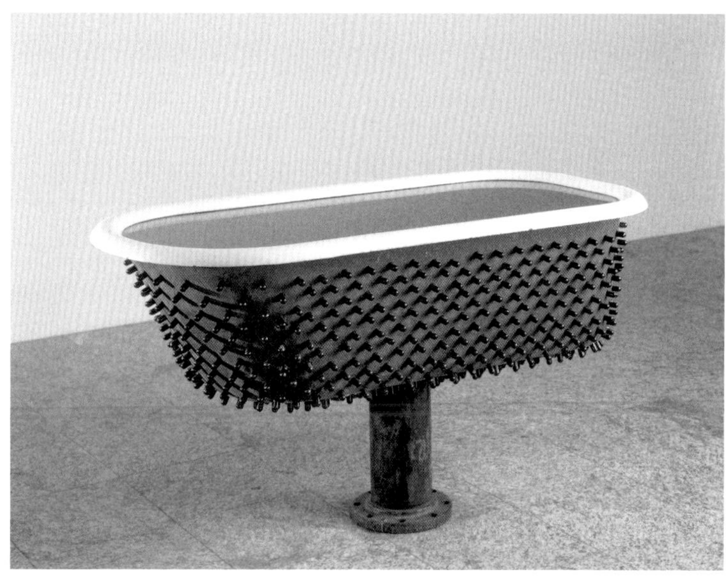

Fig. 2. Charles Ray. *Tub with black dye*, 1986. Tub, glass test tubes, pipe, dye, 33½ × 59 × 30 in. (85 × 150 × 76 cm). Prada Foundation, Milan

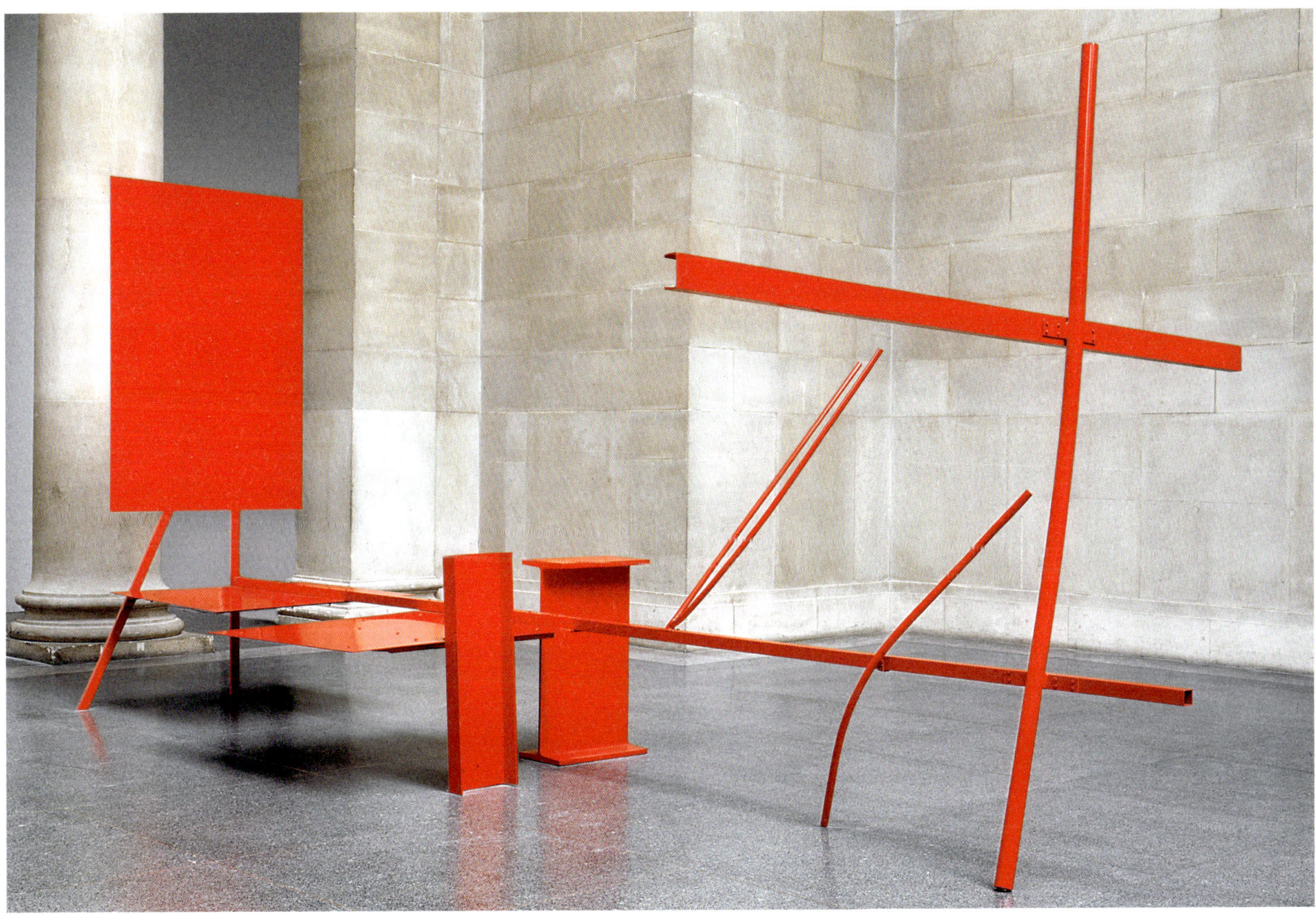

Fig. 3. Anthony Caro (British, 1924–2013). *Early One Morning*, 1962. Painted steel, aluminum, 9 ft. 6 in. × 20 ft. 4 in. × 11 ft. (289.6 × 619.8 × 335.3 cm). Tate, London, Presented by the Contemporary Art Society, 1965 (T00805)

representation. It was this three-dimensional "picture" that served as the basis for the cot's fiberglass pattern.[8] (*Tractor* [2005; pl. 6], a topographically complete object modeled on a disused tractor, was developed in a similar manner.[9]) The cot that appears in the various editions of *Mime* is therefore a copy of an interpretation of a particular cot, which is itself nothing more than a mass-produced object based on an industrial pattern. The nature of Ray's creative activity means that every version of *Mime* is virtually identical to but also subtly different from the others (see fig. 28).[10]

Beginnings

Born in Chicago in 1953, Ray took to the arts in early adulthood, joining the studio program at the University of Iowa in 1971. Under the tutelage of Roland Brenner, a disciple of abstract sculptor Anthony Caro (fig. 3), and Hans Breder (fig. 4), who oversaw the school's intermedia program, Ray began a lifelong engagement with high modernism, on the one hand, and cross-disciplinary practice, on the other.[11] After receiving his BFA, he spent a year at the University of Kentucky, where he met Siah Armajani, a visiting artist with whom he developed a friendship that helped shape his notion of "the civic."[12] Later Ray transferred to the Mason Gross School of the Arts at Rutgers University. His tenure overlapped with Op artist John Goodyear, his supervisor, as well as Geoffrey Hendricks and Robert Watts, members of the transnational network known as Fluxus. Under the watch of these very different artists representing a wide range of approaches, Ray avidly explored process-based sculpture and performance throughout the 1970s.[13] In 1981, two years after completing his MFA, he joined the faculty at the University of California, Los Angeles. The city has been his home ever since.

From the beginning of his career, Ray has investigated the fundamental conditions of sculptural language. Even when staging live events, his approach to art has been deeply sculptural. Appropriately, he is primarily celebrated today for his three-dimensional work, which explores a wide range of subjects, assumes an astonishing variety of forms, and experiments with numerous materials and techniques. Despite this diversity, Ray's work has addressed a consistent set of formal, structural, and thematic concerns, so much so that any effort to periodize his fifty-year career risks reifying difference, especially between abstraction and figuration, attributes of which are shared by all of the artist's sculptures. Throughout, Ray has tested the limits of what sculpture can be and what can be sculpture, expanding, even radicalizing, the medium.

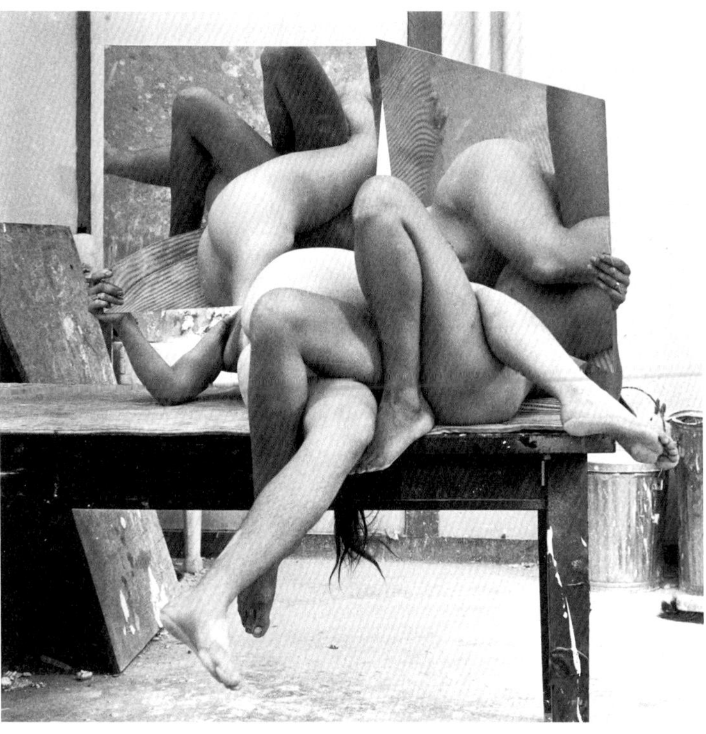

Fig. 4. Hans Breder (American, born Germany, 1935–2017). *Body/Sculpture*, 1972. Gelatin silver print, 9¾ × 9¾ in. (24.8 × 24.8 cm). Smithsonian American Art Museum, Washington, D.C., Gift of the artist (2013.50.3)

One of the through lines in Ray's career is a concept closely related to patterns: that of pictures. Indeed, the artist's fascination with patterns is part and parcel of his long-standing investment in pictures, both of which are fundamentally related to the operations of reproduction and repetition.[14] For the artist, pictures, like patterns, serve as both a means to an end and as subject matter in and of themselves. Ray's early performances, for example, in which he treated his body like so much clay, a material to be wrapped and hoisted, bent and folded, were staged mostly for the benefit of the camera. *Untitled* (1973; pl. 12) and *Plank piece I and II* (1973; pl. 10), for instance, survive solely as photographs: they are now apprehended specifically as representations.[15] In addition to creating sculptures entirely for the purpose of being photographed, as with his self-portrait *No* (1992; pl. 1), he has transformed photographs into three-dimensional installations, as with *Yes* (1990), which features a picture of the artist hallucinating on LSD, the image set into a convex frame that has been covered with a bowed sheet of glass and mounted on an identically curved wall.

There is an even more fundamental connection between pictures and sculptures, however. In a 2007 interview, Ray described his various source materials, from mannequins and automobiles (fig. 5) to toys, trees, and other works of art (pl. 19),[16] as *images*—objects so thoroughly acculturated that they have shed their material substrate and exist in the popular imagination solely as disembodied representations. "I'm using these images, things from my life, from the world, as a way to think," Ray has stated. "I'm not thinking about mannequins, or fire trucks, or trees. I'm thinking about sculpture. I have to wonder what it would be like to be free of these external images. But I don't know if it's possible for me, and they do bring a richness."[17] In other words, the images or "cultural givens" he references are mostly additive, even if they are secondary to the sculptures themselves.[18] (Some of the artist's physical materials, such as Pepto Bismol and newspaper ink, are also "images" or "cultural givens" as defined here.[19]) For Ray, the challenge is making something *sculptural* from the "richness" that images provide. Overall, pictures and sculptures are fundamentally, if problematically, entwined in the artist's work, exemplifying a tension also at play in his oeuvre's relationship to patterns.[20]

Interestingly, Ray matriculated from graduate school in 1979, at the exact moment when both pictures and sculptures were enjoying something of an artistic and theoretical renaissance. That year's Spring issue of *October*, for instance, featured Douglas Crimp's essay "Pictures," the title of an eponymous exhibition Crimp organized in 1977, alongside Rosalind Krauss's "Sculpture in the Expanded Field." By using the word "pictures" to describe the paintings, sculptures, films, and photographs featured in his show, Crimp sought "to convey not only the work's most salient characteristic—recognizable images—but also and importantly the ambiguities it sustains."[21] The recognizable images of which Crimp speaks, seen in work by the likes of Jack Goldstein (fig. 6), Troy Brauntuch, and Cindy Sherman, are all borrowed from preexisting sources—patterns, of a sort—and transformed in the process of quotation. What results are pictures that comment on the mechanics of representation as much as they do on issues such as gender, sexuality, and subjectivity. Ray was never a formal member of the so-called Pictures generation, but Crimp's essay nevertheless constitutes one of the conditions of possibility for the emergence of his work, especially as it relates to images and patterns.[22]

For her part, Krauss provided a structuralist reading of the changes that had occurred in sculpture since the late 1960s. This period is most closely associated with postminimalism, when sculptors started to operate beyond the four walls of the studio and gallery; adopted increasingly informal arrangements of ever more unconventional materials; and experimented with a wide variety of tools and procedures, as seen in the output of Eva Hesse (fig. 7), Nancy Holt, and Robert Morris.[23] Ray never exhibited alongside the postminimalists, but a sculpture such as *Untitled* (1973; fig. 8), in which a two-ton wrecking ball was dropped on a steel plate, parallels the work of these contemporaries, especially in its emphasis on tension, suspension, instability, and process.[24] Process is a concern of Ray's that persists in the present, as seen in *Mime*, which bears evidence of both its

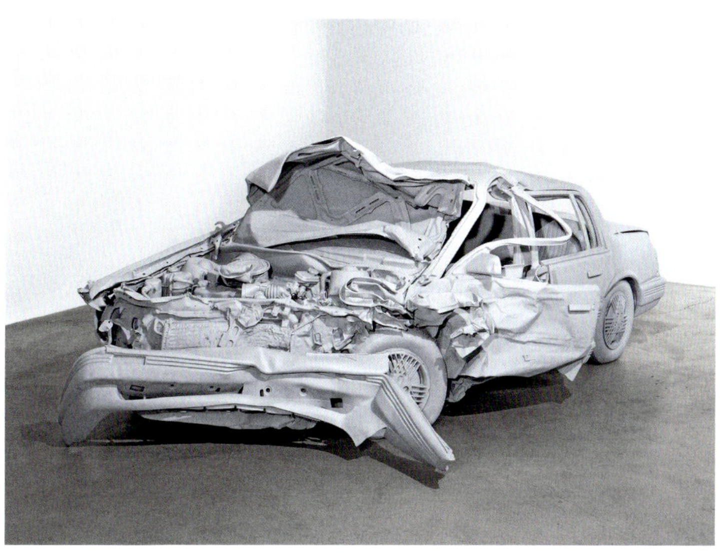

Fig. 5. Charles Ray. *Unpainted sculpture*, 1997. Painted fiberglass, 60 in. × 78 in. × 14 ft. 3 in. (152 × 198 × 434 cm). Walker Art Center, Minneapolis, Gift of Bruce and Martha Atwater, Ann and Barrie Birks, Dolly Fiterman, Erwin and Miriam Kelen, Larry Perlman and Linda Peterson Perlman, Harriet and Edson Spencer with additional funds from the T. B. Walker Acquisition Fund, 1998 (1998.74.1–.85)

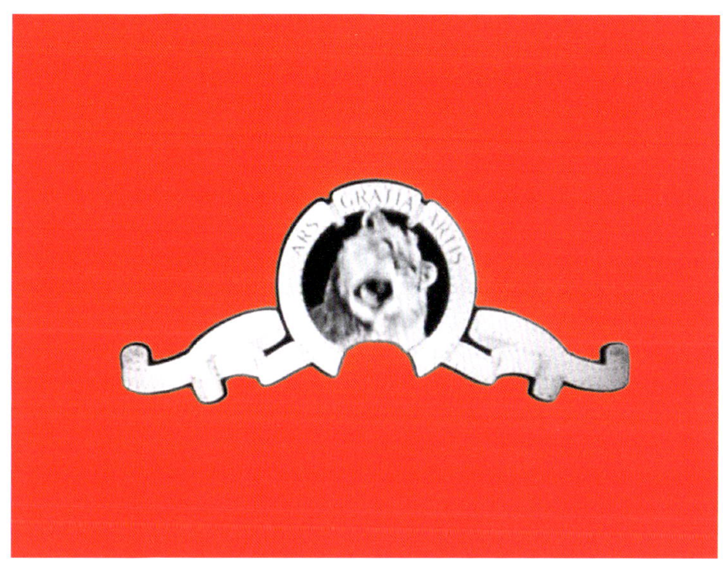

Fig. 6. Jack Goldstein (American, 1945–2003). *Metro-Goldwyn-Mayer*, 1975. 16mm film, color, sound, 2 min. Whitney Museum of American Art, New York, Purchase, with funds from the Film and Video Committee and the Director's Discretionary Fund (2003.220)

production and its assembly. Importantly, both Crimp and Krauss characterized their respective objects of inquiry as postmodern, insofar as they emerged after the end of modernism and its various shibboleths, especially rule-bound self-referentiality and medium specificity.[25] Overall, Ray's work was formed in the crucible of these two currents of postmodernism, sitting squarely at the intersection of the historical developments diagnosed by Crimp and Krauss.

In 1981, two years after Ray graduated from Rutgers and moved to Los Angeles, Krauss published "The Originality of the Avant-Garde," which brings Crimp's concept of pictures to bear on sculpture writ large. Her essay begins with a consideration of the posthumous casts made from Auguste Rodin plasters that the artist left to the French state. In what sense, the critic queries, can these casts be considered original, produced as they were after Rodin's death? This question turns out to be a red herring: the more pressing issue, Krauss argues, is the authenticity of sculptural casts in general, which are essentially three-dimensional facsimiles of preexisting patterns.[26] The critic ends her discussion with none other than Sherrie Levine, one of the artists showcased in Crimp's exhibition, known for photographing copyrighted prints by artists like Edward Weston, thereby collapsing the distinction between original and copy, author and pirate. In a conclusion with great bearing on Ray's practice, Krauss ultimately argues that sculpture and photography share much the same ontological status. Endowed with the "ethos of reproduction," both mediums are defined by their ability to facilitate the creation of copies.[27] Sculpture and photography are therefore inextricably related to the category of the pattern and to the operation of patterning, a connection Ray simultaneously exploits and explores.

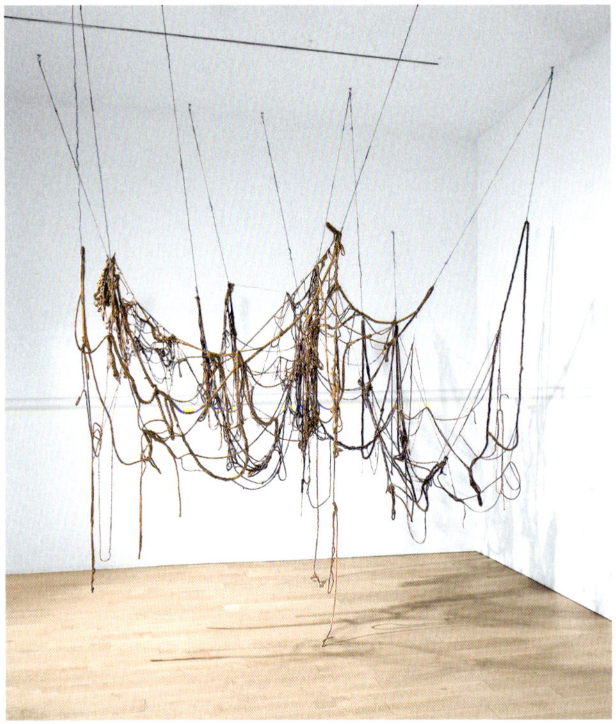

Fig. 7. Eva Hesse (American, born Germany, 1936–1970). *No title*, 1969–70. Latex, rope, string, wire, dimensions variable. Whitney Museum of American Art, New York, Purchase, with funds from Eli and Edythe L. Broad, the Mrs. Percy Uris Purchase Fund, and the Painting and Sculpture Committee (88.17a–b)

The Self

One of Ray's most persistent patterns—the basis for multiple works in a variety of media—is himself. The artist's physical self makes appearances in performances like *Untitled*, of 1973 (pl. 12), and photographic series like *All my clothes*, from the same year.[28] Ray's body continues to appear in works from the late 1970s and 1980s, but only as a part-object, with portions obscured or effaced by elements in wood or metal, as in *Shelf* (1981; fig. 9). Here, the artist is set into a wall-bound shelf that bisects his neck, visually severing his body, which is nude, from his head, which is painted the same shade of gray as the shelf and the objects it supports. Besides objectifying the very seat of consciousness and abstracting the figure as a whole, the paint effectively drains both life and authenticity from the artist.

Of works such as *Shelf*, Ray once said, "I became an image. An image in a larger configuration."[29] Soon after, the artist began to privilege his identity over his body, approaching the

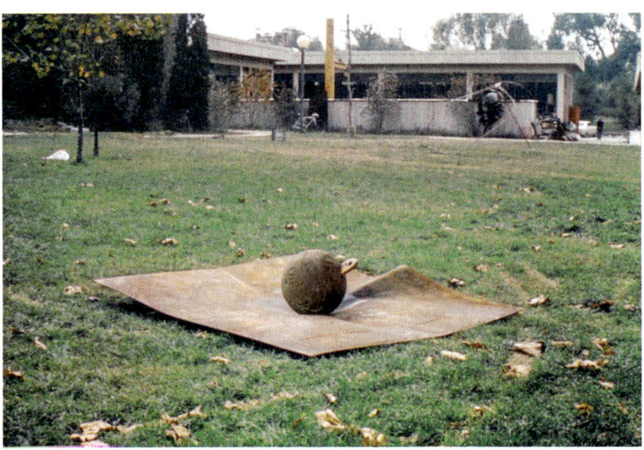

Fig. 8. Charles Ray. *Untitled*, 1973. Steel plate, two-ton wrecking ball, 24 × 72 × 72 in. (61 × 183 × 183 cm)

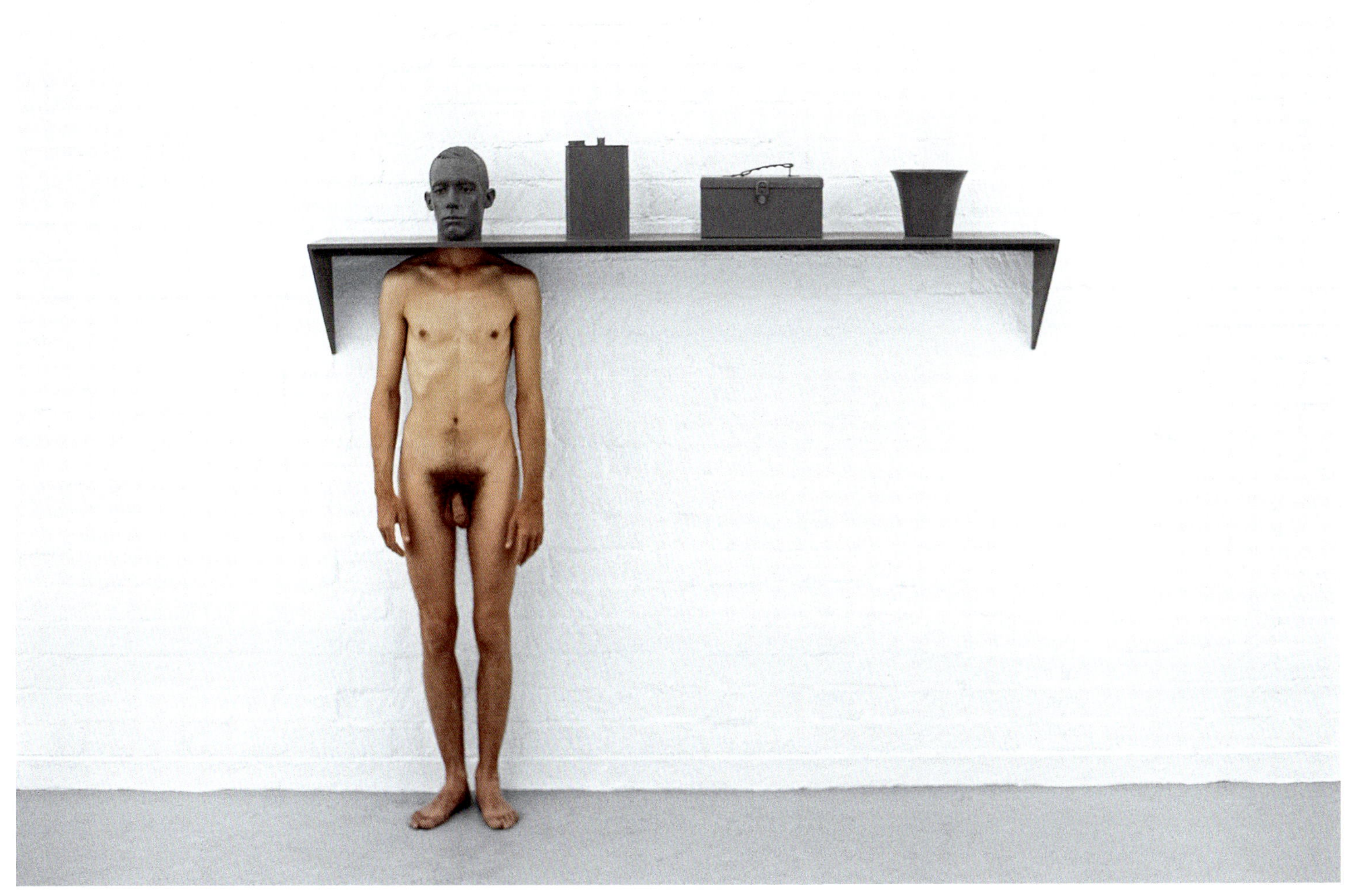

Fig. 9. Charles Ray. *Shelf*, 1981. Steel, painted found objects, human body, 71 × 78 × 10 in. (180 × 198 × 25 cm)

self not as a physical entity but as a disembodied pattern to be repeated and appropriated.

Key to this body of work is a secondary pattern, that of the mannequin. Take *Self-portrait* (1990; fig. 10), for instance, the first in a series of adulterated self-portraits—adulterated because the "selves" in question are nothing more than three-dimensional simulations.[30] Consisting of a mannequin to which Ray added, with the help of a commercial mannequin maker, a representation of his own head, and which he dressed with an exact replica of his favorite sailing outfit, *Self-portrait* upends the tradition referenced in its title.[31] Historically, artists have been associated with authenticity; the presumed singularity of the maker secures the originality (not to mention the exchange value) of the work of art. Conventional self-portraits, such as those by Rembrandt and Velázquez, play an important role in confirming the artist's pedigree. They are able to do so, however, only by effacing their status as pictures, as representations. The precise opposite is true of *Self-portrait*, which flaunts its inauthenticity. Here, Ray recedes dramatically from view, disappearing into a maze of facsimiles, with copies piling up on top of copies. Wherever the artist's true self might lie, it certainly isn't in this three-dimensional picture patterned as much on an artificial, mass-produced version of a human being as it is on its subject. Ray takes aim at the myths that artists, male artists specifically, have accrued in an even more provocative work titled *Male mannequin* (1990), a generic mannequin to which he attached a cast—a portrait—of his own genitals, surrounded by real pubic hair. *Male mannequin* parodies the equation of creative genius and masculine prowess, artistic mastery and sexual potency—a cultural pattern that has long underlain Western art history—implicating the artist in the process.

No (pl. 1), a photograph of a fiberglass mold of Ray's head and upper torso, painted a brownish-beige color and embellished with a wig and the artist's own shirt and glasses, followed two years later.[32] The artist styled his double with the intention of having its picture taken by a professional portrait photographer, adopting gestures specific to the genre, including crossed arms and a distant gaze. With its studio lighting and colored backdrop—chosen by the photographer—*No* patterns itself on the kinds of photographs found in homes and break rooms around the country. The year 1992 also saw the creation of Ray's most complex self-portrait, *Oh! Charley, Charley, Charley . . .* (fig. 11), in which eight nude, three-dimensional facsimiles, all patterned on mannequins and cast from body molds, engage in an autoerotic orgy.[33] The sex, however, turns out to be just as lifeless, just as dysfunctional, as the figures, none of which actually touches or penetrates any other. While the artist is multiplied in *Oh! Charley, Charley, Charley . . .* , he is constructed in *Puzzle bottle* (1995), a diminutive glass bottle containing a three-dimensional self-portrait comprised of puzzle pieces. Here, the artist is assembled bit by bit, not unlike a car on a production line, a fitting metaphor

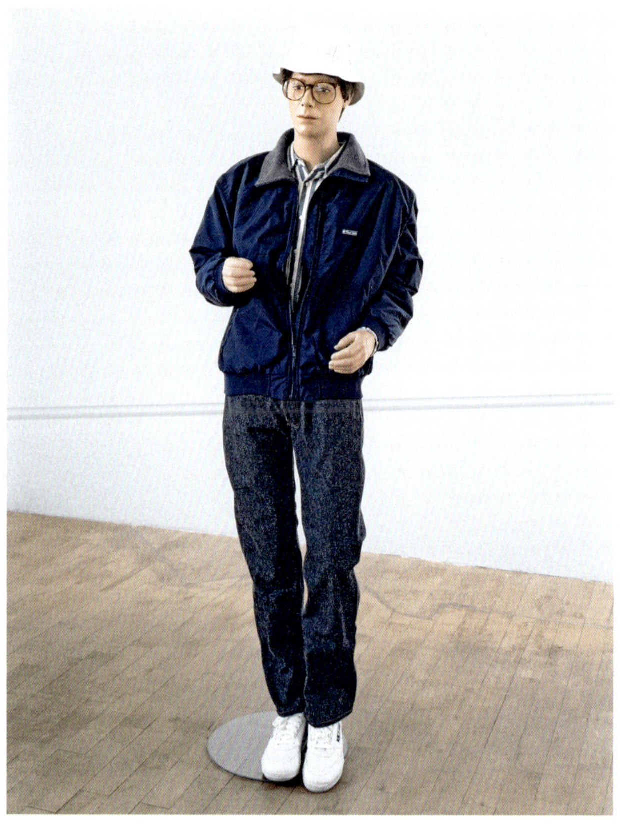

Fig. 10. Charles Ray. *Self-portrait*, 1990. Painted fiberglass, clothing, eyeglasses, hair, glass, metal hardware, 75 × 26 × 20 in. (191 × 66 × 51 cm). Orange County Museum of Art, Santa Ana, Calif., Museum purchase (1990.002)

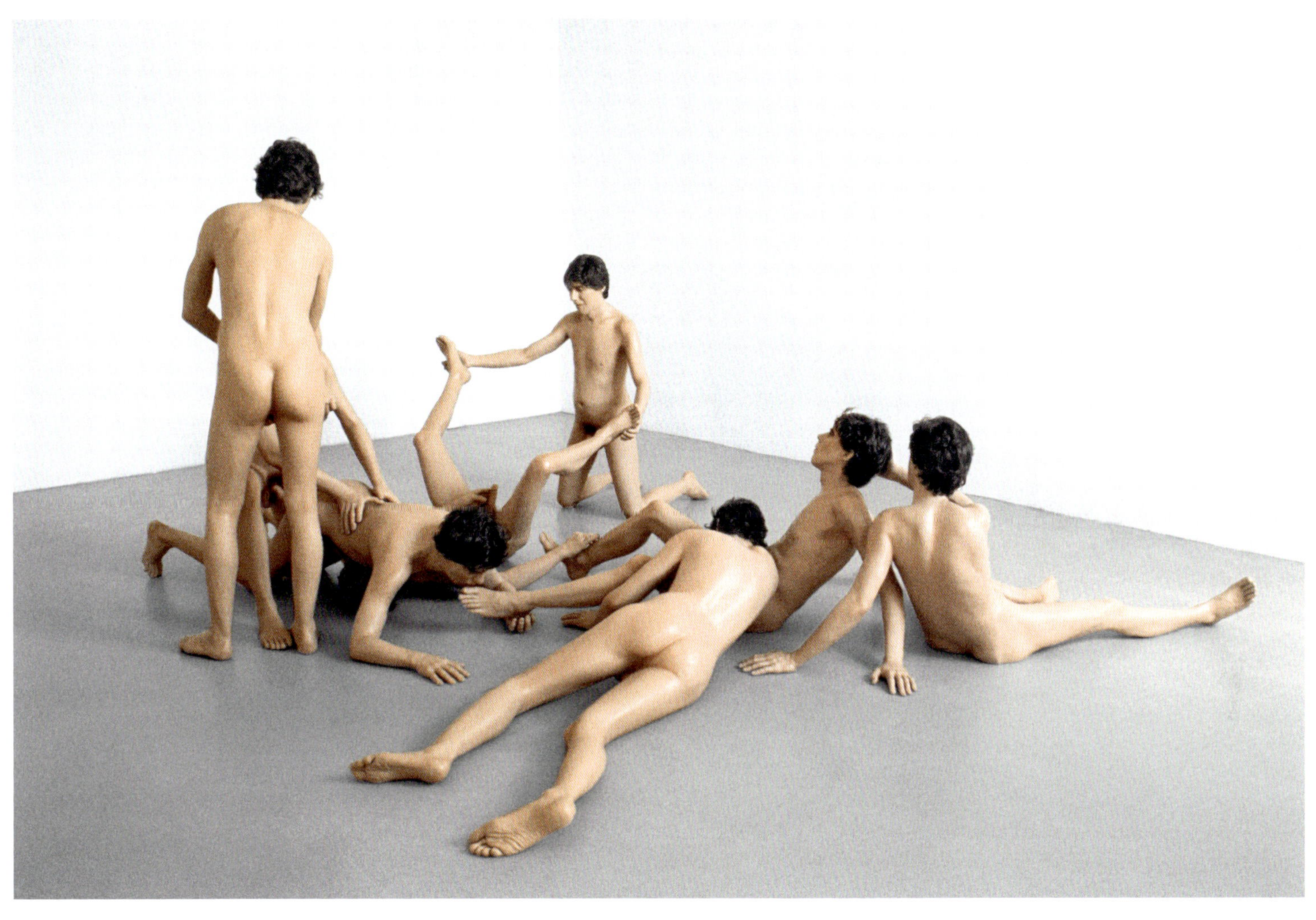

Fig. 11. Charles Ray. *Oh! Charley, Charley, Charley . . .*, 1992. Painted fiberglass mannequins, hair, 72 × 180 × 180 in. (182.9 × 457.2 × 457.2 cm). Rubell Museum, Miami, Rubell Family Collection

for the displacement of subjectivity and authorship found throughout Ray's work. A more recent sculpture, *Clothes pile* (2020), made of painted aluminum and patterned on a wrinkled pile of the artist's own castoffs, deposes Ray entirely, with only a ghostly residue of his physical self remaining.

In 2014 Ray completed another self-portrait, *Horse and rider* (fig. 13). Standing just over life size, the work is patterned on the long-standing tradition of equestrian statues, most of them erected in honor of White men such as Marcus Aurelius (fig. 12), Napoleon, Robert E. Lee, and John Wayne (fig. 27) and the imperialist ventures and military campaigns they waged, whether on battlefields or screens.[34] These sculptures yoke power to the performance of singularity and authenticity, not to mention Whiteness and masculinity, themselves patterns with immense cultural currency. In *Horse and rider*, Ray takes aim at these and other prototypes. Bereft of the pedestal that typically elevates such works physically and symbolically, the protagonists have been drained of energy, dynamism, and prowess. Instead of the emphatic diagonals and phallic verticals of earlier equestrian statues, Ray's is comprised of a series of arcs and curves, from the horse's neck to the artist's slumped shoulders, that direct the viewer's gaze downward. Additionally, all four of the horse's feet are planted firmly on the ground. The artist's left hand is raised, but the reins are conspicuously absent, further diminishing the potential for movement, an effect intensified by the stainless steel out of which the sculpture has been machined. The overall impression is of inertia, not heroism, exhaustion, not hyperbole. Although *Horse and rider* turns the history of the equestrian statue on its head, its position seems to be more anxious than critical, as if it were, to borrow from Sigmund Freud, not quite finished mourning its lost object—an increasingly beleaguered yet still formidable model of White masculinity, one of many cultural patterns, including the self-portrait, that Ray subjects to appropriation and revision.[35]

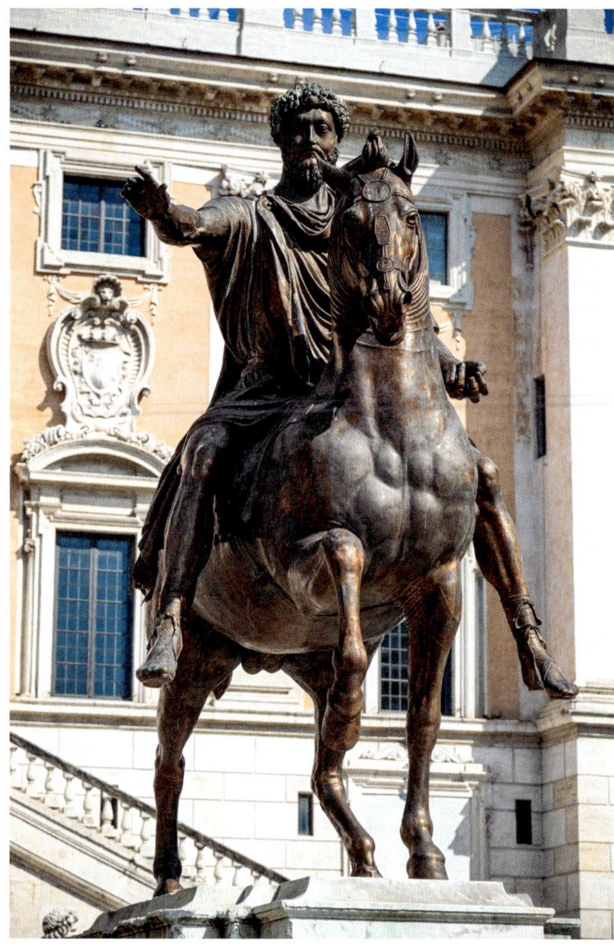

Fig. 12. Equestrian statue of Marcus Aurelius, 1981 replica of A.D. 161–180 original. Bronze, H. 13 ft. 10⅞ in. (424 cm). Piazza del Campidoglio, Rome, original in the collection of the Capitoline Museums, Rome

The Body

In the early 1990s, the mannequin—especially its more conventional, ubiquitous manifestation, what Ray has called the "Sears standard"—served as the artist's most prominent pattern.[36] Above all, the mannequin is a representation not of a human being, but of a prototype. Three-dimensional replicas of socially acceptable archetypes, mannequins constitute a collection of cues, codes, and contracts—patterns—that together signify a "typical" person. Insofar as they reflect and codify dominant standards of sex, gender, race, and beauty, mannequins are ideological objects par excellence. Race is especially key to the optics and politics of such figures, which have historically linked desirability to Whiteness. Even today, rare is the mannequin with dark "skin." In societies founded on White supremacy, the

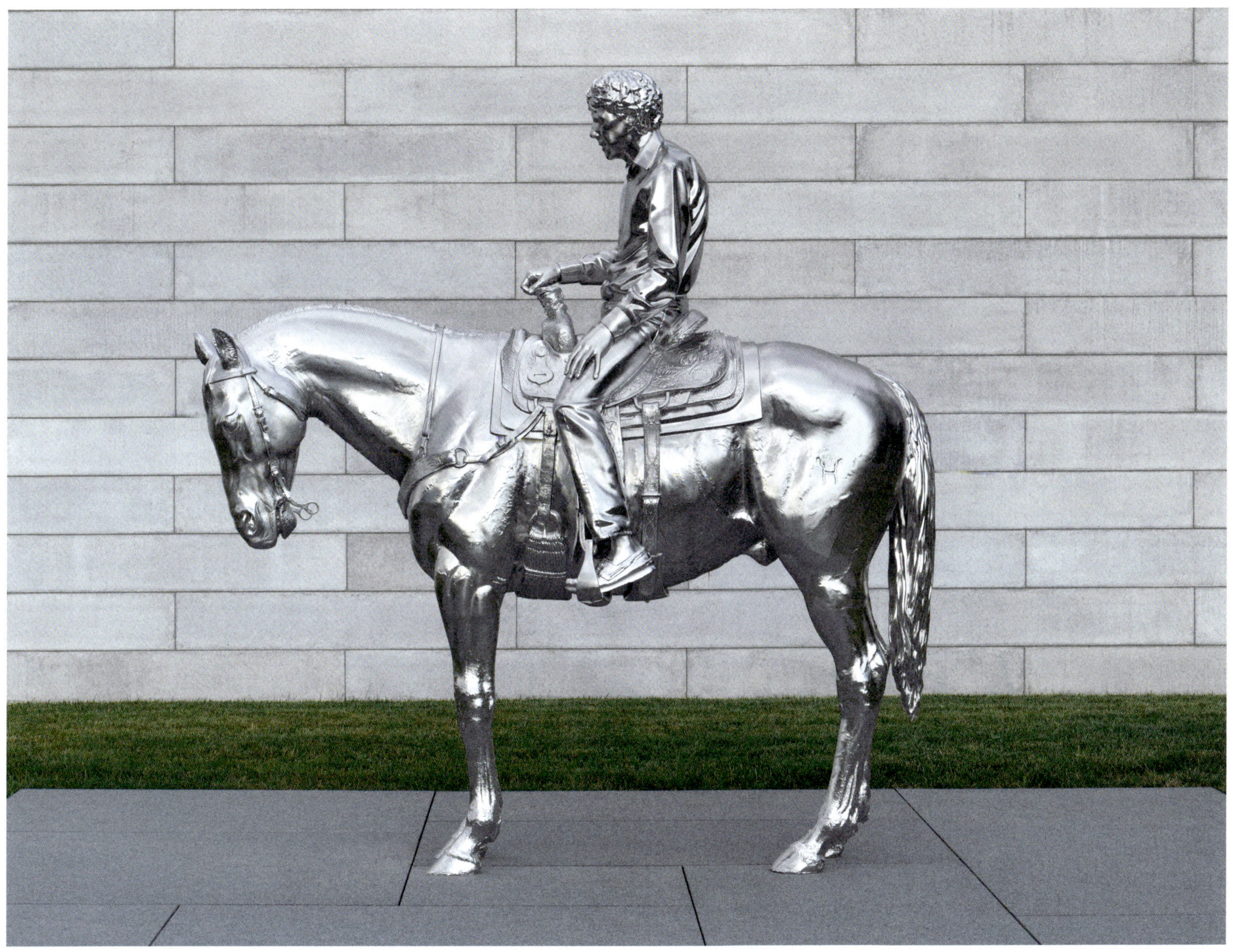

Fig. 13. Charles Ray. *Horse and rider*, 2014. Stainless steel, 9 ft. 1½ in. × 40 in. × 8 ft. 9⅞ in. (278 × 102 × 269 cm). Glenstone Museum, Potomac, Md.

mannequin tells us, "generic" is broadly equated with White and "average" with light.

For the most part, Ray takes the mannequin as he finds it, choosing to alter only its sculptural attributes. Signifiers of Whiteness as well as masculinity and femininity and maleness and femaleness remain intact. Neither they nor the relations of power they sustain are overturned. That said, the mannequin is a wily thing—likewise any sculpture that takes it as a pattern. Indeed, the very nature of the mannequin—its insistent inauthenticity—throws all givens into doubt, an effect Ray deliberately exploits. Race, gender, and sex are not so much depicted in the artist's sculptures of mannequins as they are represented, at a triple remove, no less: what denotes Whiteness isn't skin (an unreliable index of race to begin with), but an acrylic-based paint made of natural and synthetic ingredients that Ray sourced from the mannequin manufacturer Decter.[37] Likewise, what denotes maleness and femaleness isn't flesh (similarly an unreliable index of gender) but fiber-reinforced plastic.

In *Self-portrait*, Ray hewed fairly closely to the rules governing mannequins, but this would quickly change. In 1992 he began experimenting more freely with the mannequin as both an idea and an object, which is to say as a pattern. That year he debuted *Fall '91* (fig. 14), sometimes referred to as "The Big Lady," a sculpture with the appearance of a mass-produced White female mannequin, base plate and all.[38] Ray increased the proportions of the mannequin by one-third, exploiting to both sculptural and psychological ends the discrepancy between apparent and actual size. From a distance, *Fall '91* conforms to the height of a typical mannequin, which is that of an average woman.[39] During the course of approach, however, it appears to grow at the same time viewers feel as if they're shrinking.[40] Eventually, all ninety-six inches of the Big Lady bear down. Her size should not be mistaken for political authority, though. Any power she appears to wield is an illusion, a function of the spectator alone, whose fantasies fill the void of the discarnate vessel in front of them.[41]

Boy (pl. 16), from the same year, moves in a slightly different direction. A representation of a representation of a boy, the sculpture is patterned on a mannequin endowed with the features and proportions of a prepubescent White male but with the height of an adult man, specifically Ray. *Boy* is dressed in an outfit more appropriate to a toddler living in the 1940s, the knee-high socks and sandals especially anachronistic. In this case, the artist orchestrates a highly uncanny gap between age, size, and appearance; cognitive dissonance ensues. Equally unsettling are *Boy*'s vacant eyes, simpering smile, and extended arms, which in this context seem more threatening than welcoming. Each of these decisions serves to deprive Ray's sculpture of the innocence traditionally associated with childhood and Whiteness, both of them conventions, or patterns, with which Ray has long been interested.[42]

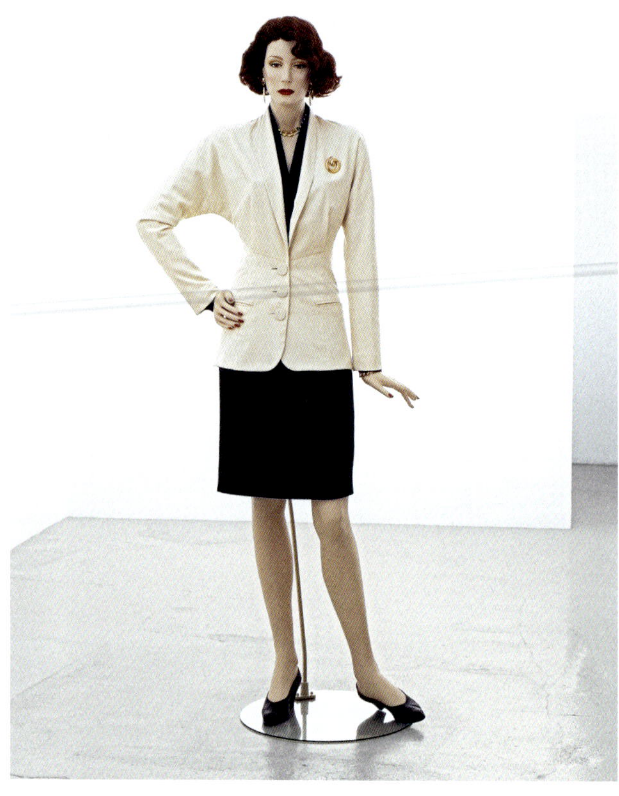

Fig. 14. Charles Ray. *Fall '91*, 1992. Painted fiberglass, hair, clothing, jewelry, glass, metal hardware, 96 × 26 × 36 in. (244 × 66 × 91 cm). Glenstone Museum, Potomac, Md.

The multipart *Family romance*, of 1993 (pl. 14), strays even further from the template of the mannequin, reworking a wide variety of other discursive patterns in the process. While *Boy* and *Fall '91* are best described as sculptures of mannequins, *Family romance* and *Oh! Charley, Charley, Charley . . .* are sculptures of *figures*—some of Ray's earliest, in fact. If they resemble mannequins, it is mostly because the artist was still relying on the technology of mannequin-making. Eventually, he would identify new means and new materials, as in *Aluminum girl* (2003).[43] The title *Family romance* alludes to "Family Romances," a 1909 essay by Sigmund Freud on interfamilial conflict,[44] as well as to "family values," a slogan instrumentalized to hyperbolic and hypocritical ends by President George H. W. Bush in the early 1990s.[45] *Family romance* travesties a familiar archetype—the White, heteronormative family. It is comprised of four units: father, mother, youth, and toddler, all of them nude. The figures retain a few distinguishing attributes, but otherwise they read as a chain of three-dimensional paper dolls. All are the same height, making them either too tall or too short for their age. The overall arrangement is strict, repetitive, and modular: the figures face forward, their hands joined to one another in a gesture drained of affection and intentionality. In leveling difference and banning emotion, Ray upends the hierarchy of roles, responsibilities, and relationships that governs patriarchal families. He effectively deprivileges both desire and maternity as well: logic bests passion, while mechanical reproduction trumps procreation. *Family romance* is a figurative sculpture with the serial logic of a Donald Judd (fig. 15) and the uncanny charge of a Surrealist sculpture by Salvador Dalí, proving that repetition and pathology are but two sides of the same coin.[46] Insofar as they dramatize their own artificiality, *Self-portrait*, *Male mannequin*, and *Family romance*, among others, also decouple the human from the "natural." They present selfhood as a cultural artifact, a function of society, similarly denaturalizing sex, gender, and race, disidentifying them with biology.[47]

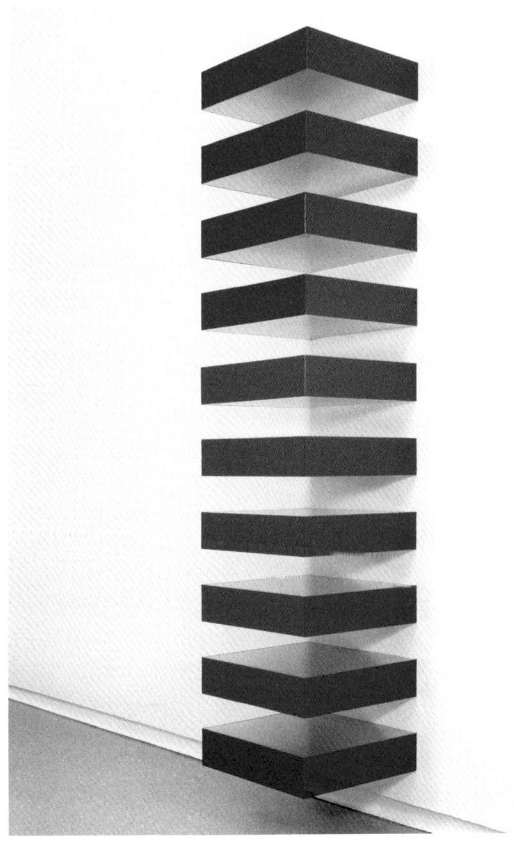

Fig. 15. Donald Judd (American, 1928–1994). *Untitled*, 1970. Stainless steel, Plexiglas, 10 parts, 6 × 27 × 24 in. (15.2 × 68.6 × 61 cm) each. Museum of Contemporary Art Chicago, Gerald S. Elliott Collection

The Mimic

After completing *Family romance*, Ray abandoned the mannequin as a pattern and a technology. He continues to sculpt figures, but he references different prototypes and utilizes different materials and forms of production. Still, there are as many similarities as disparities in his work from the 1990s and 2000s, as demonstrated by *Mime* (2014; pl. 17). Here, a male figure modeled on professional mime Lorin Eric Salm lies on a cot, his right arm thrown over his head and his left hand resting on his left thigh. The mime's chest is inflated ever so slightly, just enough to imply the activity of breathing and the presence of intentionality. Although quite different in appearance, *Mime* is in many ways an extension of *Boy* and *Self-portrait*, insofar as it shares their emphasis on abstraction, reification, mimesis, and theatricality.[48] Much links the mime and the mannequin ontologically as well. First and foremost, they are patterns that pattern themselves on human beings. Lodged at the heart of the mime and the mannequin is a fundamental contradiction: each simulates life, and in so doing drains it of precisely what makes it "lifeful," which is to say, its "aliveness."[49] In *Mime*, Ray seizes on this contradiction, using sculptural means to create layers of uncertainty and illusion. The status of the figure, for instance, is unclear. Is he a mime who is sleeping? Is he a mime who is miming sleep? Given the resemblance of sleeping to dying, he might also be a mime who is miming the onset of death. Or perhaps he is a mime who is miming representations of dead and dying figures. After all, Ray's mime mimics a gesture repeated across classical, Renaissance, and neoclassical sculptures of wounded and deceased warriors (fig. 16).[50] So common is this pose, it has achieved the status of a pattern. With *Mime*, Ray has orchestrated a sculptural event with a range of equally plausible, simultaneous meanings and temporalities, thanks in large part to his reliance on patterning.

Mime is also one of the artist's most self-referential sculptures, with the loop between form, medium, and content closed tight. As art historian Richard Neer and others have noted, miming and sculpting are fundamentally imitative activities, making *Mime* as much about sculpture as it is about anything else.[51] (Neer's argument inadvertently recalls Krauss's 1981 essay, and her case for the fundamentally photographic conditions of sculpture, based as both mediums are on repetition and reproduction.) For their part, sleeping and dying are both liminal states of being, with life suspended between consciousness and unconsciousness. Suspension is also key to the art of miming, involving as it does the postponement of action and the temporary deferment of movement. It was this exact tension that Ray sought to capture in *Mime*, which arrests the human figure in time and space just as it hinders the resolution of meaning, leaving the precise nature of the mime's comportment open to interpretation.[52]

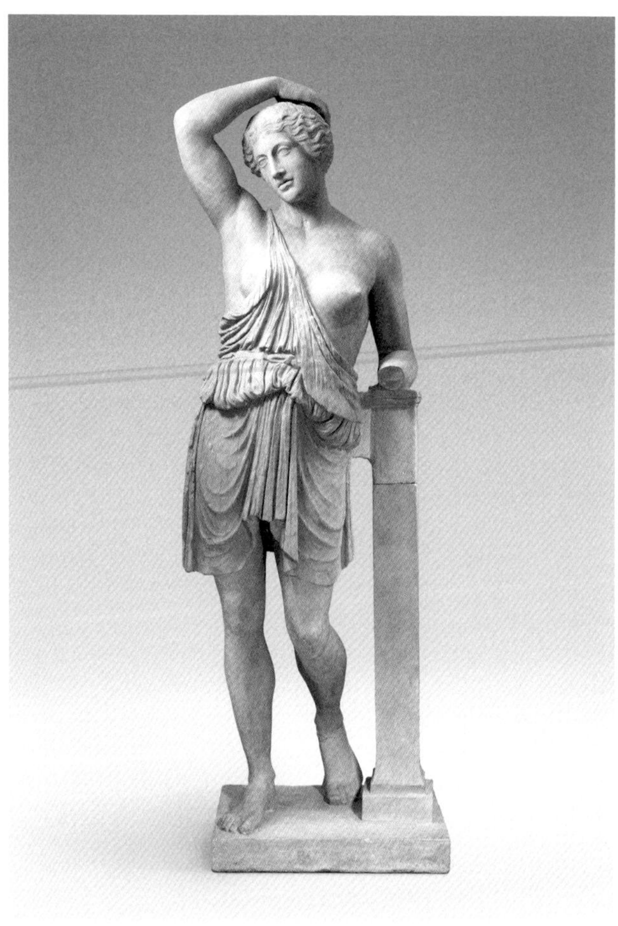

Fig. 16. Marble statue of a wounded Amazon. Roman, 1st–2nd century A.D. Marble, H. 80¼ in. (203.8 cm). The Metropolitan Museum of Art, New York, Gift of John D. Rockefeller Jr., 1932 (32.11.4)

The Pair

Between 2009 and 2021, Ray completed three sculptures that together make up a triumvirate linked to a single pattern, Mark Twain's novel *Adventures of Huckleberry Finn*, published in the United States in 1885. The first, *Boy with frog* (pl. 9), from 2009, is only loosely attached to the book.[53] According to Ray, the work refers indirectly to the character Huck, whose preoccupation with the natural world is evident throughout *Huckleberry Finn*.[54] *Huck and Jim* (2014; pl. 7) and *Sarah Williams* (2021; pl. 18), on the other hand, reinvent two specific moments from the novel: the former from chapter 19, when Huck and Jim debate the origins of the stars while floating down the Mississippi River on their raft, with Jim suggesting the moon might have laid them the way a frog lays eggs; the latter from chapter 10, when Jim advises Huck to dress as a girl so he might pass undetected into Missouri to gather information about the ongoing search effort. "Sarah Williams" is the moniker Huck assumes upon donning his disguise, making the name a double fiction: a persona assumed by Huck, who is himself an invention of Twain's imagination. With an identity as unstable as its gender, Sarah Williams is the kind of pattern that has long intrigued Ray. Indeed, one of the reasons the artist focused on this particular moment in the novel was the "transgression of Huck's cross-dressing."[55]

Both *Boy with frog* and *Huck and Jim* originated as commissions for civic spaces, the former from the French collector François Pinault for the Punta della Dogana, in Venice, and the latter from the Whitney Museum of American Art, for the plaza outside its building in the Meatpacking District.[56] When asked about his reasons for choosing *Huckleberry Finn* as a point of departure for the Whitney commission, Ray spoke of his desire to synchronize form, content, and site. More specifically, he wanted to make an emblematically American sculpture for the country's most prominent museum of American art.[57] Written by an author born in the United States, *Huckleberry Finn* is most certainly an American novel—a great American novel, according to T. S. Eliot—but that's not all that makes it distinctly American.[58] First and foremost, *Huckleberry Finn* is a novel about America in which slavery plays a central role.[59] More than just a backdrop, slavery—that most morally reprehensible of institutions, what some have called the country's original sin—is one of the book's central protagonists, self-consciously so.[60]

Equally American are the book's many incongruities, some of them historical, others political. For instance, *Huckleberry Finn* sprung from the imagination of a White man whose biological family owned slaves but whose father-in-law, Jervis Langdon, was an abolitionist; Twain also endorsed the oppression of Black people as a boy but called out racial violence as an adult.[61] In addition, while the novel is set in antebellum Missouri, it was written during the waning years of Reconstruction, in the 1870s and 1880s, as the promise of Black liberation clashed with the legalization of segregation, racial violence, and voter suppression.[62] Perhaps most importantly, the story revolves around a fraternal but asymmetrical relationship between a poor White boy escaping an abusive father and an enslaved Black man en route to the free states. Linked by their shared experience of cruelty and their common desire for independence, Huck and Jim are friends, but they are by no means equals: Huck's race entitles him to powers that Jim's does not, among them the power White people legally wielded over Black people in the 1840s.[63] Huck periodically lords this authority over Jim, indulging in callous jokes and tricks. The tension between homosocial solidarity and cross-racial conflict comes to a head in chapter 31, when Huck decides to "steal" Jim out of slavery, but only after an agonizing internal debate, during which he very nearly leaves him with the family to whom he'd been sold by a swindler.[64] Huck ultimately makes the right, the just, decision, but only out of a sense of responsibility to Jim.[65] For Huck, bondage and racism are givens, natural like the weather. Not once does he question either their existence or their future. Huck might permit Jim his freedom, but he never actually repudiates slavery, nor does he recognize his own prejudice, a conflicted perspective born at least in part of America's conflicted relationship to race during the nineteenth century. (In many ways, the character of Huck embodies the country's own racial fault lines and blind spots, perhaps intentionally, as Ralph Ellison has argued.[66]) Overall, *Huckleberry Finn* presents bondage and racism as unresolved moral dilemmas, and in grappling with them as it does, it denaturalizes them ever so slightly, but without critiquing them outright. This insight was one of the origins of novelist Toni Morrison's incisive 1996 response to the book, which she described as both "amazing" and "troubling."[67] For Morrison, *Huckleberry Finn* occasioned a great many literary satisfactions, but also alarm, discomfort, and "muffled rage, as though appreciation of the work required my complicity in and sanction of something shaming," particularly the frequent humiliation of Jim, likewise the "secrecy in which Huck's engagement with . . . a racist society is necessarily conducted."[68] That said, she ultimately appreciated the novel's "ability to transform its contradictions into fruitful complexities and to seem to be deliberately cooperating in the controversy it has excited. The brilliance of *Huckleberry Finn* is that it *is* the argument it raises."[69]

Importantly, neither *Huck and Jim* nor *Sarah Williams* actually illustrates *Huckleberry Finn*. The novel is treated like all of Ray's patterns, as conceptual and sculptural raw material, with each work taking what it wants, adapting in the process. *Huck and Jim* consists of two male figures, an adolescent and an adult, both about twice life size, identifiable through the sculpture's title. Ray used a young White male model for Huck and an older Black male model for Jim. Like most of Ray's figures, they are shown in a state of acute absorption.[70] Huck bends forward as if to scoop an object off the ground, but his hand remains empty, leaving the item's identity a mystery.[71] Jim stands upright and stares out at a distant point—concerned, perhaps, with what the artist has described as "the greater implications of their journey down the river."[72] Ray's Jim bears little resemblance to the character in Twain's novel. The latter is little more than a compilation of stereotypes through which Jim's humanity, to paraphrase Ellison, barely manages to emerge, an effect enhanced by the book's original illustrations, which devolve into racist caricature.[73] In the sculpture, Jim is stoic, confident, and self-possessed, reminiscent in many ways of an ancient Greek or Roman statue.

Huck and Jim are both depicted nude, without much fanfare or narrative grandstanding.[74] In fact, the characters could often be found without clothes in the novel, hardly needing them while floating on a raft or camping on Jackson Island in

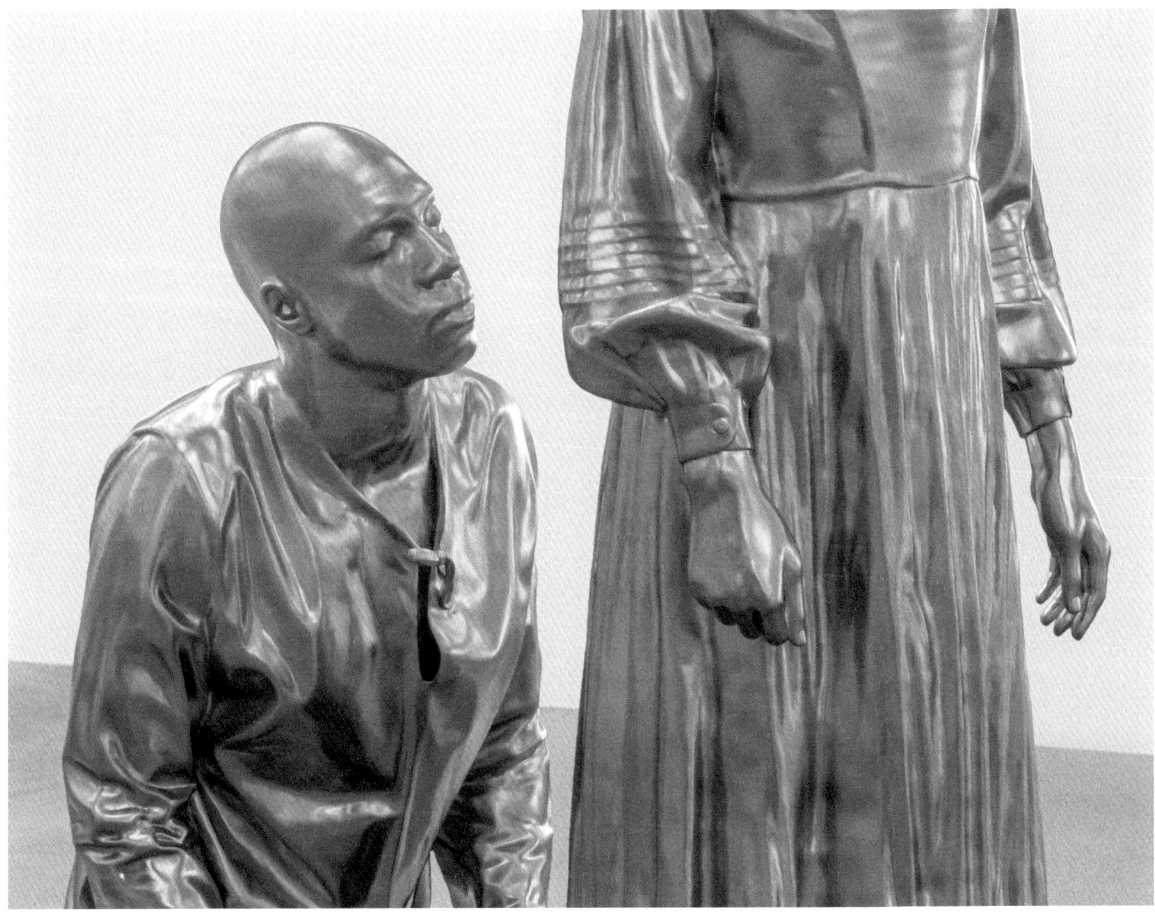

Fig. 17. Charles Ray. *Sarah Williams*, 2021 (detail of pl. 18)

the 1840s.[75] Ray, who has been exploring the nude figure since the 1980s, thought nudity suited the sculpture's original site, a fountain whose waters would have evoked the Mississippi River. Fountain or not, what signals homosociality in Twain's novel reads as potentially homoerotic in Ray's sculpture. The proximity of the two figures—their relationship to one another in space—has the effect of recoding their nudity. The act of bending over, for instance, thrusts Huck's bottom upward and his head downward, an entirely innocent gesture if not for the exposed penis to his immediate left. A similar connotative shift occurs in the case of Jim's nudity: considered in concert with Huck's and endowed with all the authority of a classical statue, it becomes charged with homoerotic potential.[76] What makes this undercurrent troubling, though, is not the specter of queer, cross-racial desire, but that of an intergenerational bond between an adolescent and an adult.

Sarah Williams likewise depicts both Huck and Jim, also modeled on a young White man and an older Black man, respectively (fig. 17). Ray has described the sculpture as "a joint task between two figures," with Huck and Jim collaborating on the creation of the Sarah Williams persona.[77] The composition is loosely patterned on an illustration by E. W. Kemble from chapter 10 of the novel's first edition, in which a smiling Jim kneels behind an impish Huck, shortening his companion's calico gown with a fish hook.[78] Very little else links sculpture and illustration, though. In *Sarah Williams*, Huck is pensive, his head bent and his eyes closed. Jim, coiled with anticipatory energy, stares directly into the swell of Huck's backside, leaning forward and turning his head slightly, his right thumb and finger pressed together as he prepares to raise the hem of Huck's dress. Action has been deferred, with the focus on looking, not doing, as it was in the illustration.[79] Again, an otherwise fraternal relationship appears to have been queered, making a potential couple out of a pair, generating what Ray has described as a "layered dynamic that the viewer is allowed to pass through."[80]

The versions of *Huck and Jim* and *Sarah Williams* featured in this exhibition were machined out of stainless steel. The material works in concert with the sculptures' form, composition, and subject matter, playing a key role in what and how they mean. Most importantly, Ray relies on stainless steel to temper verisimilitude with abstraction. Shiny and semireflective, stainless steel resists legibility, simultaneously dazzling and confusing the eye. It also dematerializes, even liquidizes, the surfaces of the sculptures, especially *Sarah Williams*'s dress, whose many folds and creases create pockets of light and shadow.[81] The effect is both kinetic and changeable, like waves lapping along a shoreline. Ray has often spoken about Twain's evocative descriptions of the Mississippi River, which might very well have been at play here (fig. 18). In choosing to render the figures out of this particular material, Ray also takes racial difference, at least at the level of skin color, out of the equation. Not only have Huck and Jim been cut from the same cloth, so to speak, they have been cut from a cloth of no single hue. Unlike marble or plaster, stainless steel mirrors its surroundings, making it effectively polychromatic. At some level, therefore, the racial identity of Ray's figures is multiple and inexact.

In 2014 Ray wrote of his desire to "create [in *Huck and Jim*] a relationship of sculptural events,"[82] more specifically, to express sculpturally "a complexity in the relationship between Huck and Jim that is American in the deepest sense."[83] In the case of both *Huck and Jim* and *Sarah Williams*, Ray does so primarily through the arrangement of the figures in space. Put simply, he choreographs relations by choreographing bodies, creating two sculptural dyads.[84] One set of relations revolves around the dynamic of affinity and estrangement. Of *Sarah Williams*, for instance, Ray has said that it "transform[s] . . . two people . . . into one beast or structure," compressing Huck and Jim into a single three-dimensional frame.[85] Further entangling them are the low-relief fishhook and fishing line, of which Ray has written: "The hook and line used to fit the dress to Huck's body also weave a thread into Jim's shirt, down his chest and up and out of Sarah's collar at the nape of the neck" (fig. 50).[86] As for *Huck and Jim*, Ray has compared the two figures to a "forest of limbs,"[87]

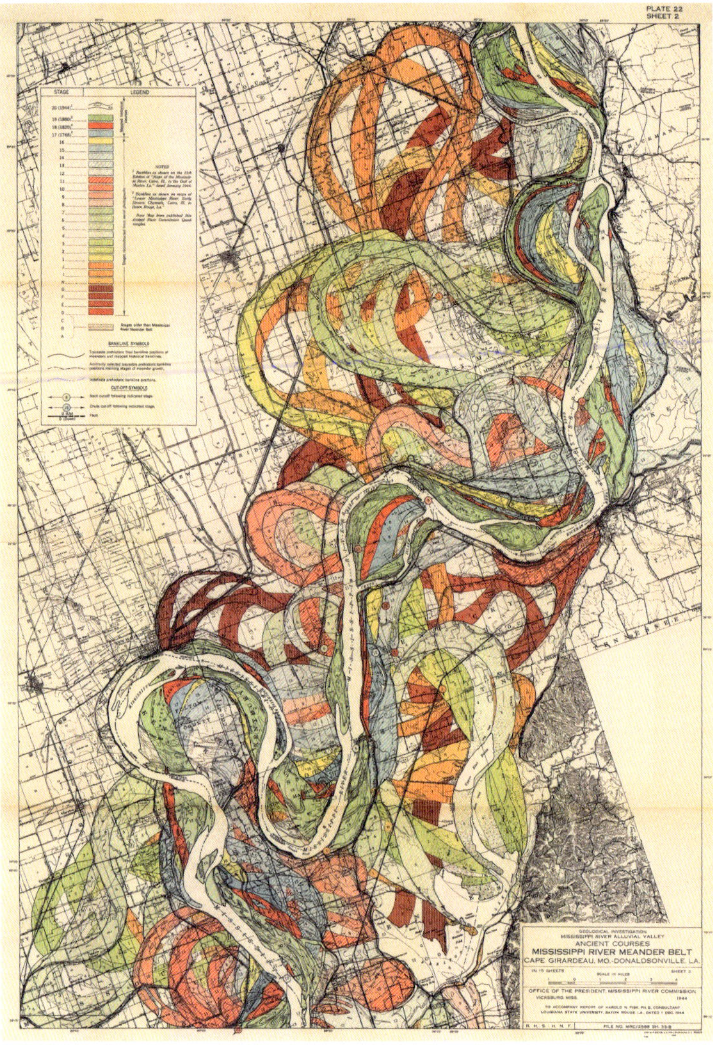

Fig. 18. Harold Fisk. Map of the Mississippi River meander belt from Cape Gireaudeau, Mo., to Donaldsonville, La., 1944

so interwoven are their parts and so confused are their external boundaries, an effect enhanced by the stainless steel from which they are machined. The medium turns both sets of Ray's sculptures into cameras of a sort: captured on their surfaces are distorted reflections of the things around them, including one another. Etched onto Huck's exterior are images of Jim and vice versa, all of them partial, abstract, and imprecise.[88] Thanks to the reflected rays of light that each seizes from the other, Huck and Jim are formally and optically entwined, just as they are ethically, politically, and structurally interconnected in Twain's novel.[89] Put another way, each unit—each character—serves as figure to the other's ground, as image to the other's backdrop. They are legible individually only by virtue of their visual, spatial, and conceptual affiliation.

That said, none of the figures lock eyes with each other, nor do they touch. Missed opportunities for contact abound, as in *Huck and Jim*, where Jim's hand hovers over Huck's back (fig. 46).[90] Both "tender" and "tentative,"[91] this gesture is meaningful precisely because it *isn't consummated*,[92] expressing sculpturally the very real limitations to cross-racial solidarity. Morrison has written eloquently about the precarity that haunts Huck and Jim's relationship, explaining that theirs was a fraternity "doomed to separation," thanks to America's strict racial hierarchy.[93] Equally "American in the deepest sense" is the dialectic of domination and subordination, power and privilege baked into the works at the sculptural level. Signs of racial difference might have been tempered in both works, but signs of racial hierarchy persist, thanks mostly to the orchestration of the figures relative to one another, especially in the case of *Sarah Williams*, where Jim lowers himself to the ground, putting himself at Huck's service. Here, Ray concretizes distinctly racial—and emphatically American—relations of equality and inequality.

Ray is no less suspicious of moralizing and didacticism than was Twain, who famously begins *Huckleberry Finn* with this warning: "Persons attempting to find a motive in this narrative will be prosecuted; persons attempting to find a moral in it will be banished; persons attempting to find a plot in it will be shot."[94] Like Twain, Ray studiously avoids taking explicit positions. ("Selfishly, I'm not a political person," he has said, a deeply political statement in and of itself.[95]) From the very beginning, though, he has sculpted subjects charged with social, political, and ethical import, refusing at the same time to "short circuit" what he calls "meaning machinery."[96] For him, sculpting is a way of thinking, a "way into the world."[97] Similarly, each of Ray's sculptures functions as a kind of philosopher's stone that holds the viewer's attention, indefinitely prolonging the interpretative process.[98] "I don't want the work to answer the question it poses," he has said.[99] When his sculptures provoke, as they always do, that provocation derives not just from the orchestration of sculptural means like surface and steel, space and mass, but also from the deft selection of patterns and the adroit use of the process of patterning.

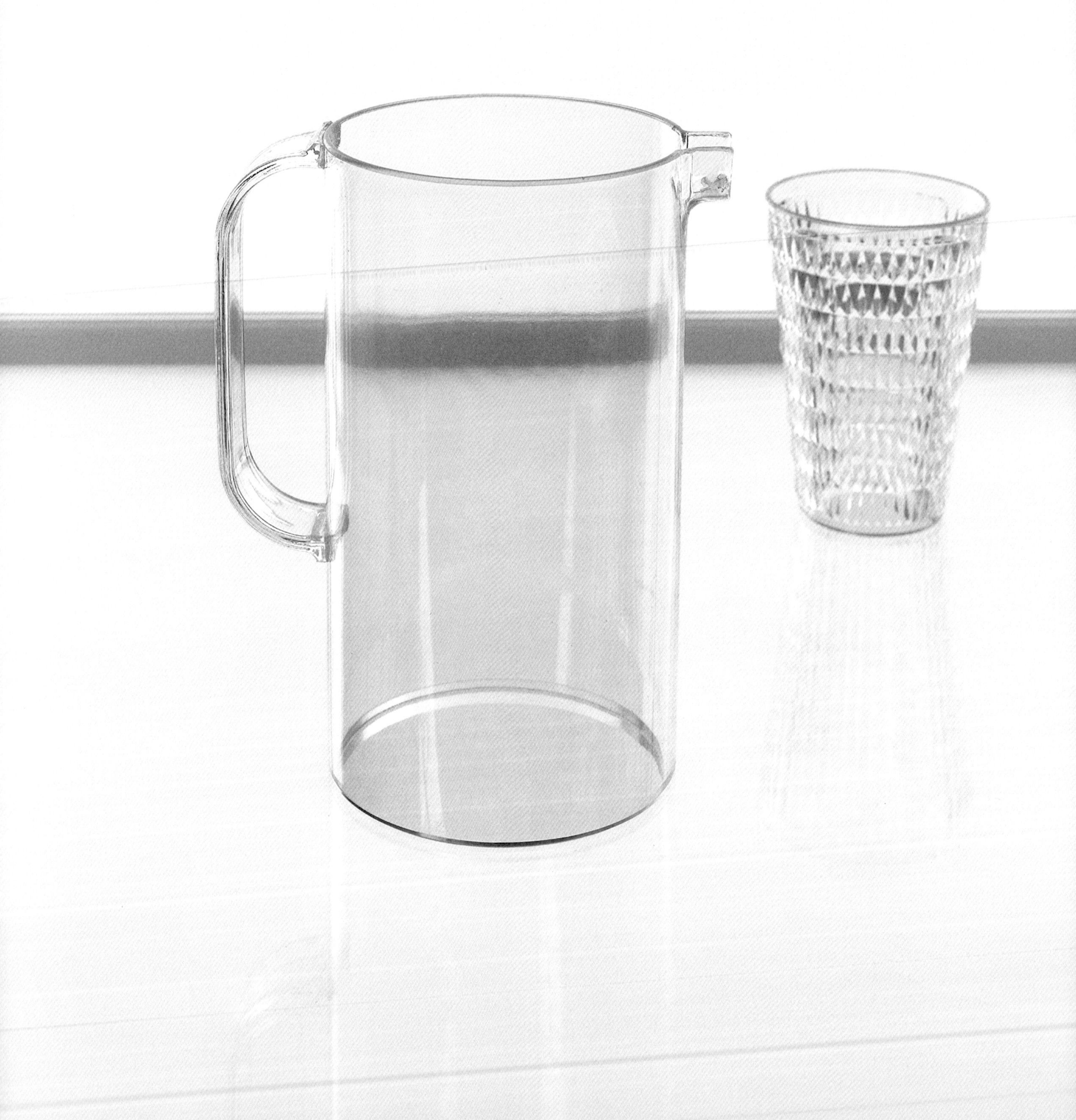

Holding Space

Brinda Kumar

Modalities of touch are bound up with the spatial, conceptual, optical, material, and even temporal dimensions of Charles Ray's sculptures, and it is at the intersection of these that meaning emerges for the artist. Touch plays a myriad of roles in Ray's practice, from informing and nuancing the conditions of making to mediating the encounter with his work. His reflections on process reveal how haptic modes of ideation feature deeply in his artistic approach, and he is consistently alert to his materials' tactile valences. Furthermore, manifesting as points of contact as well as pointed absences, touch in Ray's sculptures directs space at the same time as it describes subject matter and its narrative limits.

Ray most directly calls out a tactile aspect in what he refers to as his handheld pieces: *Chicken* (2007; pl. 2), *Handheld bird* (2006; pl. 3), and *Hand holding egg* (2007; pl. 4). The three intimately scaled sculptures are closely linked in concept and material articulation. *Handheld bird* was initially a study for *Chicken*; Ray later decided to finish it as a complete work on the suggestion of scholar Michael Fried.[1] *Hand holding egg* also emerged tangentially, from a fragment of a larger unrealized sculpture based on his goddaughter holding an egg, made around the time he was conducting research for *Chicken*.[2]

The composition of *Hand holding egg*—a lightweight and fragile cast of a child's hand cupping an eggshell with an unevenly cracked opening—suggests potential and growth, but also evacuation. It becomes a trace object, which the artist likens to "an old bleached bone in the desert," adding, "the egg is empty and the beast is long gone."[3] The choice of porcelain, a dermal medium that is both delicate and strong and traditionally

Fig. 19. Charles Ray. *Table*, 1990 (detail of pl. 8)

used for vessels, here holds air and light. Hand and egg merge where their edges meet, creating one continuous, connected hollow and articulating an internal space that allows light to shine through the break in the egg's shell and touch the inner surface of the child's hand—like a periscope. (Ray's approach here also harks back to an earlier work, *Table* [1990; fig. 19], where the bases of pitchers, jars, and glasses—all themselves objects to be grasped—are fused with the surface of the table on which they rest, creating forms through which the eye can travel and space can flow.)

As indicated by its title, *Handheld bird* is the only one of the three sculptures that is explicitly intended to be held as well as seen, thus twinning two modes of sensory perception (fig. 20). The painted steel fetal form is connected to a long history of sculptures that are meant to be grasped by the viewer, from Renaissance bronzes to Japanese netsuke to Bauhaus "hand sculptures."[4] Ray has remarked that the viewer's hand is a base for the work, though it is not static or neutral—it can cradle and gently turn the piece.[5] This movement allows for the simultaneous optical and tangible traversal of the sculpture's smooth surface, with its rounded forms and shallow recesses. It also enables a sense of the object's surprising weightiness and the perception of gradual changes in its temperature as the metal responds to the warmth of the holder's touch. Yet the titular bird is no incipient being, no recent hatchling—instead, its folded joints, tubular shanks, and barely etched beak are presented as a precise composite of bulges and crevices. The sense of the avian form thus comes into focus obliquely, incidentally, and through the subtle interplay of visual and haptic cues—it is felt even as it fades, sharpening and softening at the same time.

Chicken, the smallest of the three works, compresses and fuses the spatial and tactile conditions of the two others. The fetal form was precisely modeled in clay, with every detail from ribbed claw to feathery appendage articulated, and then fired in porcelain. This internal structure was eventually encased in a stainless-steel shell, and the bird's still-forming body, with a single immature talon and tightly squashed folded wing, can only partially be seen through a crisp-edged round cutout. The emphatic, impossible circularity of the hole indicates that it is not a natural rupture of the encasement.[6] Recalling (but also departing from) the kind of opening seen in *Hand holding egg*, the hole in *Chicken* makes vision possible while also circumscribing it.[7] Equally, it may present as an orifice with all the possibilities of fleshly, sensual engagement of an opening in the body. Or perhaps—with Henry Moore and Barbara Hepworth (fig. 21) in mind—the circular puncture that invites optical and spatial passage (or even the physical exploration of its inner form) may be Ray's take on what he has described as his modernist forebears' "sculptures with holes."[8]

In discussing the work, Ray notes, "*Chicken* pits two forces against each other. The curiosity of the viewer is met by

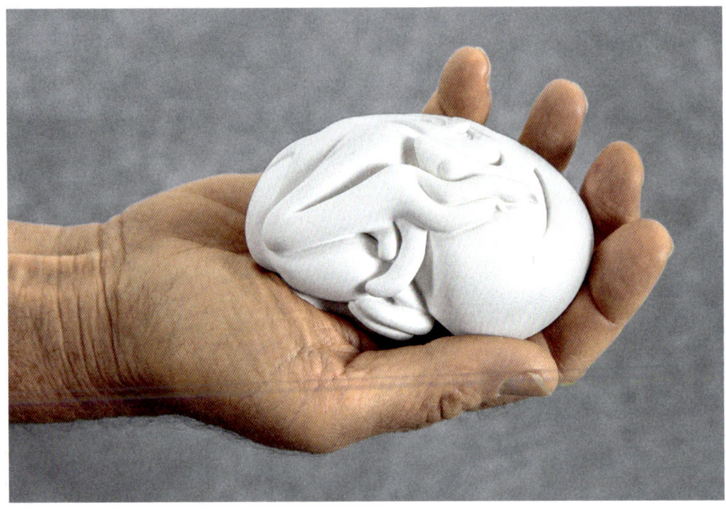

Fig. 20. *Handheld bird* (pl. 3) in Ray's hand

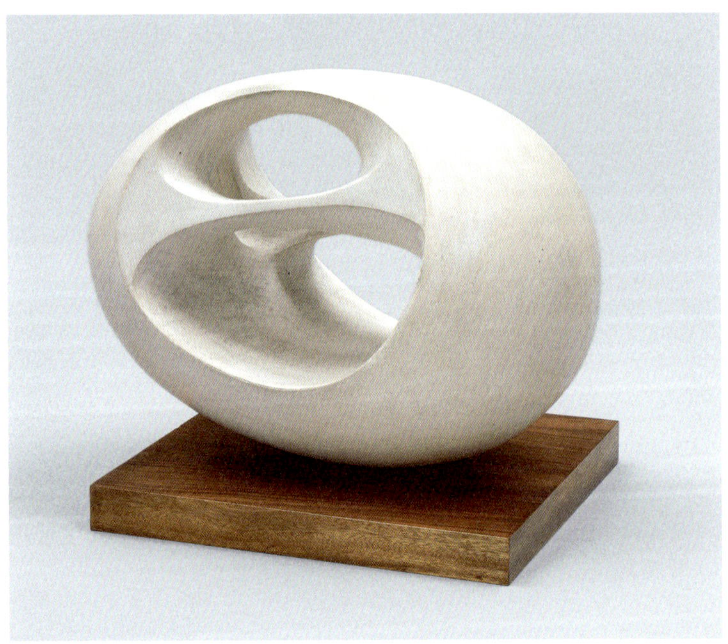

Fig. 21. Barbara Hepworth (British, 1903–1975). *Oval Sculpture (No. 2)*, 1943, cast 1958. Plaster on wood base, 12⅞ × 15¾ × 11⅞ in. (32.8 × 40 × 30 cm). Tate, London, Presented by the artist 1967 (T00953)

the energy of the chicken birthing out."[9] To have "met" in this context suggests a range of possible interactions and other dual forces at work, from formal counterforce and balance to material encounter and contact. With its prominent oculus, the work initially invites and even privileges visual engagement, but it simultaneously relies on the eye's extra-optical readings of its haptic valences.[10] Although the points of contact are not visible, for Ray the hole is critical for what he understands as the sculpture's armature—a key term that describes his approach to the structural and philosophical articulation of form in space—for it is through that mathematically precise hole, and within the shell that *holds* the bird and the space around it, that the space inside and outside the work are linked.[11]

These points of contact between space and form are crucial to Ray's conception of sculpture. He has noted this for a range of works, from *Family romance* (1993; pl. 14)—"you can find the meaning of this sculpture where the hands come together"[12]—to *The new Beetle* (2006; fig. 22), which unfurls around "the juncture between the hand and the car."[13] Such contact nodes also connect Ray's practice to that of Anthony Caro, especially the latter's creation of sculptural forms through the precise fusing of constituent elements. The implied tactility that is part of some of Caro's abstract sculptures—the incorporation of a door handle and other manual tools in his Table Pieces (fig. 23), for instance, which scales them to the human hand and relates them to the body—is something that Ray is alive to as well. At the same time, however, the irreducibility of Caro's pieces to the meaning of their constitutive parts enables Ray to reaffirm that his own sculpture, including the works that feature bodies, is invested in abstraction above all else.[14]

Nevertheless, the significance of points of contact between figures and objects inevitably animates a reading of Ray's sculpture through narrative and subject matter (much as the artist himself eschews such an approach). In parsing the role of touch in these instances, certain themes and through lines of interest become evident. A fascination with the formative conditions of childhood (and the memory of it), for example, recurs across many sculptures in which touch can function mnemonically.[15] These include the numerous instances of children holding their playthings—the car, the sword (fig. 24), the frog (pl. 9), the reins of a pet pony (*Girl on pony*, 2015), and even the empty eggshell. At other times, the objects meant to be held, to be moved in space—the toy tractor (*Father figure*, 2007), the broken action figure's foot (fig. 25)—in turn become the basis for further sculptures, solitary monuments to a way of haptically engaging with, molding, and understanding the world.

Yet just as often there are instances of bodies and hands that are emphatically *not* touching, *not* grasping, *not* holding, and for Ray it is in this articulation of the interstices of material forms that sculpture emerges. Notably, the artist often employs tactile verbs when describing modes of spatial displacement that are

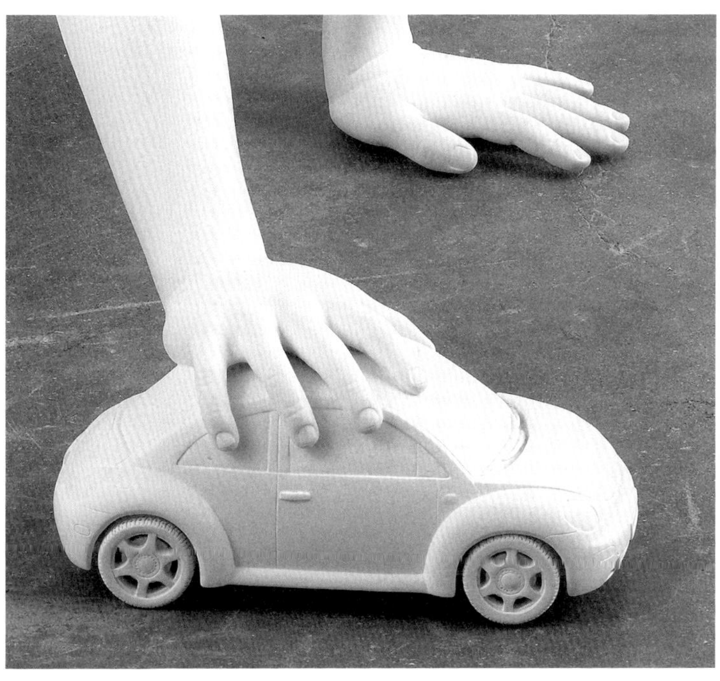

Fig. 22. Charles Ray. *The new Beetle*, 2006. Painted stainless steel, 21 × 34½ × 28½ in. (53 × 88 × 72 cm). Glenstone Museum, Potomac, Md.

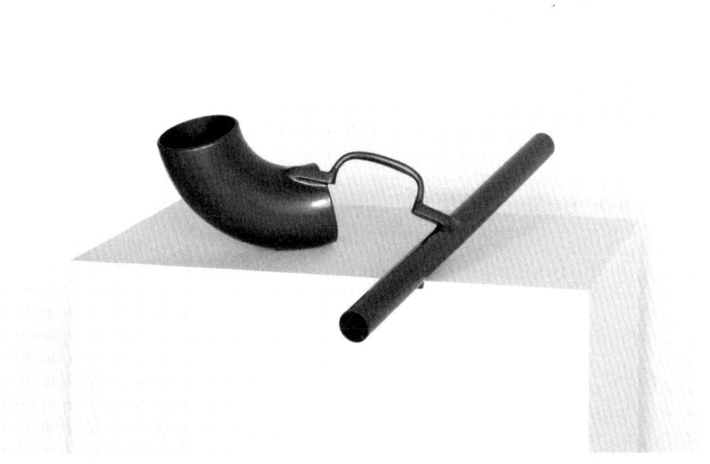

Fig. 23. Anthony Caro (British, 1924–2013). *Table Piece XXII*, 1967. Painted steel, 10 × 31½ × 27 in. (25.4 × 80 × 68.6 cm). Caro Family Collection

key to his process: "I see sculpture as using space, bending it, modeling it, manipulating it."[16] He is drawn to lessons from the history of Western sculpture, observing once that "the abstract notion of an intrinsic space is what allows me to look at both ancient and contemporary sculpture as working on the same problem."[17] This careful orchestration of the space between and within figures is where the meaning of sculpture arises for Ray (whatever additional signification it may present as well). The visual entanglement but careful avoidance of actual contact between bodily forms in a work like *Oh! Charley, Charley, Charley . . .* (1992; fig. 11) has been compared to the relationship between the six figures that share a plinth in Auguste Rodin's *The Burghers of Calais* (1889).[18] Ray himself considers Rodin's use of space between the not-touching figures in *Burghers* as crucial to its sculptural achievement.[19]

Such space is also present in Ray's recent works featuring paired figures. Based on characters drawn from Mark Twain's *Adventures of Huckleberry Finn*, the bodies in *Huck and Jim* (2014; pl. 7) and *Sarah Williams* (2021; pl. 18) are simultaneously separated and bound by the space between them. These instances of barely but not quite touching take on further meaning—a suspension of intimacy (fig. 46). Do the acts of *not* holding here involve *with*holding?[20] In *Huck and Jim*, the figure of the young boy bends and cups his hands *as if* he were holding something. Inspired by an exchange between the characters in the book, Ray originally rendered Huck in the act of scooping up frog spawn, but he eventually removed this element.[21] While editing the surface of a sculpture to sharpen or smooth out details is not uncommon in the artist's process, the element's excision here signals not just a further shift away from narrative adherence but also a tangible disappearance, underscoring Ray's wariness of attaching subjective meaning to his work, which may always slip through one's fingers. This haptic displacement can also be understood as a counterpoint to the kinds of removal present in sculptures like *Hand holding egg* or *Handheld bird*. While in the former the hollowed-out interior creates a structure through which space can flow, in the latter it is the hand, with its implied presence indicated by the title, that is (always) missing.[22]

Similar absences or deletions are also conspicuous in *Horse and rider* (2014; fig. 13) and *Shoe tie* (2012; fig. 26), both modeled on Ray himself. *Horse and rider* nods to a range of equestrian sculptural precedents, but perhaps most immediately for the Los Angeles–based artist, to a locally recognizable landmark—the sculpture of the Hollywood legend John Wayne made by Harry Jackson (1984; fig. 27). Unlike the figure of Wayne, who sits confidently astride a steed stepping forward in response to the rider, Ray's figure is slouched on an obdurate horse, raising his hand somewhat limply, as if to clasp what are, in fact, missing reins. As with the frog spawn, the sense of the absent form creates the space to consider the sculpture beyond its narrative—a deferment of fixed meaning.

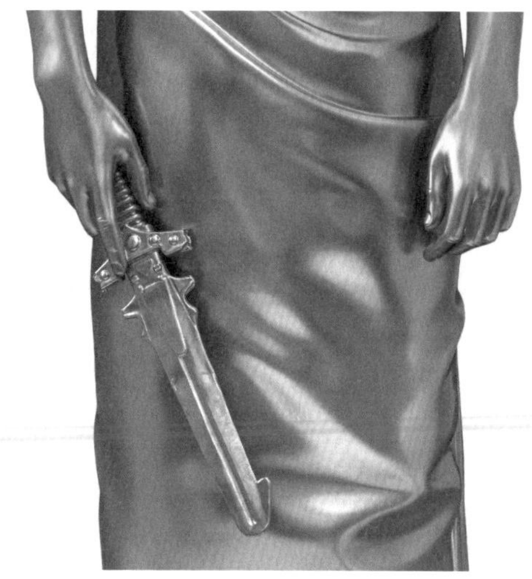

Fig. 24. Charles Ray. *School play*, 2014 (detail). Stainless steel, 76 × 23 × 15½ in. (193 × 59 × 40 cm). Collection Glenn and Amanda Fuhrman NY, Courtesy the FLAG Art Foundation

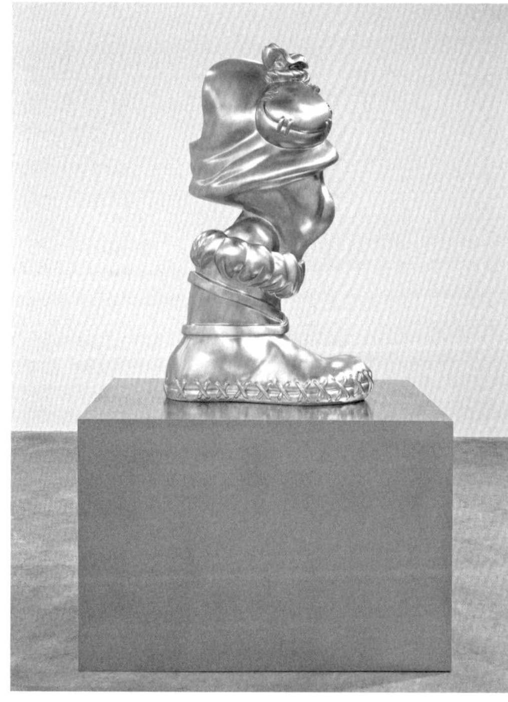

Fig. 25. Charles Ray. *Future fragment on a solid base*, 2011. Aluminum, 82¾ × 48 × 36 in. (210.2 × 122 × 91.4 cm). Collection Glenn and Amanda Fuhrman NY, Courtesy the FLAG Art Foundation

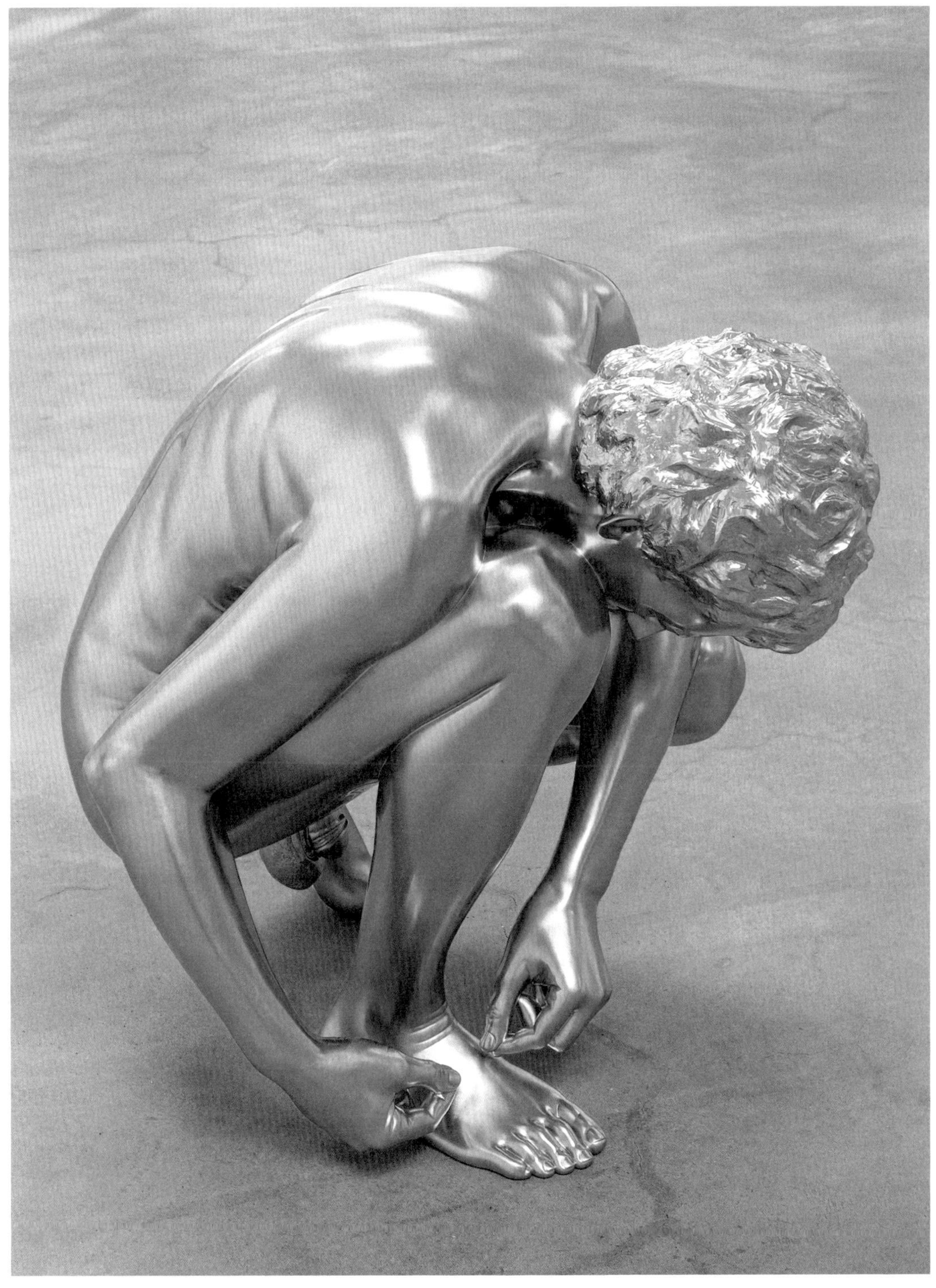

Fig. 26. Charles Ray. *Shoe tie*, 2012. Stainless steel, 28⅞ × 29¼ × 23½ in. (73.3 × 74.3 × 59.7 cm). Collection of James and Dana Tananbaum

Ray described the genesis of *Shoe tie*, a stainless-steel sculpture of a naked figure crouching to tie a shoe that isn't there, in one of his routine predawn hikes: "One morning, while retying my shoe on the trail in the dark, I speculated that if a ghost were to tie his shoe he wouldn't need to have a shoe. I don't believe in ghosts, but the logic of the thought stayed with me. Eventually I saw this gesture as a sculpture."[23] In this description, Ray's aesthetics of touch, of haptically intuiting sculptural potential *in the dark*, at a time of visual abeyance, seem to connect with the eighteenth-century German philosopher Johann Gottfried Herder's ideas challenging the precedence accorded to vision in the understanding of the plastic arts. Herder affirmed that the approach to sculpture was extra-optical, necessarily exceeding vision and a single viewpoint, and opened up the space for the role of touch in arriving at and aesthetically appreciating sculptural form.[24]

With their absent reins and shoes, the figures in both *Horse and rider* and *Shoe tie* have been described as pantomiming.[25] Yet for Ray, the simple conjunction of a hand gesture and a missing prop does not alone constitute the conditions for miming (as pantomiming is better understood in this context). Indeed, such comparisons distract from Ray's interest in the art of miming and its potential for conveying corporeal presence in space, and by extension in miming's relationship to his own practice. An admirer of the great French mime Etienne Decroux, Ray finds resonance in the former's statement that "all drama is the drama of gravity."[26] So it is unsurprising that the role of gravity, and of suspension in particular, was of fundamental importance when Ray embarked upon *Mime* (2014; pl. 17), a sculpture of a figure lying on a cot, its eyes closed.

Arriving at the structure of *Mime*, a work that exists at the threshold of miming and sleeping, meant understanding the kinesthesia of those two (pre)conditions. In terms of the former, as Ray succinctly put it, "The armature of miming is suspension," both in its gravitational and ontological senses.[27] The model for the sculpture, professional mime Lorin Eric Salm, recalled, "He wanted me to create a pose of sleeping and yet to be suspended in my position of sleeping. . . . I may have lifted certain parts of myself off the cot, but I wasn't necessarily conscious of which parts actually separated themselves from the cot. It may have just happened that way, or for all I know that could have been a decision Charley made somewhere in the process *to create space where there wasn't one*. I honestly don't know."[28] The recumbent figure in *Mime* achieves a state of suspension by simultaneously giving in to and resisting gravity, apparent in a host of details. He sinks into the cot, creating bulges on its underside, and at the same time his limbs suggest an uplift—from the lightly resting, partially raised knee, elbow, and hand on his left side, to the perplexingly perpendicular foot and forearm held aloft on his right. The dynamics of space are described by these multiple points of contact—of parts touching and not touching.

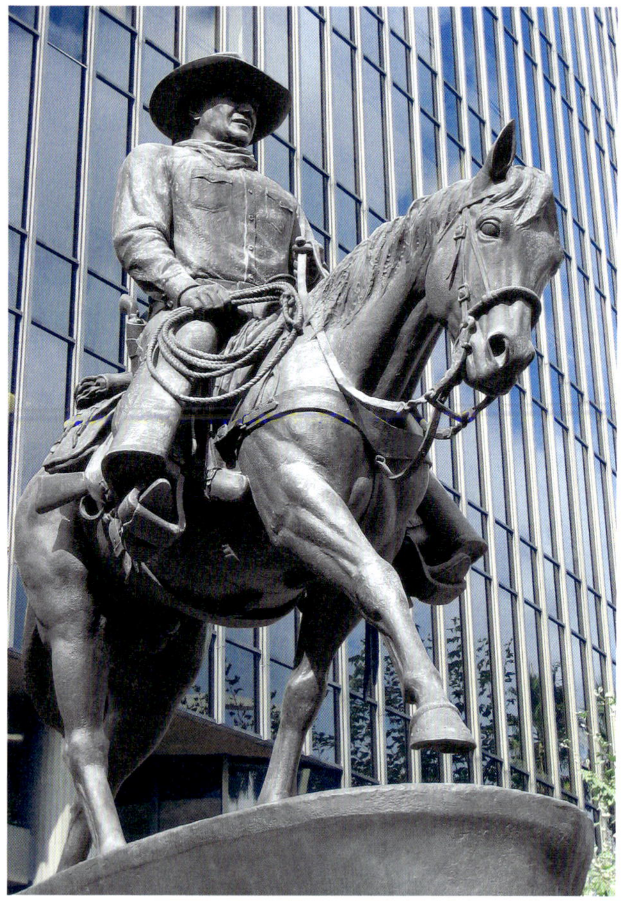

Fig. 27. Harry Jackson (American, 1924–2011). *John Wayne*, 1984. Bronze. Wilshire Boulevard, Los Angeles

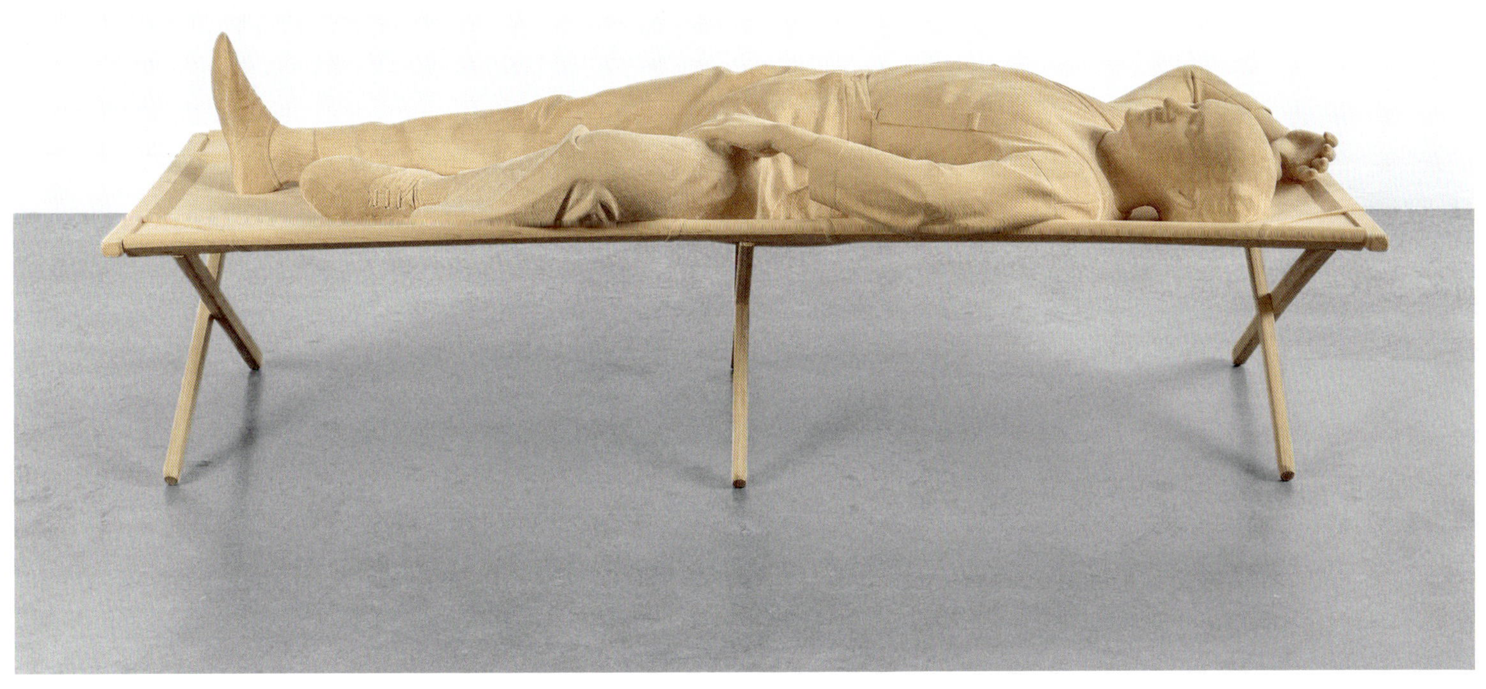

Fig. 28. Charles Ray. *Mime*, 2015. Cypress, 22 × 79 × 26 in. (55.9 × 200.7 × 66 cm). Glenstone Museum, Potomac, Md.

Insofar as the figure is shown sleeping (or pretending to sleep), the suspension of visual perception and by extension consciousness, a condition of darkness or even temporary blindness, is also implicit in *Mime*.[29] (These conditions link the sculpture to the genesis of *Shoe tie* as well.) It is thus not simply the closure of eyes but rather "the total kinesthetics of the sculpture that links to sleep or wakefulness" that is evident in the figure's holding and releasing of tension at the same time.[30] With his innate potential for bodily movement, gesture, and touch, the figure of the mime, especially presented as sleeping, underscores the importance of other modes of sensorial engagement in the creation and understanding of the sculpture.

The making of *Mime* offers yet another way of considering how tactility operates in Ray's practice: through his approach to materials. Using the same pattern, the artist simultaneously produced cypress wood (fig. 28) and aluminum iterations, which he understands not as merely two different versions of the same sculpture, but as separate sculptures altogether. Their material differences necessitated a distinct arrival at form. In the case of the former, master wood-carver Yuboku Mukoyoshi and his workshop in Osaka chiseled laminated timbers of Japanese cypress (hinoki). For the aluminum sculpture, robotic hands made the various parts that would eventually be mechanically fastened together, with seams still visible, to form the finished work. Both were made through the subtractive processes of carving and machining, with tools—ranging from manually wielded chisels to digitally deployed instruments—serving as extensions of the human hand to excise matter. These shared principles aside, Ray is also alive to the transformations that arise from different conditions of creation, which may also explain why he sees the works as discrete. In discussing the wood *Mime*, Ray acknowledged the kinship between material and conceptual processes: "Carving, too, can be a kind of miming. . . . Both crafts carve so close to the surface of their topology. A slip of the carver's hand is a stumble in a mime's performance. . . . I broke the boundary . . . by superimposing the craft of my subject upon the craft of making. This exchange of crafts is the *meaning* of the work."[31]

In this intertwining of making and material toward the production of meaning, with no element, no detail too minor for consideration, Ray draws upon lessons learned from his deep study of archaic sculpture. He describes the haptic as formational in the creation of ancient kouros figures (fig. 29), observing that the process of gradually using successively smaller and finer punches eventually brought about "a democracy of parts because you have to build the whole thing all the way around in the third dimension. And that comes not just from its materiality but also from its making, which is so directly connected to its material."[32] In other words, through its making, the potentiality of material, of matter, is made active, i.e., it is in its matter*ing* that the object is set in motion through time by the (extended) hand of the sculptor, suspending or deferring fixed meaning,

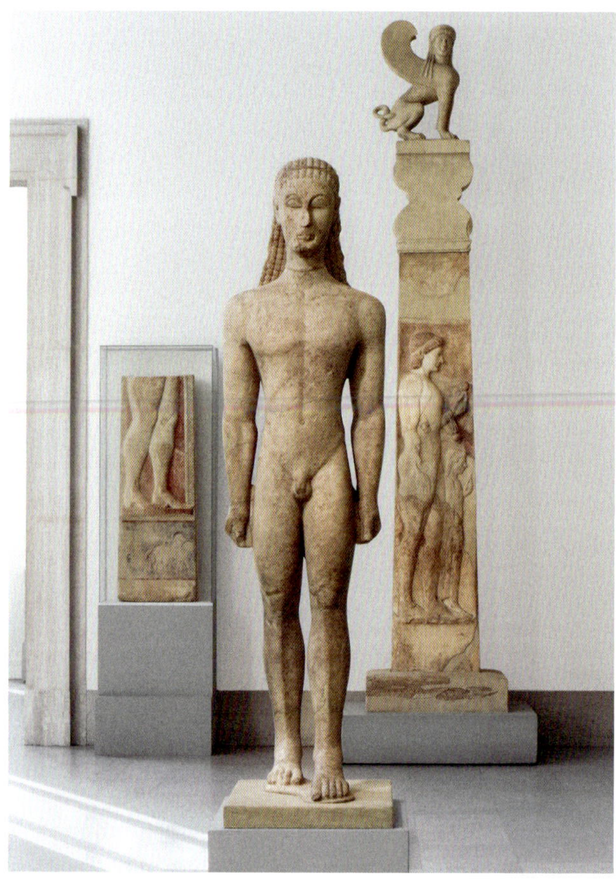

Fig. 29. Statue of a kouros (youth). Greek, Attic, ca. 590–580 B.C. Marble, 76⅝ × 20$\frac{5}{16}$ × 24⅞ in. (194.6 × 51.6 × 63.2 cm). The Metropolitan Museum of Art, New York, Fletcher Fund, 1932 (32.11.1)

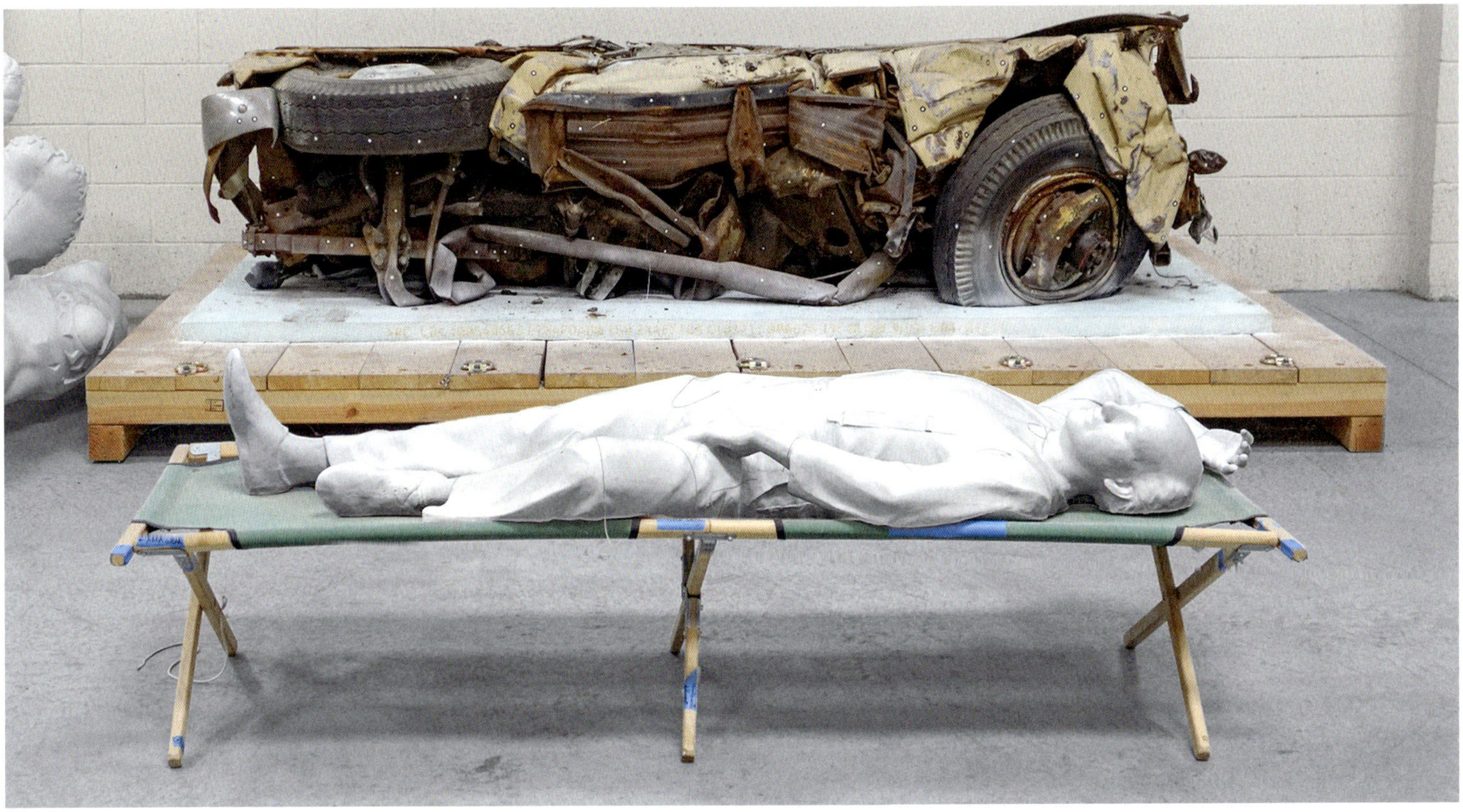

Fig. 30. Plaster pattern of *Mime* (pl. 17) on an army cot in front of Ray's baled Chevy pickup truck in his studio, 2013

which lies perennially on a horizon that may be seen but not be fully grasped.

In a photograph from Ray's studio, the pattern of the human model that formed the basis of the *Mime* sculptures is placed on a real camp bed in front of the artist's mechanically crushed Chevy pickup truck—itself the basis for another sculpture (fig. 30). This pairing simultaneously gestures toward implied futurities of the finished works and shared premises in sculptural conception—the latter indicating an understanding of carving as a tangibly directed manipulation of space through the displacement of material.[33] The role of touch thus emerges subtly, even obliquely, but pervasively, as informing the formal and conceptual conditions that intertwine in Ray's processual arrival at sculptural form. During a recent conversation, Ray shared a photograph of another sculpture in progress, showing a hand grasping a beer can. As with *Handheld bird* or even with the hand of *Mime* (fig. 31), this sample may one day be a finished work itself, but for now it remains brimming with sculptural potential.[34] "Have you ever squeezed the space out of an empty can? Where does the space go? This simple action is the beginning of my sculpture."[35]

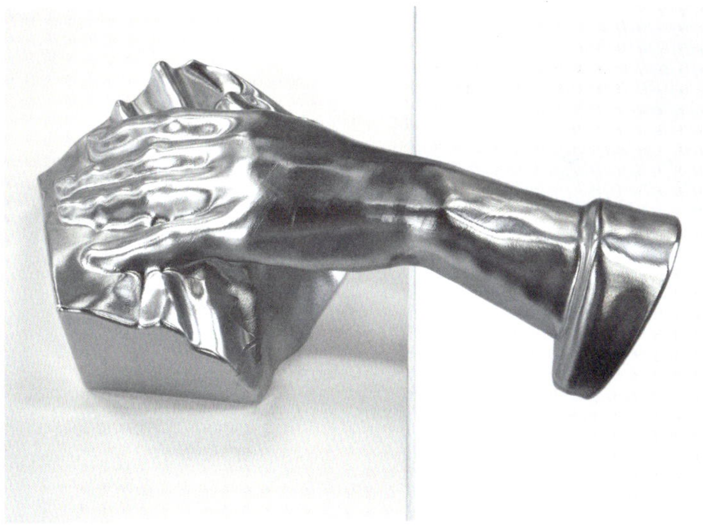

Fig. 31. Charles Ray. *Study for a sleeping mime*, 2012. Aluminum, 4¼ × 12½ × 7 in. (10.8 × 31.8 × 17.8 cm). H. Gael Neeson Collection

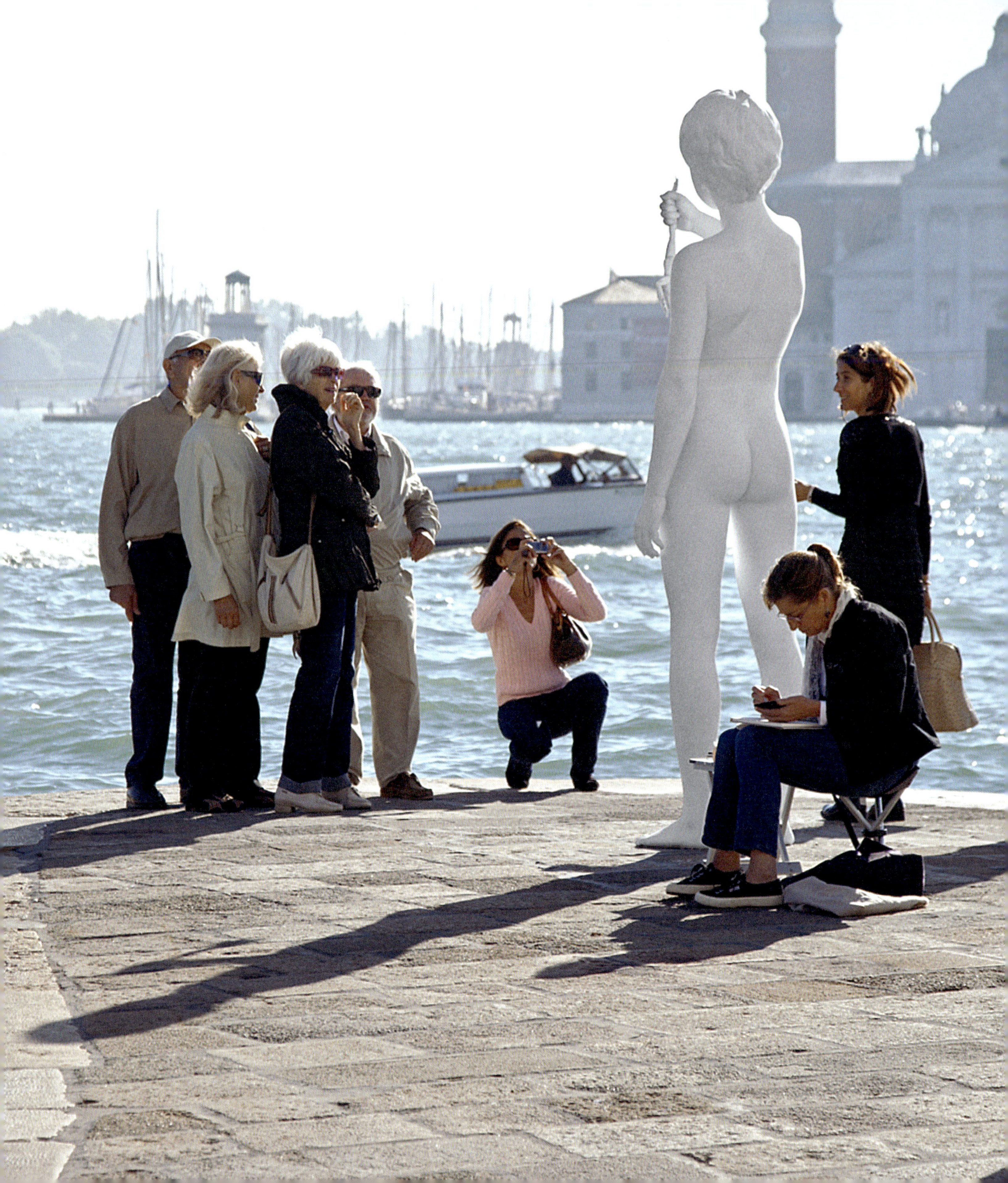

Sculpture in a Cultural Square
Charles Ray in Conversation with Hal Foster

Hal Foster
How did you and the curator, Kelly Baum, decide on which pieces to include in the show?

Charles Ray
Kelly wanted to include work from every decade: starting from the 1970s, when I was young, the ’80s, ’90s, and into this century. Kelly had a wish list; I added to it. She took away from it, and I did too.

Do you see these pieces as representative of each decade? Are they exemplary? “Prime objects”?

I don’t believe in prime objects per se. There are more popular works and less popular, but that changes. And at different times and in different ways I have a different relationship to the work. The selection was also complicated by what was available. Before the pandemic my shows at the Centre Pompidou and Bourse de Commerce and at The Met were a year apart. Now they’re a month apart, so work in Paris can’t be shared with The Met and vice versa.

There are two big galleries (fig. 33). How did you decide on the ensembles of pieces? The arrangement isn’t chronological.

Initially I had a room downstairs off the Greek and Roman galleries. It connects two areas of the museum, and Kelly and her department chair, Sheena Wagstaff, liked that conceptually. We were going to extend the show throughout the whole museum. Sometimes I was for this and sometimes I was against it. Eventually we moved the show upstairs into its current location.

So why these particular pieces in these particular groupings?

Kelly saw *Huck and Jim* (2014; pl. 7) and *Sarah Williams* (2021; pl. 18) as anchors to the show. That desire positioned *Huck and Jim* in the first room and *Sarah Williams* in the second. The other works, while orbiting these two sculptures, were positioned according to a visual poetics. There wasn’t a hard conceptual blueprint or thesis. I did want to have *No* (1992; pl. 1) at the entrance. It’s an older work, a color photograph of a sculpture of me. I saw it as a didactic to the exhibition. You have to pass through that sculptural photograph to enter the show. When I made it, I was thinking about the impossibility of expression. I was a young artist trying to do a self-portrait, but the genre was in the way. Actually photography itself was in the way. I didn’t take the picture—I brought the sculpture to a photo studio that did weddings and head shots and I told them, “Just do a standard portrait of this.” They chose the blue background curtain. I look like an employee of the month!

Fig. 32. *Boy with frog* (pl. 9) installed at Punta della Dogana, Venice, 2011

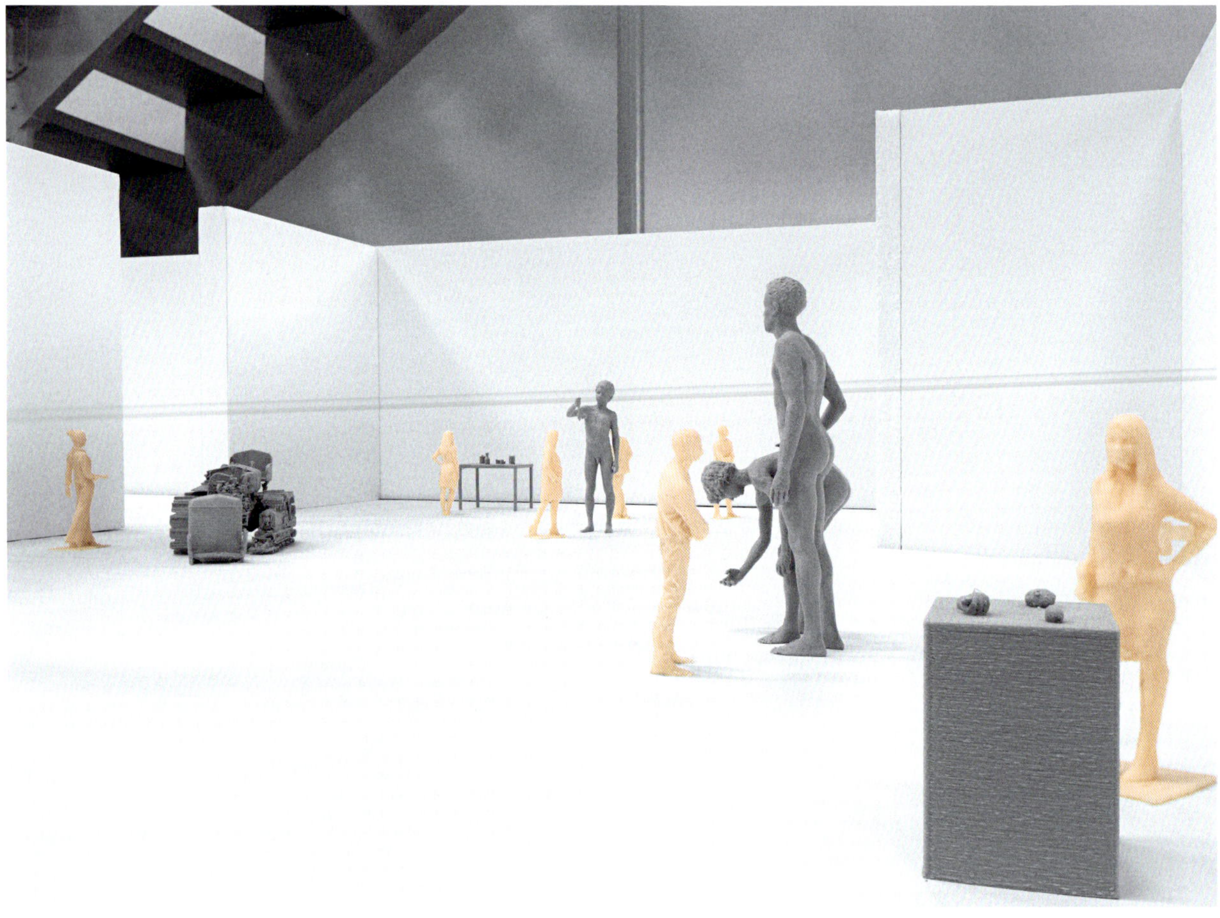

Fig. 33. Exhibition model for *Charles Ray: Figure Ground* in the artist's studio, with planned installation in progress

***No* also serves to locate you in our generation, concerned as it was with the mediation of images and a suspicion about self-expression.**

Yes, that's true, but at the same time looking at *No* is exactly what it feels like to be me. The stiffness is a proper expression, not a mediated one, for me.

The works in the first room circle around a certain theme, one of beginnings. There are the three egg pieces, and *Huck and Jim* reprises a moment in Mark Twain's *Adventures of Huckleberry Finn* when they debate the origin of the stars. *Tractor* (2005; pl. 6) stems from a memory of an object you used to play on as a little boy. I know you're resistant to themes, but is there a concern with origin stories here?

It's not the themes themselves I'm resistant to; I'm resistant to focusing on themes. Themes are like forms—meaning develops from how they are shaped. When you turn the corner from *No*, you see the three small sculptures. What about them? Birth, death. *Handheld bird* (2006; pl. 3) and *Hand holding egg* (2007; pl. 4) were studies for *Chicken* (2007; pl. 2). In *Chicken* everything centered on making the hole in the egg. The chick is complete inside the egg, but I think the sculpture dissolves in and around the hole. The mathematical definition of a hole is an object that can't be shrunk to a point. Originally the hole was sculpted as a natural-looking break in the egg, but the sculpture was static. It wouldn't dissolve because the break was an image and had a stability that was uninteresting sculpturally. I replaced the break with a portal, a round hole. It's a sculptural element, in a dynamic relationship to both the viewer and the chicken; the hole is the egg, and the sculpture becomes abstract in its dynamic. Those pieces are almost like Möbius strips in their relation to abstraction—they turn and dissolve when you pass through the hole. *Handheld bird* incorporates the viewer as a structural element. Your hand is a base, and you feel the detail as you see it (fig. 20).

Right away it also introduces the tactility of your sculpture and the relation of sculpture at large to the hand and the body. Next to it is *Huck and Jim*, which is keyed by two gestures above all—Jim with his protective hand over the bending Huck (fig. 46), Huck with his hand scooping frog spawn from the river.

Originally the Whitney Museum, which commissioned the sculpture, wanted a fountain. I was thinking the water would come out of Huck's hand and flow into a pond with eggs. I actually sculpted eggs and everything, but then realized it was a stronger fountain without water. There are two different temporal gestures in the sculpture—one past, one present, one from adolescence, one from adulthood. Like the hole in the egg, they fall through in a strange way.

What do you mean, "they fall through"?

I mean image collapses into structure, or vice versa. When I envisioned *Huck and Jim*, I saw it as one beast, orchestrated like a forest of limbs. In the novel, too, Huck and Jim are a compound object. They're one being really. There's an Anthony Caro tabletop sculpture with a straight pipe that extends beyond the edge of its base, a larger diameter elbow pipe, and a door handle that connects the two (fig. 23). It's a beautiful sculpture in part because the handle brings tactility right into it—you want to reach, grab, and hold it. I mentioned this to the art historian Michael Fried once, and he said, "Don't think about it that way. The handle is just a spacer between two abstract elements." Whether he's right or not, it flipped how I was thinking about the sculpture. When we talked about *Huck and Jim*, Kelly focused on the space between Jim's hand and Huck's back—that emptiness defines the sculpture. In fact she wanted to call the show *The Space Between*. I thought back to that conversation with Fried, and I saw that this space has no meaning. Like Caro's handle, it could be seen as a spacer connecting two sculptural elements. It's holding *Huck and Jim* together. Of course, on the topical level of the sculpture, it's a charged space. It unifies two males of different ages and different races, but my interest, like the hole in the egg, is in how the structure of this powerful narrative turns abstract. It's a sculptural interest.

The space between is often crucial in your sculpture. It's rarely null. It's also very charged in *Boy with frog* (2009; pl. 9).

When I made *Boy with frog*, I had been thinking about Giacometti and his use of armature (fig. 34). I realized that the armature of *Boy with frog* is the trajectory of his gaze—from his eyes to the frog. The whole sculpture is built around that relationship. Sure, originally

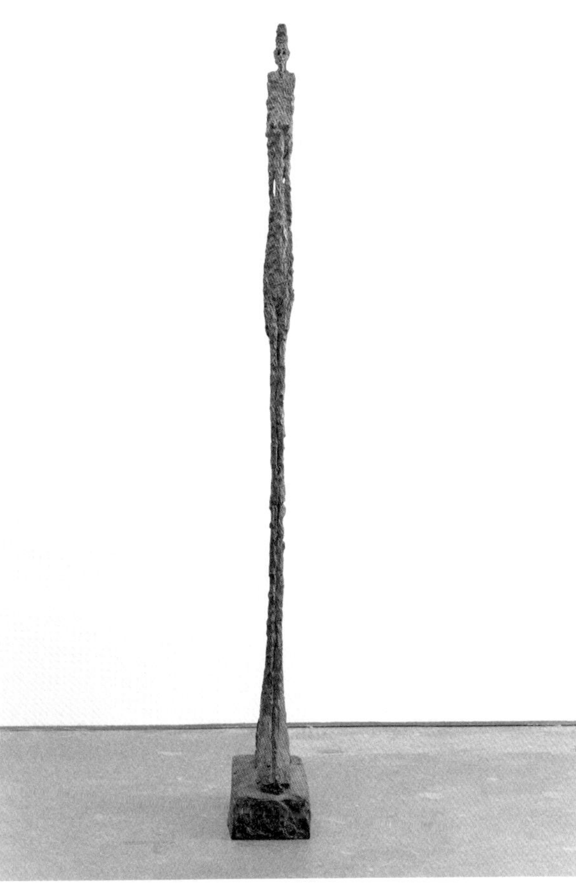

Fig. 34. Alberto Giacometti (Swiss, 1901–1966). *Standing Woman*, 1948, cast 1949. Painted bronze, 65⅜ × 6½ × 13½ in. (166 × 16.5 × 34.2 cm). The Museum of Modern Art, New York, James Thrall Soby Bequest (1222.1979)

clay was put on a steel armature, but that gaze is really the wire that the sculpture is built around in the mind.

***Boy with frog* speaks to another origin—when one first confronts the otherness of the world. As with *Tractor*, I wonder whether there's an origin story here for you as a sculptor—that sculpture begins in curiosity as well as in play, in what it is to find a thing, really see it, take it apart, put it back together, and so make another object, another space in the process.**

Making *Tractor* was a struggle; I had to change foundries in the middle of it. There's an interior to the sculpture—for me it's a transparent object. The engine, the crankcase, all the gears are within it. Originally there were sculpted flowers, too, and the tractor sat in dirt. I was interested in the space of the tractor, in its internal space as well. I was having so much trouble making it. It was so far outside of me. In contrast, *Chicken* was something really close to me. As with *Tractor*, I wanted you to see into it. Initially the egg was going to be marble. I was thinking, "Wouldn't it be beautiful to be able to carve a chicken? How far into the structure could you look?" The chicken is birthing out while you are looking in. Two energies meet on the surface of the egg, coming in and going out—a chicken coming out and a viewer looking in. When I finished the sculpture, I could hold it in my hand.

You've called *Tractor* "a philosophical object." Along with tactility, and maybe in opposition to it, that suggests transparency. "Philosophical object" almost has a Platonic intonation. That calls up *Table* (1990; pl. 8). What's the relationship of that piece to the others in the first room?

Space flows through it. The world implodes in it. There's no exterior. That's somewhat similar to the tractor. The tractor began as a jungle gym. I remember, when I was little, being pushed off a jungle gym and hitting every bar on the way down. I was thinking of the jungle gym, the playground, as our first civic space. It's where we start to socialize, where we deal with bullies, meet friends, share, climb together. I was trying to sculpt that civic space, but I kept running into genre problems. No matter what I did it looked like a bad silhouette. I tried to make it in plaster, to sculpt weeds around it. Everything was pictorial. I wanted to break it out of that, and let it tumble into its own plaza, and bring that civic place into present space. Then I remembered a tractor I played on as a kid. I

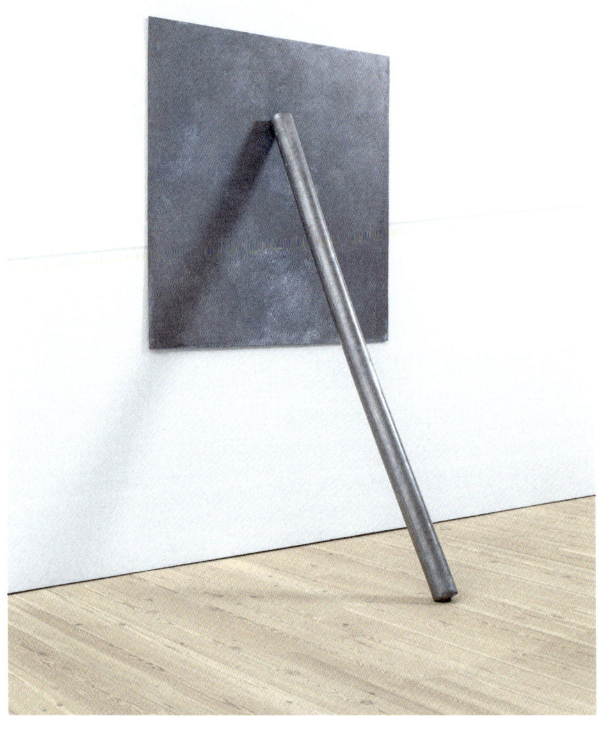

Fig. 35. Richard Serra (American, born 1938). *Prop*, 1968, refabricated 2007. Lead antimony, steel, 89½ × 60 × 54 in. (227.3 × 152.4 × 137.2 cm). Whitney Museum of American Art, New York, Purchase, with funds from the Howard and Jean Lipman Foundation, Inc. (69.20a–b)

tried to sculpt it from memory, from scratch, but that was impossible. A friend of mine said, "I know about a tractor out in the valley that somebody drove into a backyard where it blew a rod. People tried to cut it apart, and kids played on it. It's been there for fifty years." I went to see it—the tractor was as decayed as the neighborhood had become. Originally it looked like the American Dream; now it was a rough, tough place. I had the tractor pulled out, lifted onto a flatbed, and dragged back to my studio. I took it all apart and started playing with it and thinking about it. My idea shifted from the playground as a civic space to sculpture as a temporal object. I wanted people to be able to spend time with it. At first it looks like an old tractor that's been sandblasted—it's that shiny. When you get closer, it looks like I used molds to make it. Then you realize that every bolt is different and every part is handmade, that not just one person made it. Maybe fifteen different hands run through the tractor—some slack, some anal, some poetic. With even more time you realize that it's a complete, topological object, that it has an interior as well. I want you to be able to see into it without literally seeing into it. At one point there was a portal that you could open. I finally told the fabricator, "OK, now it's time to weld this portal shut." He goes, "What do you mean? No one will ever be able to see in it." And I said, "If we leave it open, that's all people will do. The sculpture will be over." I see it as a tractor in heaven.

That suggests that it's removed from our bodies too. Your earliest works in the show—the two plank pieces—foreground your body almost excessively. You become your own prop piece. What has happened to your bodily engagement with your sculpture over time?

There's a relationship to Richard Serra's prop pieces (fig. 35) in *Plank piece I and II* (1973; pl. 10), but I also see a connection to Caro. Lucy Lippard's "dematerialization of the art object" was interesting to me at that time in my life too. I'm not denying the humor, but it wasn't primary. It's not like I started out doing body art and then the body disappeared (fig. 36). My body enters the later works as well, it's just that you don't see it in the same way. Maybe my presence is also felt in the orchestration of the installations.

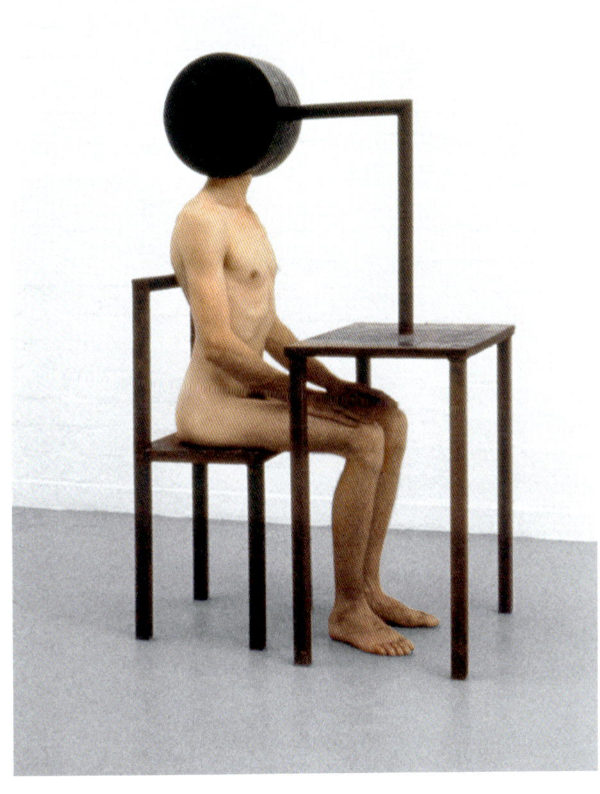

Fig. 36. Charles Ray. *The examination*, 1984. Painted steel, human body, 36 × 24 × 54 in. (91 × 61 × 137 cm)

Elsewhere you've talked about installation as a "geometry of viewing," and that, of course, involves our bodies as well as yours.

With the plank pieces my body was just there. I had a plank in the studio, and I saw my body literally enter it. Not as a conceptual gesture—it's just about my body, a plank, a wall, and the relationship between the three. Questions like "How long could you stay there?" bothered me. I was looking at it very analytically, while other people were looking at it like a car accident. "Oh, that must have hurt!" Over the years, my body has come and gone literally, but it's always there in some way. I don't see sculpture as a "practice"—I'm almost allergic to that word. My dentist has a practice; I have a behavior. For me the activity of making sculpture is a mental and physical behavior. At a certain point, I allowed my body not to enter the work, but it's still always there: looking, standing, moving, holding. It's there, too, in the gestures in the work, as in *The new Beetle* (2006; fig. 37) and *Boy with frog*. Especially with *The new Beetle*, I felt my way into it. I was sitting up and then I started sprawling out, and I wanted the piece to tail off into reality like that.

Figuration for you includes embodiment; in some ways it *is* embodiment. And it involves movement too.

We are always moving. Even when you're standing still, the space you take up is the space I would have to sculpt to get you to feel like you. If you take that and extend it in time, you have what I mean by "figuration." I see figures as manifolds—manifolds in which events occur. It's really hard to separate us from the world, from our culture. It's really hard to separate them from us, from our projections. It's one and the

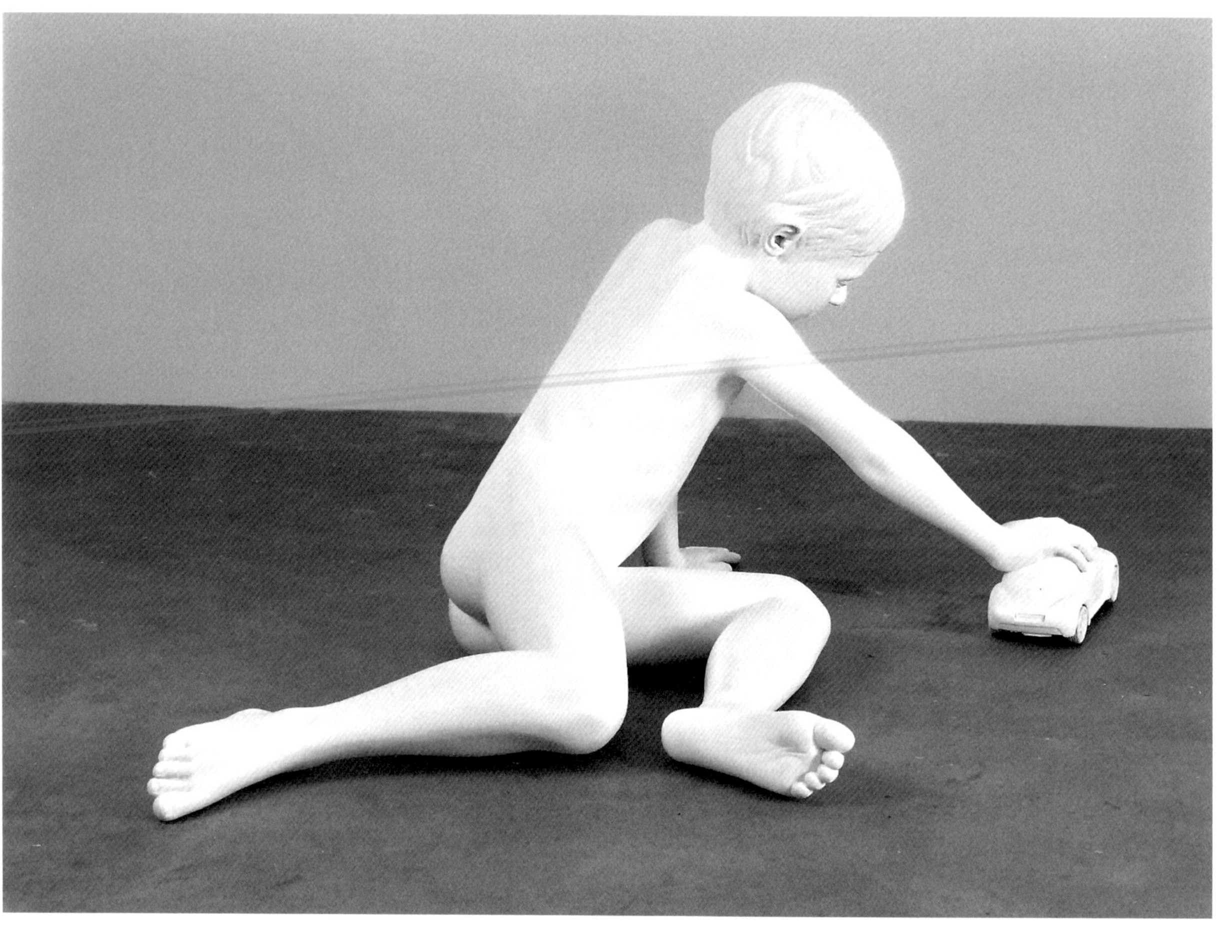

Fig. 37. Charles Ray. *The new Beetle*, 2006. Painted stainless steel, 21 × 34½ × 28½ in. (53 × 88 × 72 cm). Dallas Museum of Art, The Rachofsky Collection, Collection of Deedie and Rusty Rose, and the Dallas Museum of Art through the TWO x TWO for AIDS and Art Fund (2008.1)

same in a certain way. We are embedded. In order to really work, a figure has to reflect, has to *be*, all those things. For me figuration has to move. Not literally—not get up and walk across the room—but be animate somehow. I'm interested in the quickness of sculpture when it becomes this animate thing.

I know how important that ancient stele at The Met (fig. 38) is for you. You've talked about how the sculptural moment occurs in the space of breath—of pneuma, as you say—between the lips of the girl and the beak of the bird.

Yes, it's beautiful. I aimed for that kind of space with the hole in *Chicken*. It's space but it's solid. You can hold it, and the world implodes through it. You could hand it to an alien and say, "This is my world," and the alien would understand.

What about other allusions in your work to historical art, implicit and otherwise? There's a long history of figuration that your sculpture carries forward into our time.

That's tricky for me. People say *The new Beetle* is a twist on the ancient Roman *Dying Gaul* (1st or 2nd century A.D.). It's no such thing. People say *Shoe tie* (2012; fig. 26) is a twist on the Hellenistic sculpture *Boy with Thorn* (3rd century B.C.). It's no such thing. People say *Aluminum girl* (2003) has a contrapposto pose, but who doesn't stand like that? I never make the case that the originality of the work lies in its gestures alone.

For me the way that your work calls on a cultural repertoire of gestures and poses is a strength, not a weakness. Baudelaire called painting "the mnemotechny of the beautiful," and the art historian Aby Warburg suggested that the image is the medium through which human expressivity is conveyed across time. I think your work connects with those interests.

I guess I deny it the way I deny subject matter.

I would never say *Boy with Thorn* is the source, let alone the meaning, of *Shoe tie*.

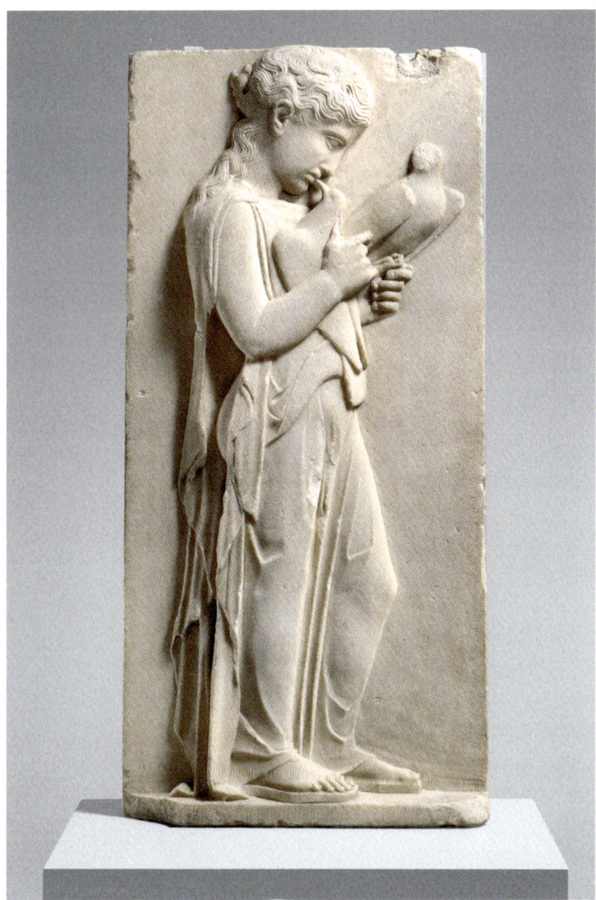

Fig. 38. Grave stele of a little girl. Greek, ca. 450–440 B.C. Parian marble, 31¾ × 15½ × 4 in. (80.6 × 39.4 × 10.2 cm). The Metropolitan Museum of Art, New York, Fletcher Fund, 1927 (27.45)

I know you wouldn't. Maybe I am defensive about those connections because they stabilize an object I'm trying to destabilize.

Your idea of figuration is to open up a space into which different allusions, meanings, and times can—to use your word—flow.

Right. I don't see it as a stable endeavor that has a single philosophical or political stance.

What about the ensemble of works in the second gallery? How did this room come together?

Kelly wanted the new piece, *Archangel* (2021; pl. 11), which originally was to be shown in Paris. I was asked to do an exhibition in Paris the same week as the terrorist attack on *Charlie Hebdo* in 2015—a collision of free speech, artistic intent, misunderstanding, and the sacredness of text. Separate cultures walking across the same city, an inability to integrate, threatened boundaries both personal and cultural, economic hardship, lies from leaders. Too many problems for one time or age to resolve. When I was asked to create an exhibit at the Pompidou, I immediately put myself in front of the iconic building, standing in the middle of the sloping plaza (fig. 47). I had a vision of the angel Gabriel alighting and slaying the prophet Muhammad's dog, inspired by a story a Muslim acquaintance once told me, about Gabriel being unable to enter Muhammad's home because he had a drawing and a dog. Culturally or historically inaccurate, the idea stayed with me. I was greatly affected by the shooting and subsequent attacks in Paris and elsewhere. I wanted to make a monument to commemorate these events for all Parisians, and I thought of an angel descending down to the unstable ground. My subject was Gabriel the archangel, known to all people of the books—the Old Testament, the New Testament, and the Qur'an (figs. 39, 40). I found this model, a beautiful young man, and put him on a box. He was holding a dog in one hand, and he had a sword in the other. I kept banging the box with a stick while he was being photographed to make him light on his feet, to make him look active rather than posed. After I sculpted it, I missed the box, so I put it back and eventually took away the sword and the dog. I thought the gesture was more than enough. The gesture became like a crucifix. I decided to carve it in wood. There's one big timber that runs from the floor up through the figure; there's one sculptural spine.

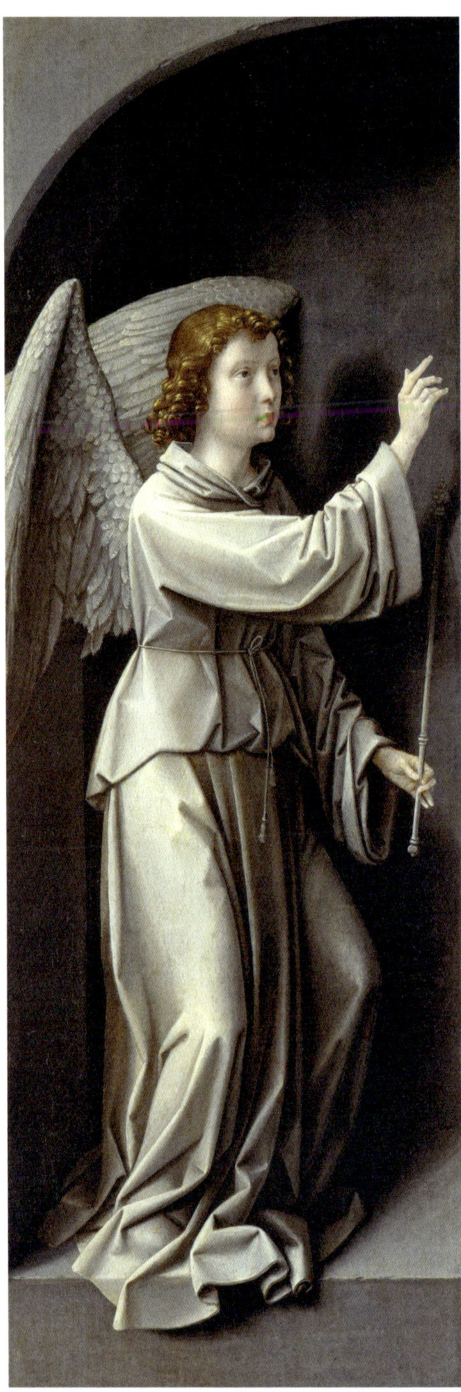

Fig. 39. Gerard David (Netherlandish, ca. 1455–1523). *Archangel Gabriel*, ca. 1510. Oil on oak panel, 34½ × 11⅝ in. (87.7 × 29.5 cm). The Metropolitan Museum of Art, New York, Robert Lehman Collection, 1975 (1975.1.120A)

Not to be too bound to subject matter, but why an archangel? That's another charged figure.

I was influenced a bit by a sculpture in Madrid (fig. 41). It's the only one I know totally dedicated to Lucifer, the fallen angel. It's Lucifer right as he's being cast out of heaven. He's just thrown down, like a big piece of clay thrown in anger on the floor. Or like a comet crashing. Maybe I was also influenced a little by all that writing by philosophers in the 1990s about Saint Paul, about the notion of his conversion—an event, a singularity.

That's a different—very punctual—kind of temporality.

Well, it's an event. It's not finished in a way. After the initial shock of terrorist events, like the one in Paris, they continue to unfold. Like the recent riot at the U.S. Capitol, they hang in the air. I love Paris and I was thinking about what kind of monument might work. Eventually, my mind drifted away from monuments, and while the title still stuck, I dropped the archangel. When I carved the figure in wood with its outstretched arms it turned into a crucifix. The flip-flops and young feet let a foot fetish drift into view. Maybe all this comes from my Catholic childhood; the idea of the archangel stemming from an old religious reader—with an image of the archangel Jophiel guarding the entrance to the Garden, the flaming sword barring us from ever returning.

There's another piece in the second room that addresses a religious, or ritualistic, moment of immense importance, an aluminum sculpture based on the marble fragments of the Great Eleusinian Relief at The Met (2017; pl. 19). The relief is about the cultivation of grain and the beginning of agriculture. Another origin piece?

Demeter is handing the boy something—maybe the grain—while Persephone is pouring something onto or into his head. The Greeks thought that life was a fluid; once it dried out, you were dead. It's a beautiful object and one of the most interesting pieces at The Met because it's hybrid. I'm interested in hybrid objects.

It's hybrid because it's a Roman copy of a Greek original?

In the nineteenth century the Roman copy existed only as ten fragments. To make them more valuable,

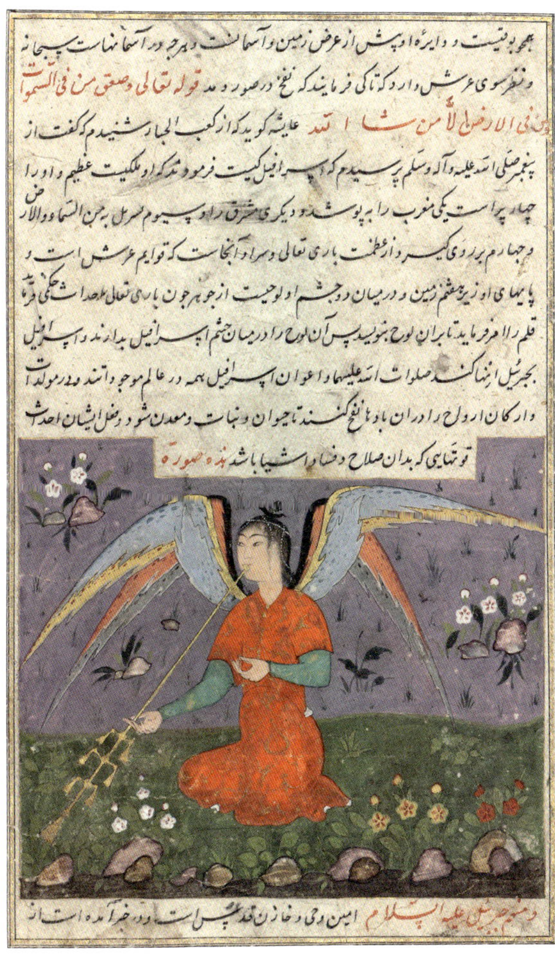

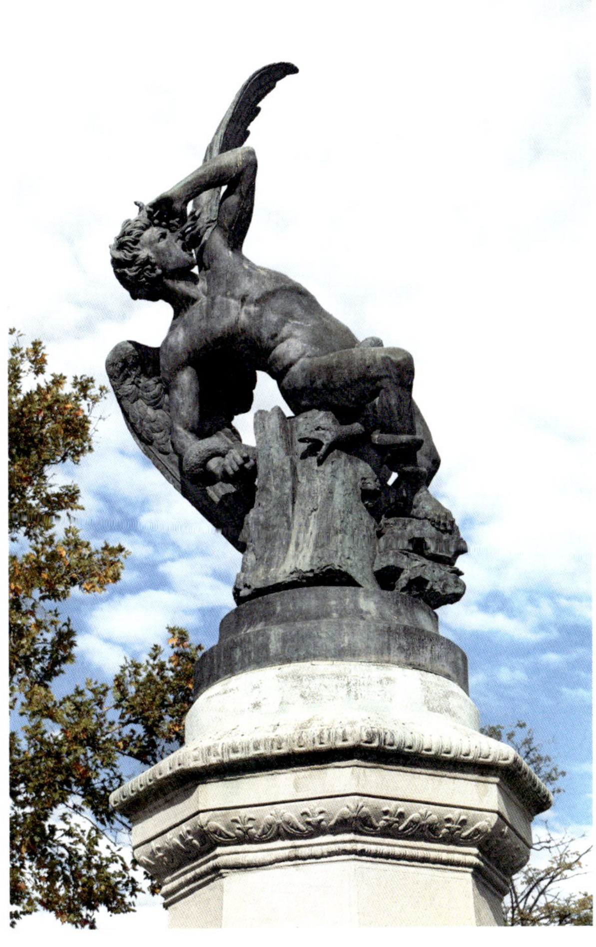

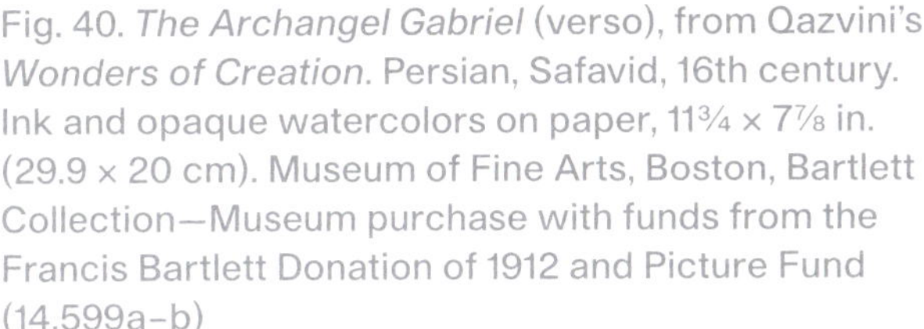

Fig. 40. *The Archangel Gabriel* (verso), from Qazvini's *Wonders of Creation.* Persian, Safavid, 16th century. Ink and opaque watercolors on paper, 11¾ × 7⅞ in. (29.9 × 20 cm). Museum of Fine Arts, Boston, Bartlett Collection—Museum purchase with funds from the Francis Bartlett Donation of 1912 and Picture Fund (14.599a–b)

Fig. 41. Ricardo Bellver y Ramón (Spanish, 1845–1924). *The Fallen Angel*, 1878. Bronze, H. 8 ft. 8¼ in. (265 cm). Museo Nacional del Prado, Madrid City Council

they were taken to Athens, where a plaster mold of the original was made, and the Roman fragments were inserted into it (fig. 42). You can see the fragments; you can also tell the differences between styles across a four-hundred-year gap in time and culture. When I remade the relief in aluminum, it became a further hybrid object. The classical art historian Richard Neer writes about how Greek sculptures bedazzled their first viewers—and how that relationship has long since changed. He saw that I put the bedazzlement back through the reflective qualities of my machined aluminum.

Neer also says that Greek sculptures were the only smooth things in a rough world. But your smooth objects enter a smooth world.

That's true, but they also introduce a displacement.

Because they draw in other temporalities?

And also because they are very heavy objects in a super-light world.

On the one hand, your sculpture is perfect—thought

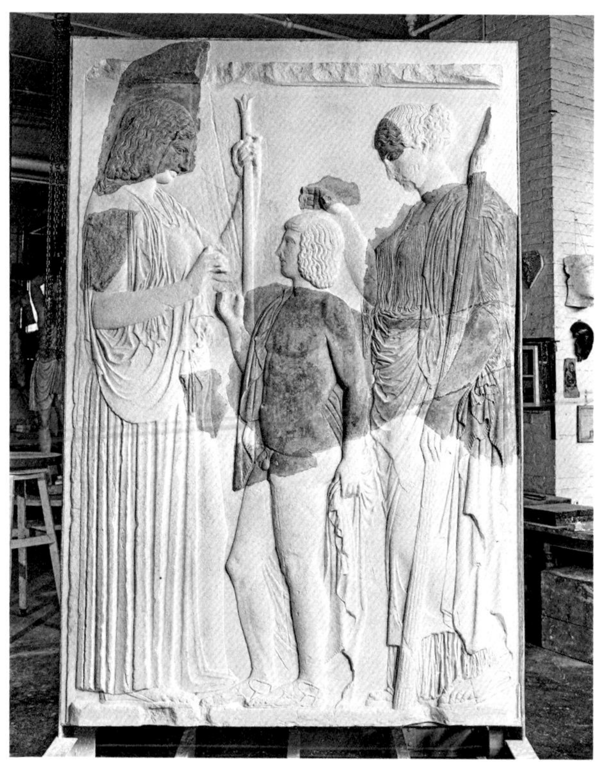

Fig. 42. Ten marble fragments of the Great Eleusinian Relief. Roman, Augustan period, 27 B.C.–A.D. 14. Copy of a Greek marble relief, ca. 450–425 B.C., found at Eleusis and now in the National Museum, Athens. The Metropolitan Museum of Art, New York, Rogers Fund, 1914 (14.130.9). Archival photograph showing the ten fragments from the Roman copy, which appear in dark gray, recently set into a cast of the original Greek relief, which appears in light gray, May 1935

through, deeply felt, expertly engineered and executed. On the other hand, it's complex, hybrid, composite physically. Composite culturally, too, so to speak. And that can lead—it has led—to controversies. The Met show comes at a time of intensive debates about public monuments and cultural appropriations. Most of the pieces in the show precede these debates, but they also flow through the work now, to use your term. How do you view these questions?

I could say they aren't mine, but they are in part; I embrace them and reject them at the same time. I think about them a lot. My father once told me that I was a good artist but I needed a great editor. Prohibitions, justified and unjustified, flow through and boil up in every cultural age. Can an artist be prohibited from entering certain cultural structures or narrative realms? An artist certainly can be criticized for subject and structure, but then we enter a complex domain. For me it is best simply to say that the artist is responsible for what he or she makes. I wasn't naive about the power of nude images of Huck and Jim, though I did take it from the book where Huck says something like, "We had no need for clothes, no how." I am aware that sexuality is suggested here, and a White boy and a Black man together is charged. But this controversial realm, whatever it is, isn't foundational to the sculpture. You have to move through it.

You do, or the viewer should, or both?

Both.

Do you mean that a controversy, when it befalls a work of art, always picks out just one aspect and locks the work in there?

No, I just mean that the foundation of the sculpture lies elsewhere.

You return to *Huckleberry Finn* with the sculpture *Sarah Williams*. It takes up a moment when Jim helps Huck cross-dress in order to sneak back into town to see whether there's any news about their escape. Here you put gender into play, but why else pick this scene?

Twain could have dressed Huck up in blackface, but he didn't. He dressed him like a girl. How subversive! And it breathes life into the novel. It also superimposes over our cultural moment now. But I don't think that the sculpture exists there, any more than I think *Huck and Jim* exists with Huck bending over and Jim standing to his side.

Many of your allusions are classical and European. These two sculptures ground your work in a key American text. Why go there in particular?

Well, it's a great book. *Adventures of Huckleberry Finn* is our *Odyssey*—the wandering, the encounters, the flow of the river, the coming-of-age of both Huck and Jim (fig. 43). During the Whitney controversy, the Mark Twain Foundation wrote me a letter. They were humorous about it, saying Twain is still stirring

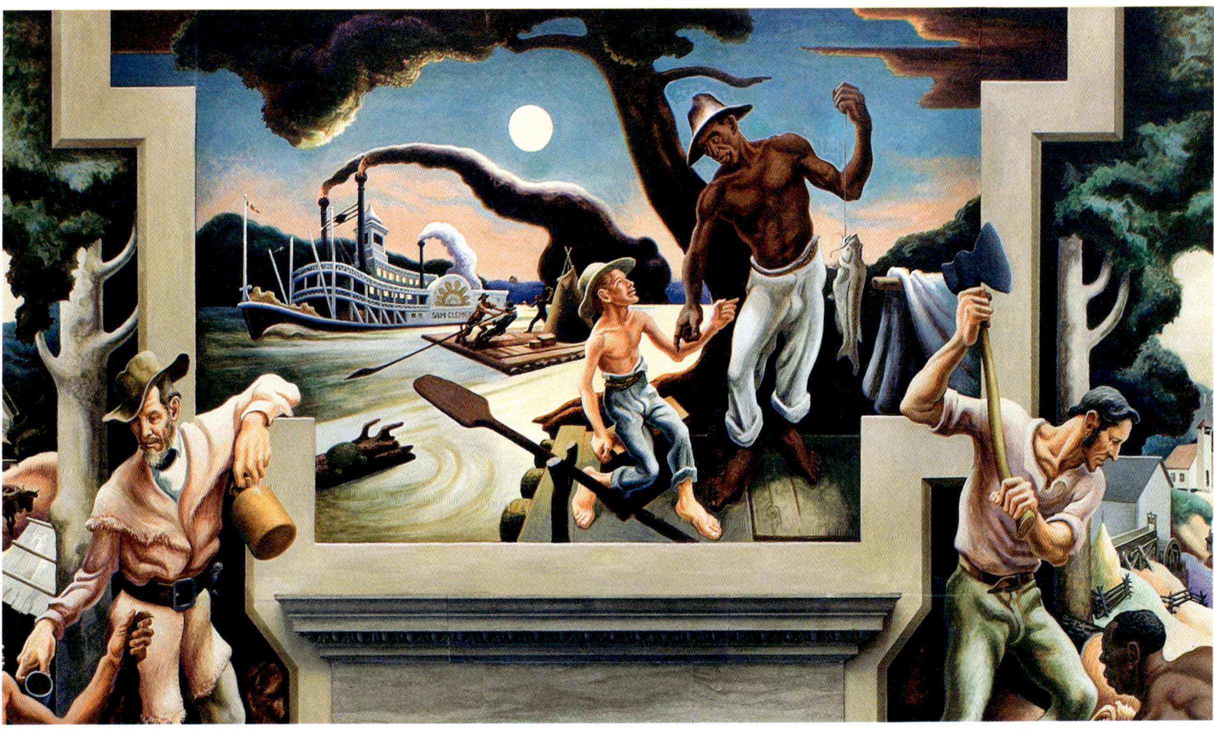

Fig. 43. Thomas Hart Benton (American, 1889–1975). Huckleberry Finn and Jim, from *A Social History of the State of Missouri*, 1935–36. Missouri State Capitol, Jefferson City

things up. The controversies never die. The book gets banned again and again. When I reentered the story, the present cultural superimpositions were obvious.

There are at least two pieces in the show that were intended for a civic realm: *Boy with frog* for the Punta della Dogana museum in Venice (fig. 32) and *Huck and Jim* for outside the Whitney Museum in New York. But one was eventually moved to another site and the other was blocked. What does that say about the possibility of reclaiming a civic dimension for sculpture today?

In some sense, I don't think they were impeded. What made *Boy with frog* civic was that it could hold its ground at the Dogana. It took a political controversy, drummed up on social media, to get it moved. But sculpturally it really held itself there.

It was embedded.

It wasn't added. It wasn't put in. It became part of the Dogana, as I was hoping *Huck and Jim* would become part of the Whitney. It would've held its ground in front of the Renzo Piano building. It would've settled in there. *Boy with frog* was lent to my show in Basel, and when I saw it inside the museum, I thought, "He's dragged the whole Dogana with him." I'm not saying I have the ability to do this. It's just something I think about and aim for—that a sculpture find its cultural square, so to speak, that it exist for people in that way in that place.

Plates

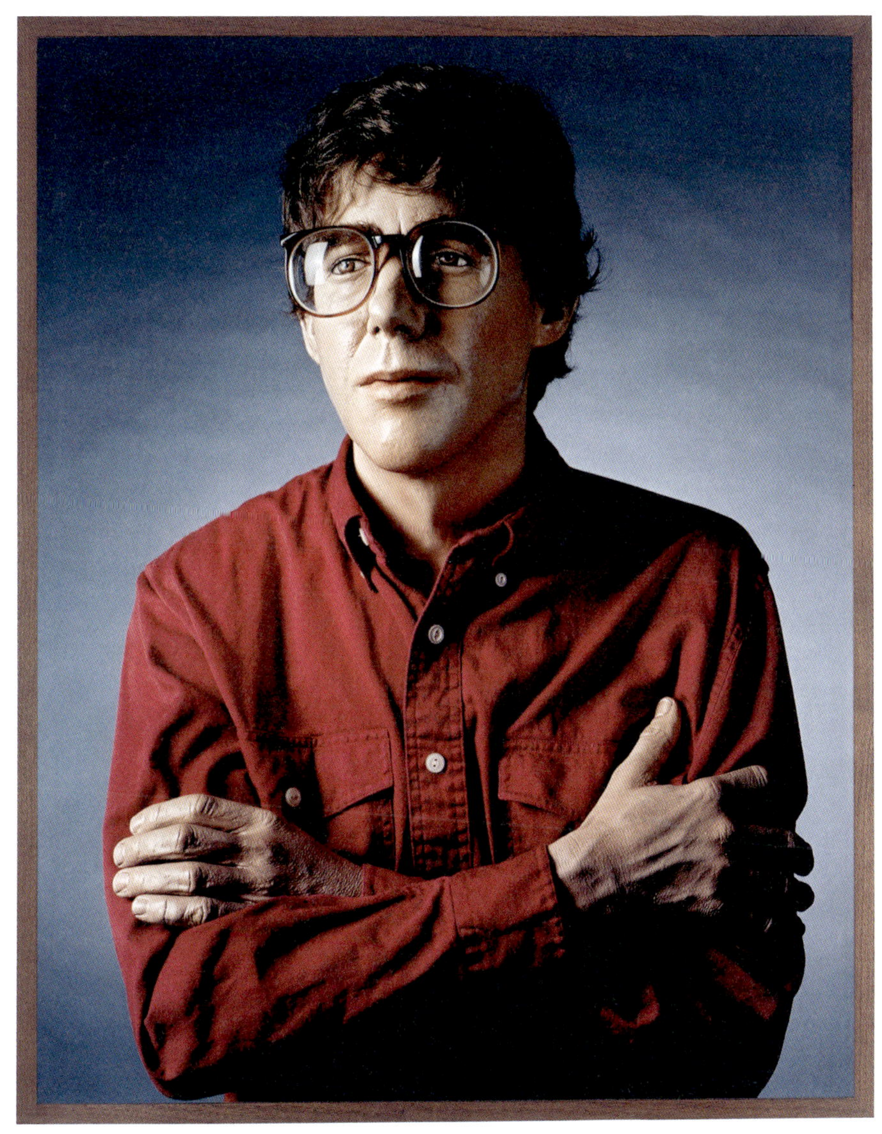

Pl. 1. *No*, 1992

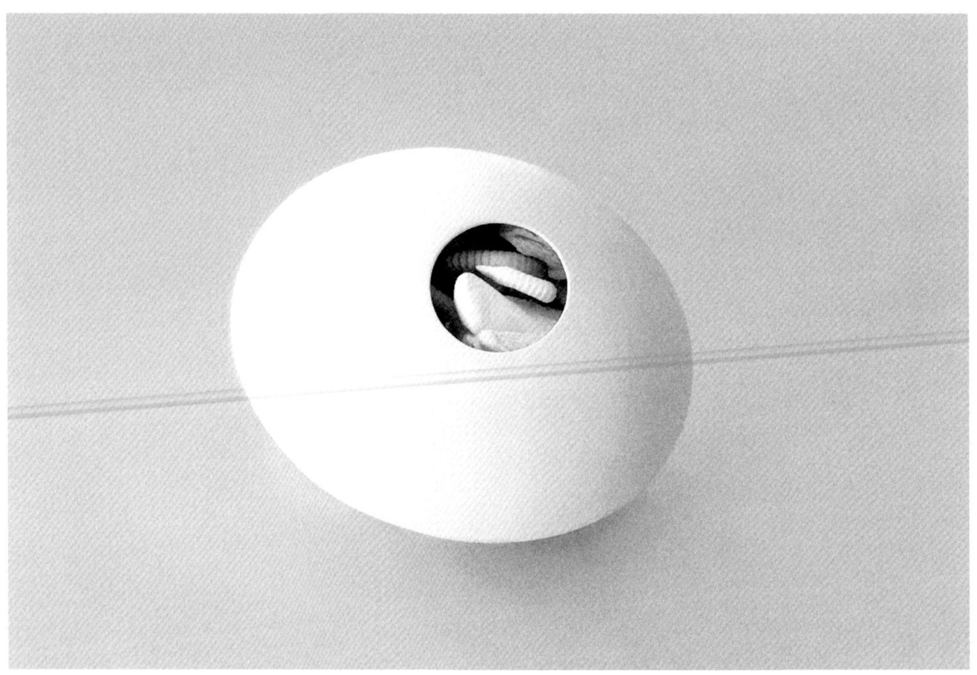

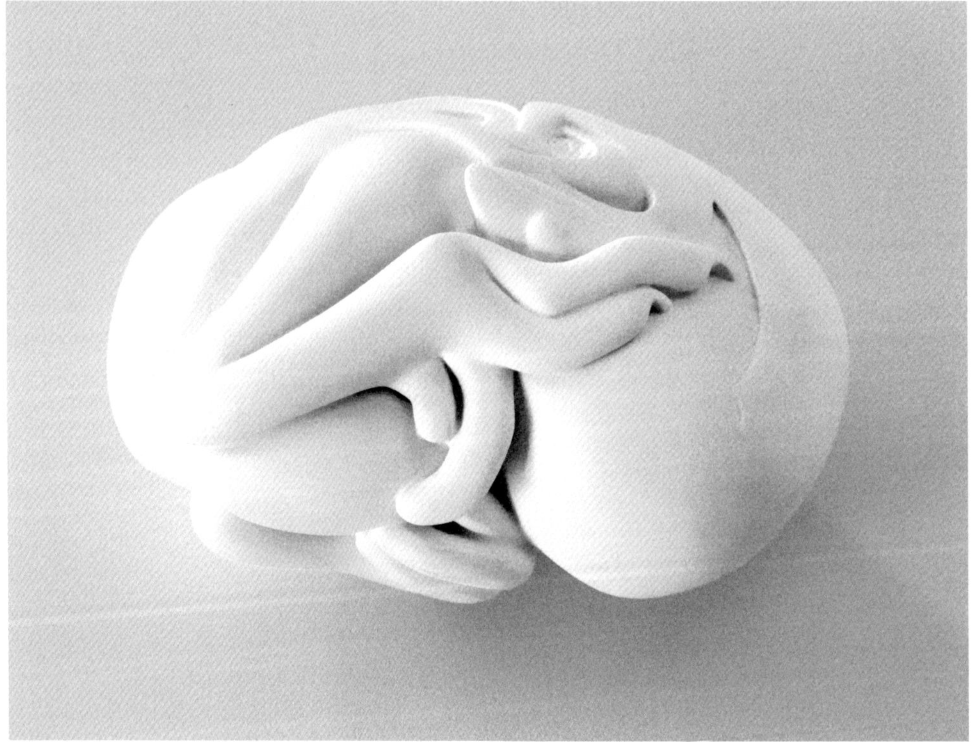

Pl. 2. *Chicken*, 2007

Pl. 3. *Handheld bird*, 2006

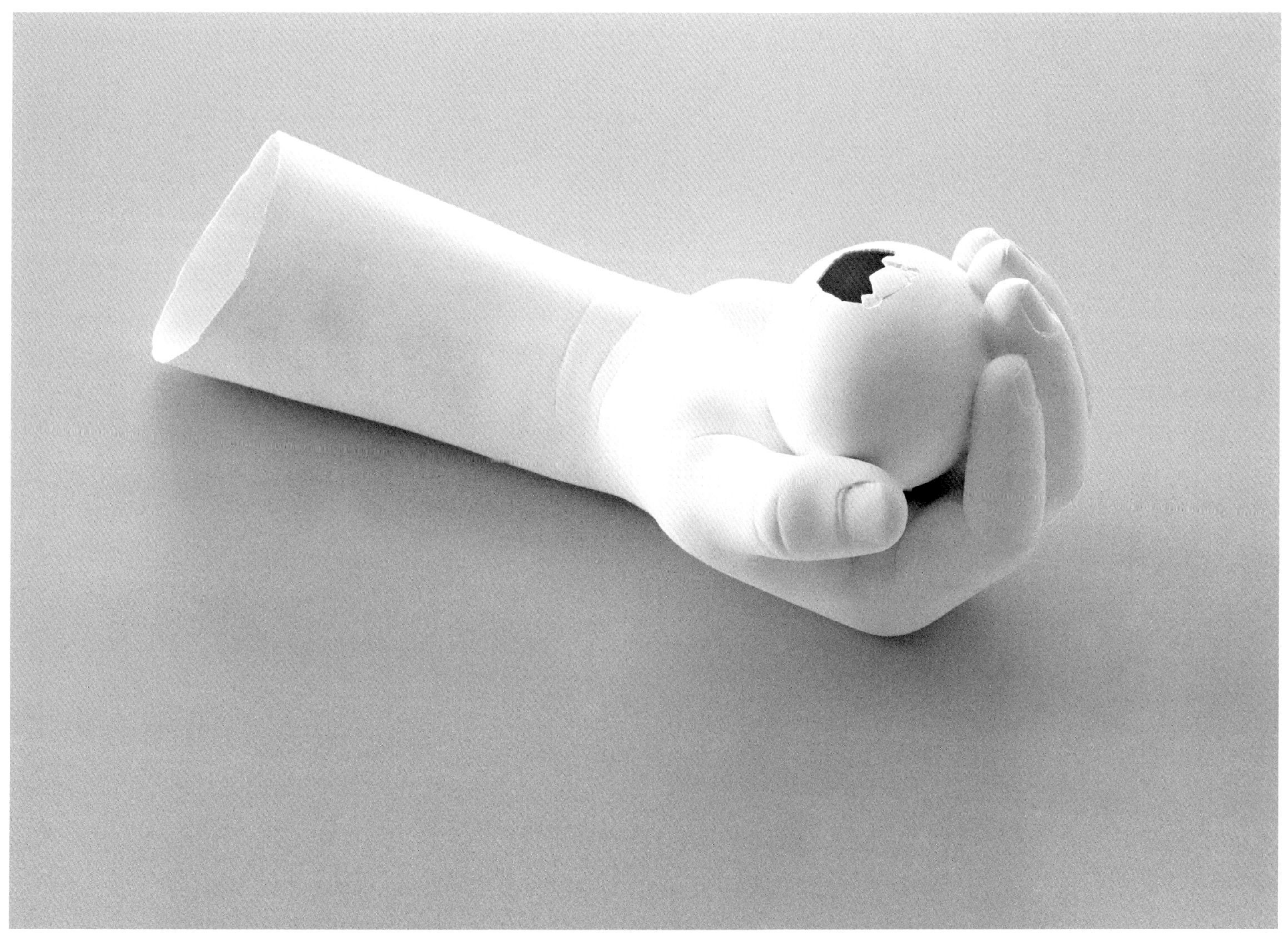

Pl. 4. *Hand holding egg*, 2007

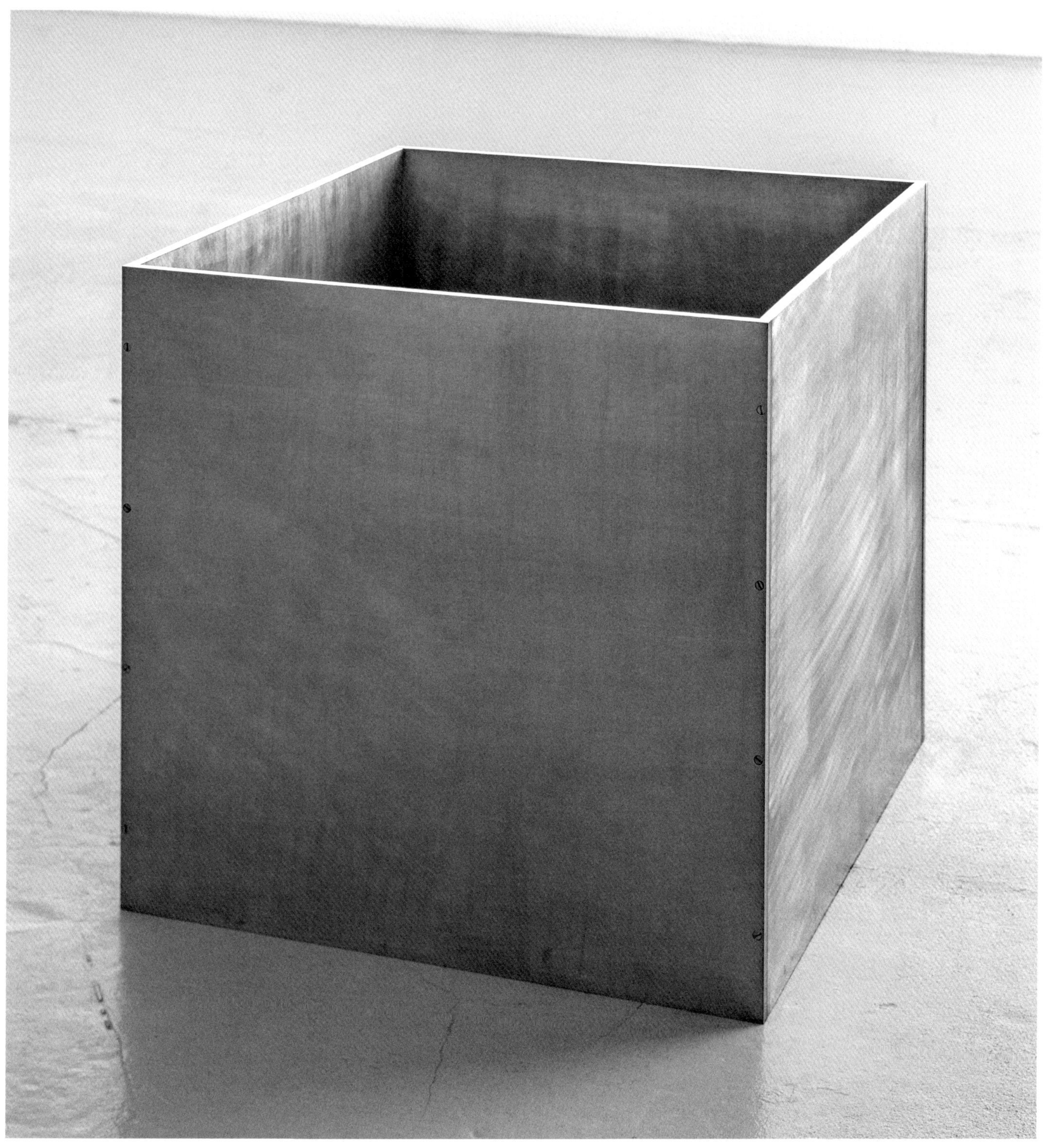

Pl. 5. *81 × 83 × 85 = 86 × 83 × 85*, 1989

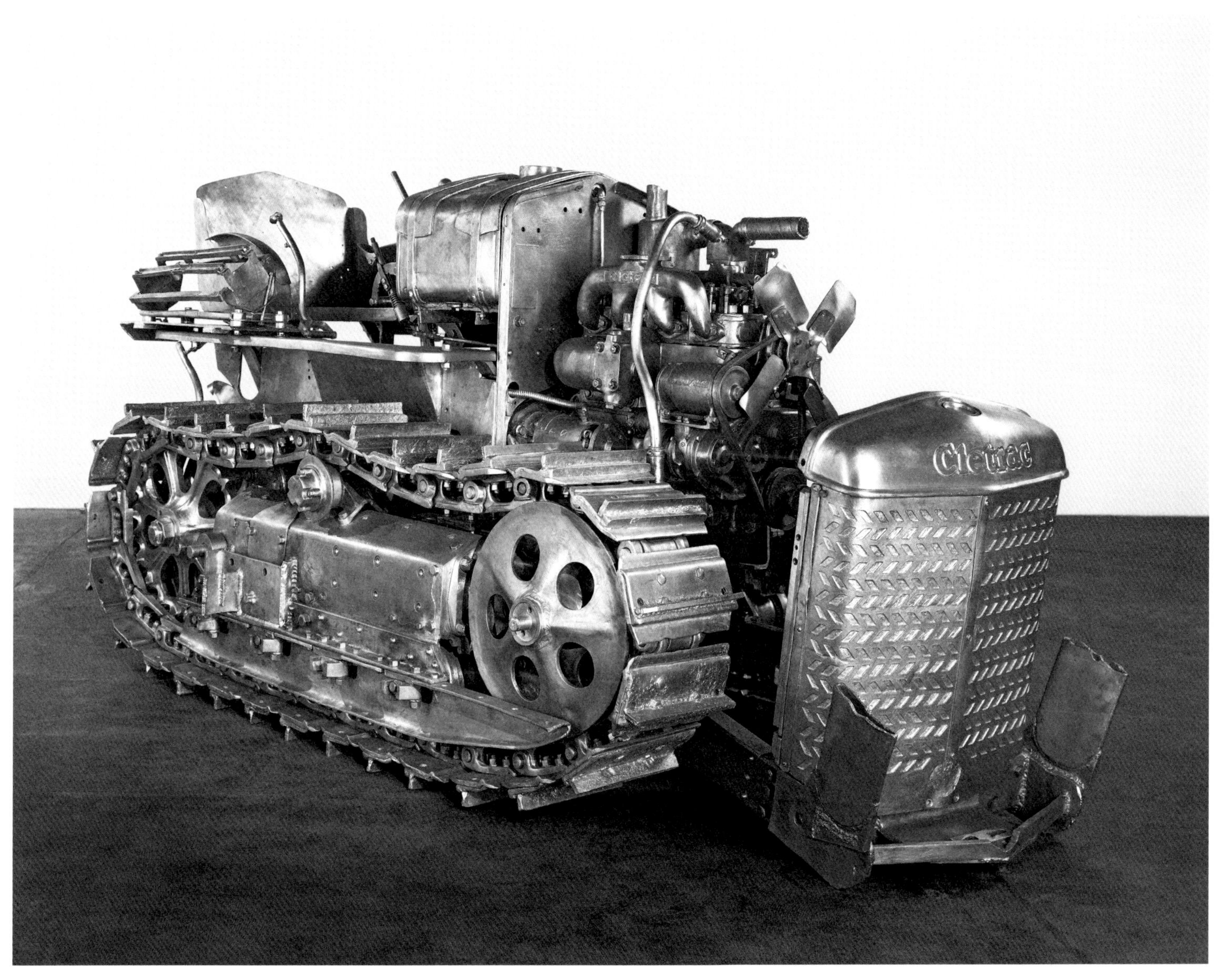

Pl. 6. *Tractor*, 2005

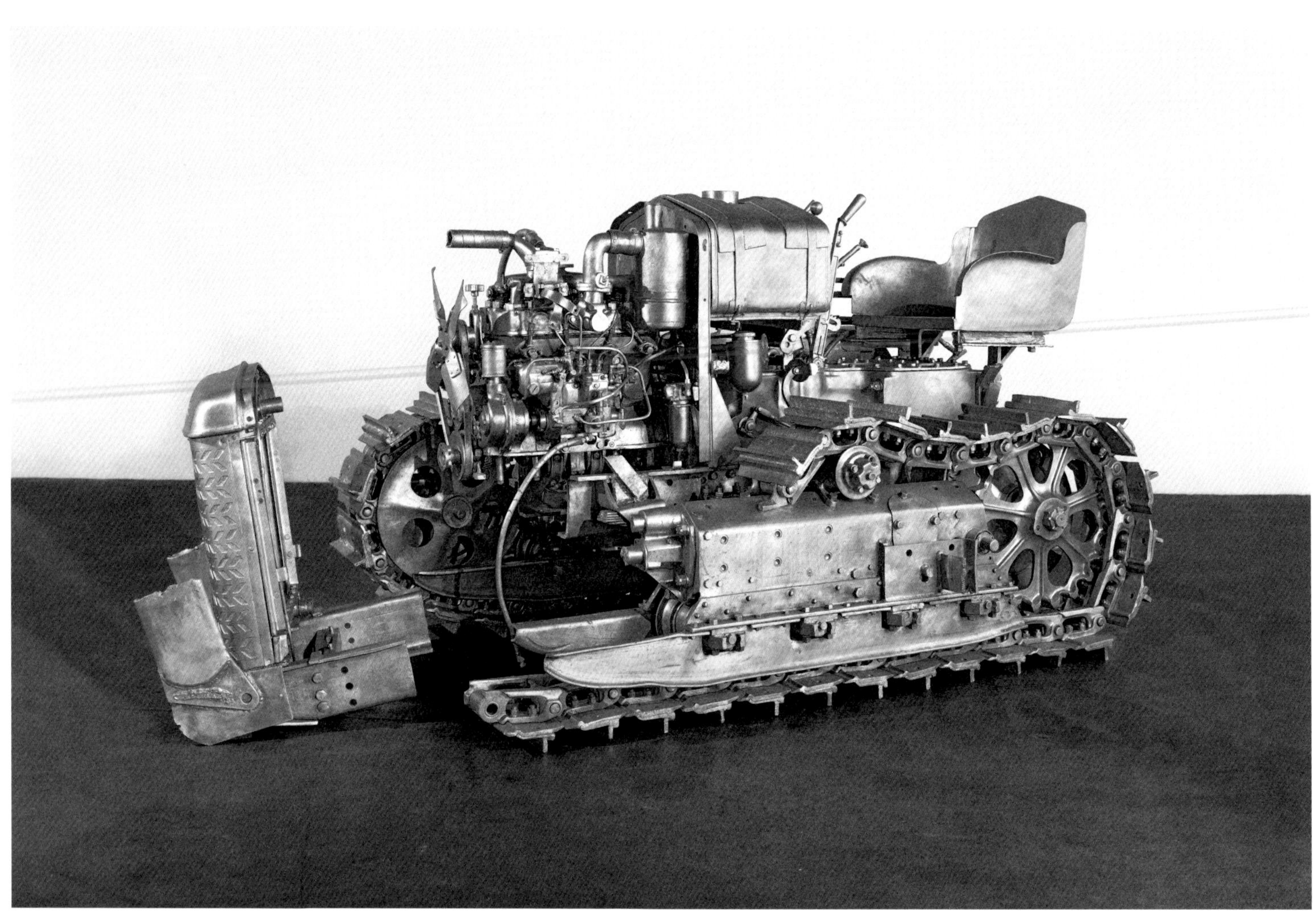

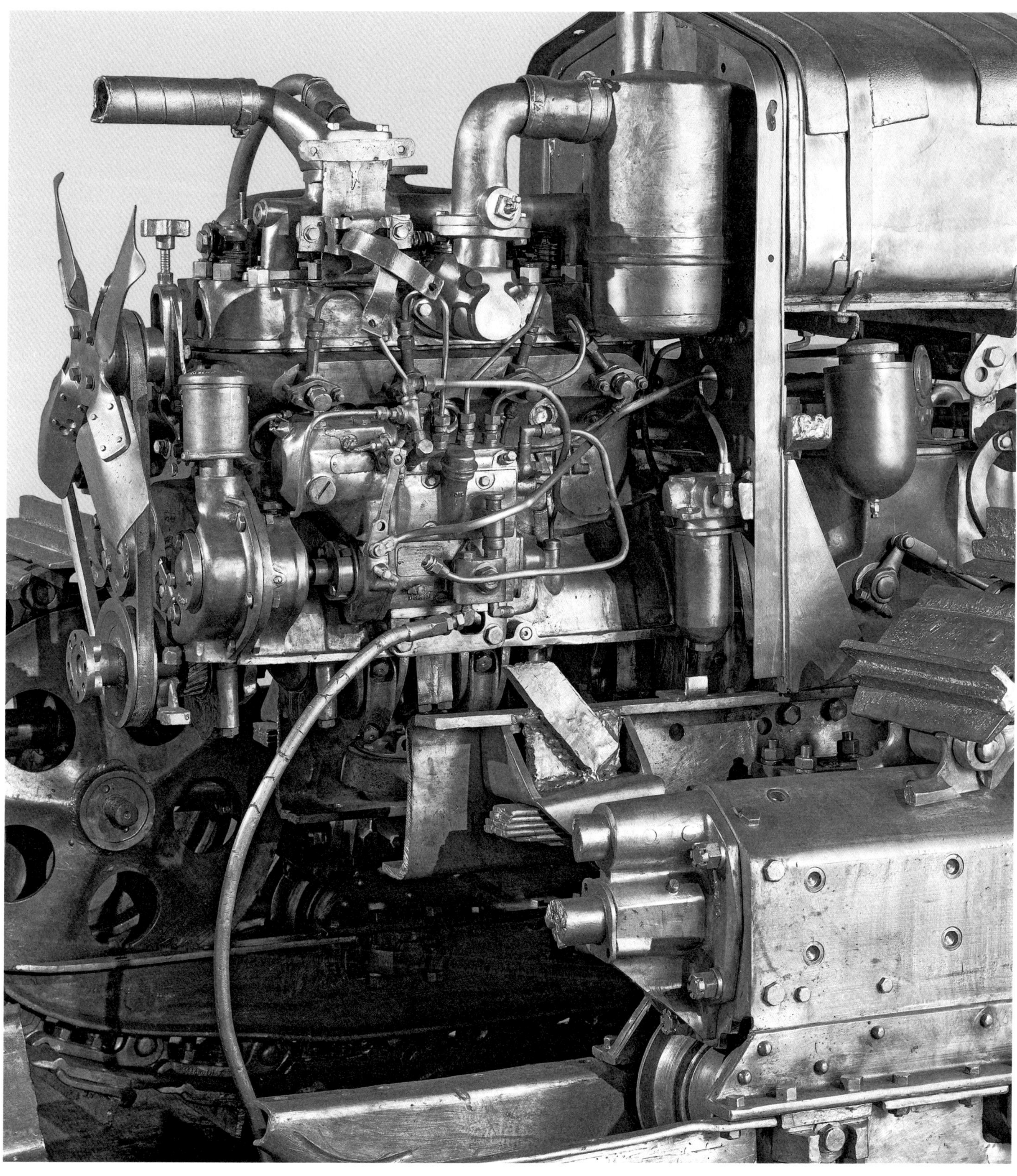

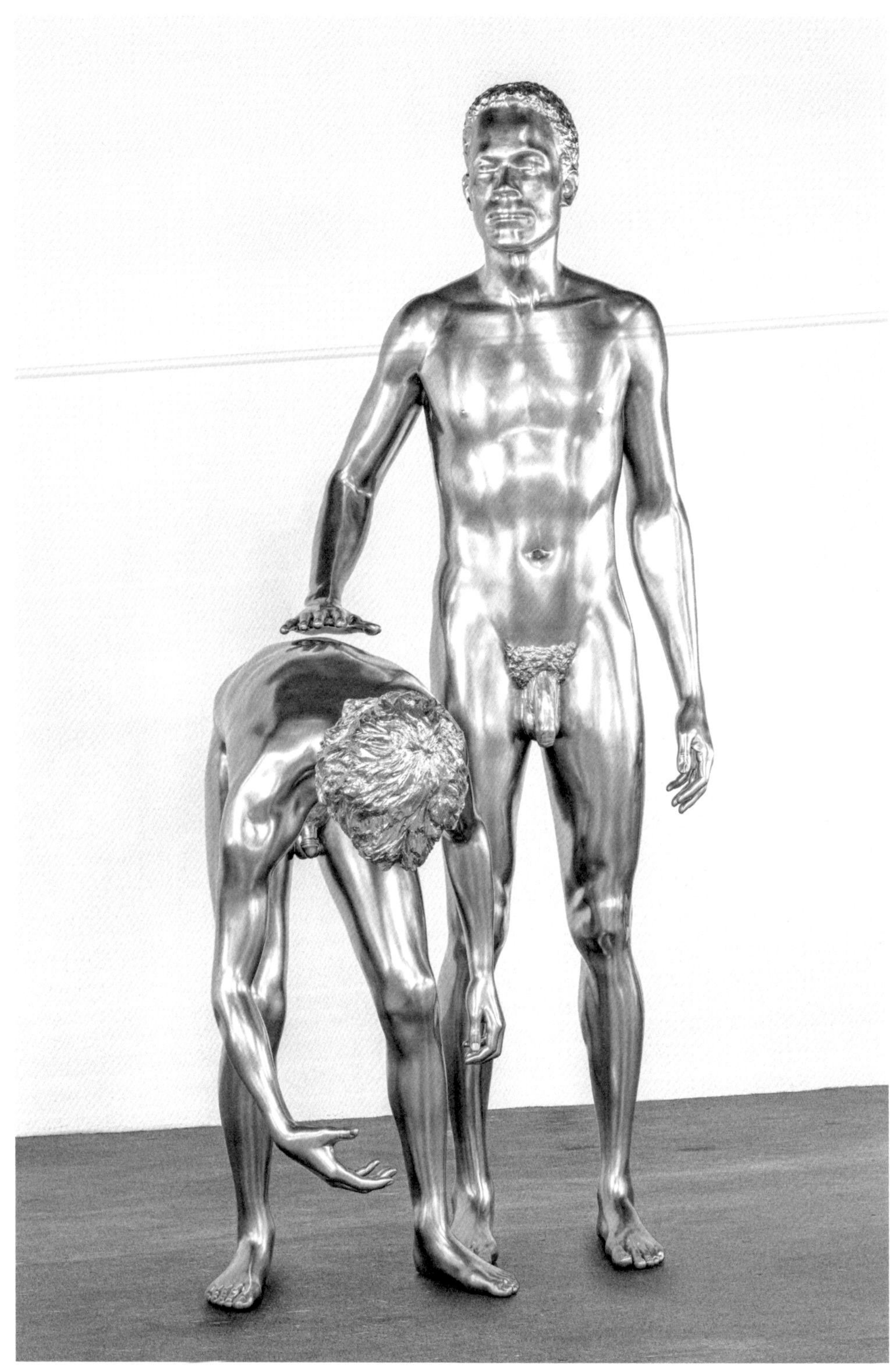

Pl. 7. *Huck and Jim*, 2014

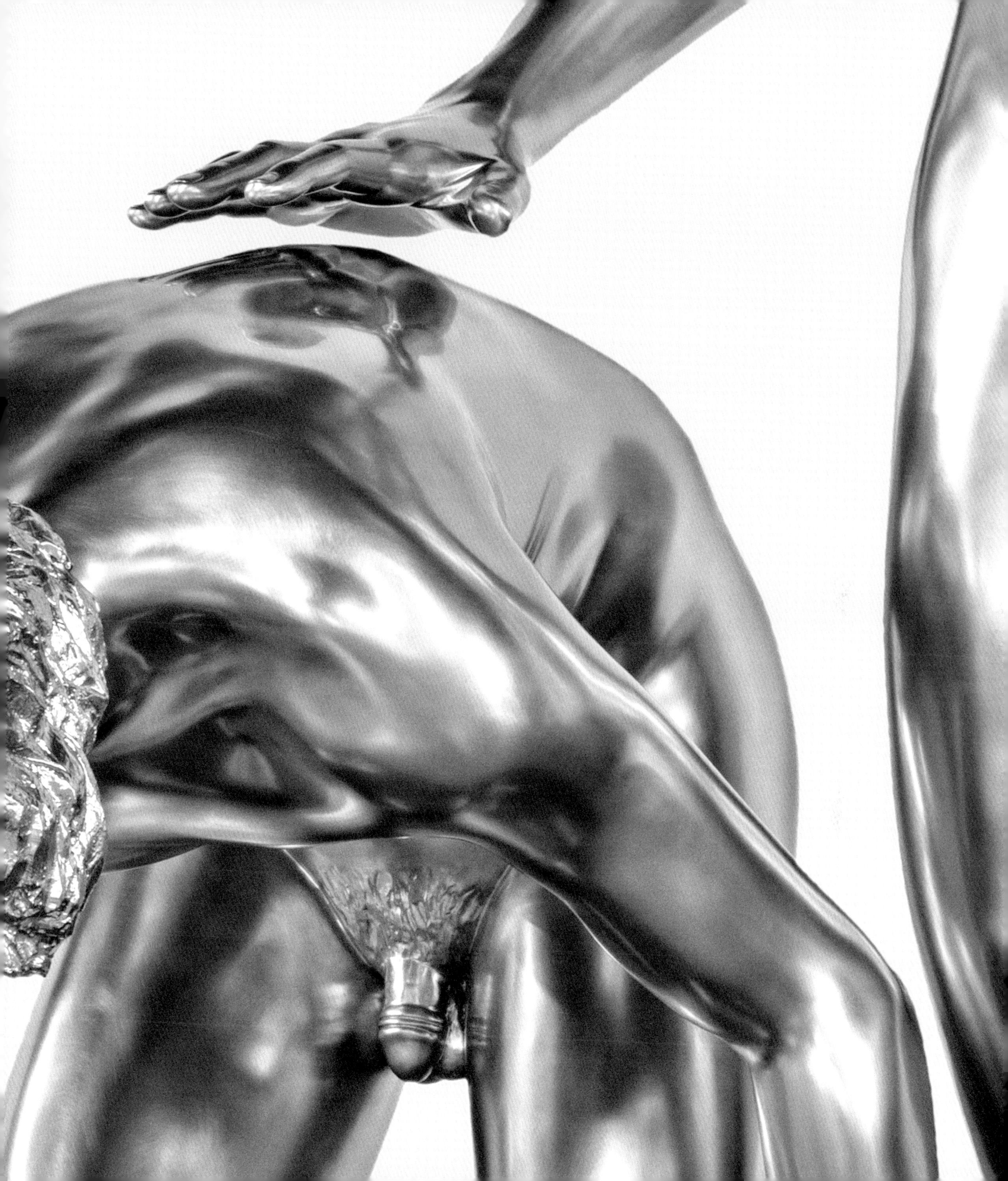

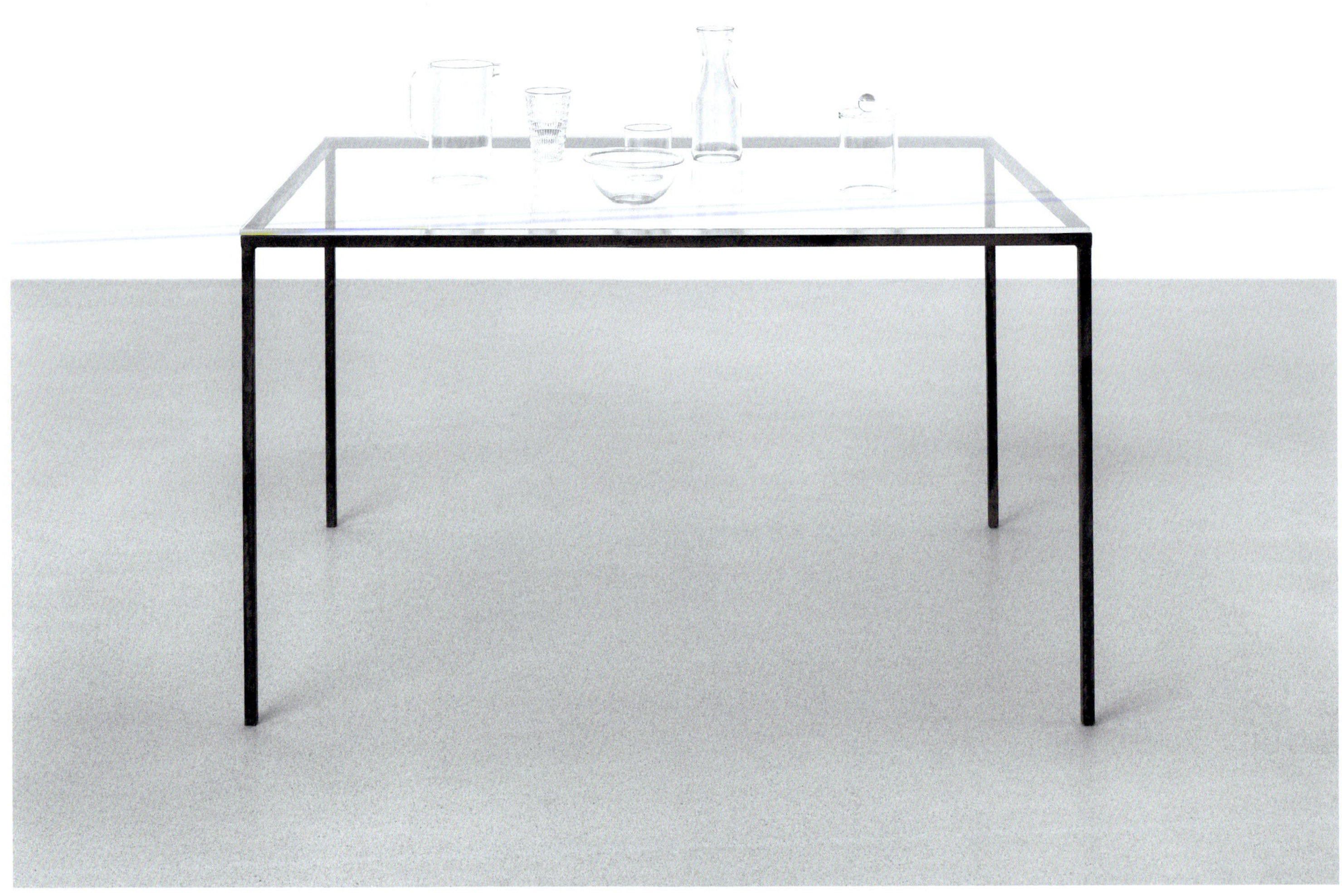

Pl. 8. *Table*, 1990

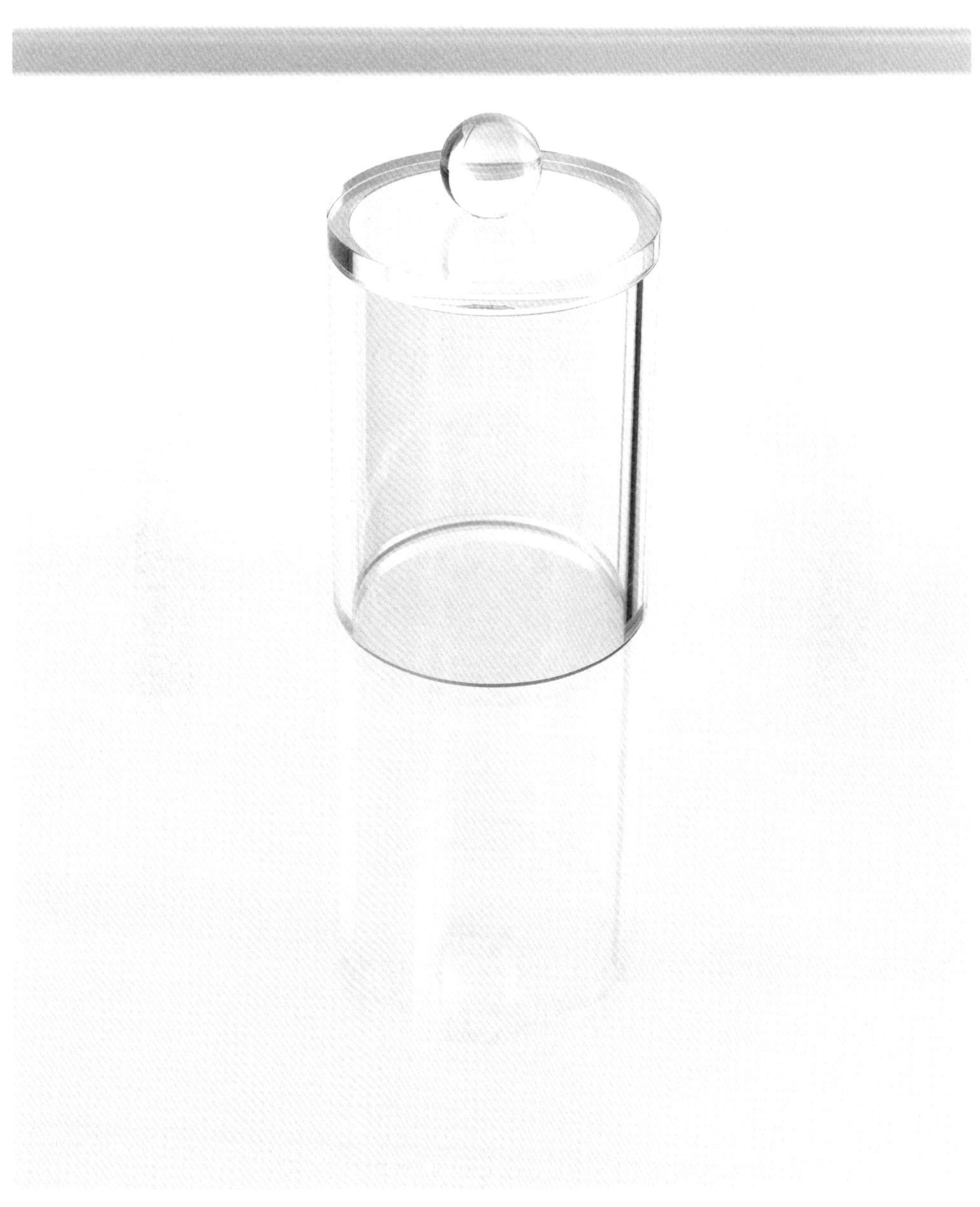

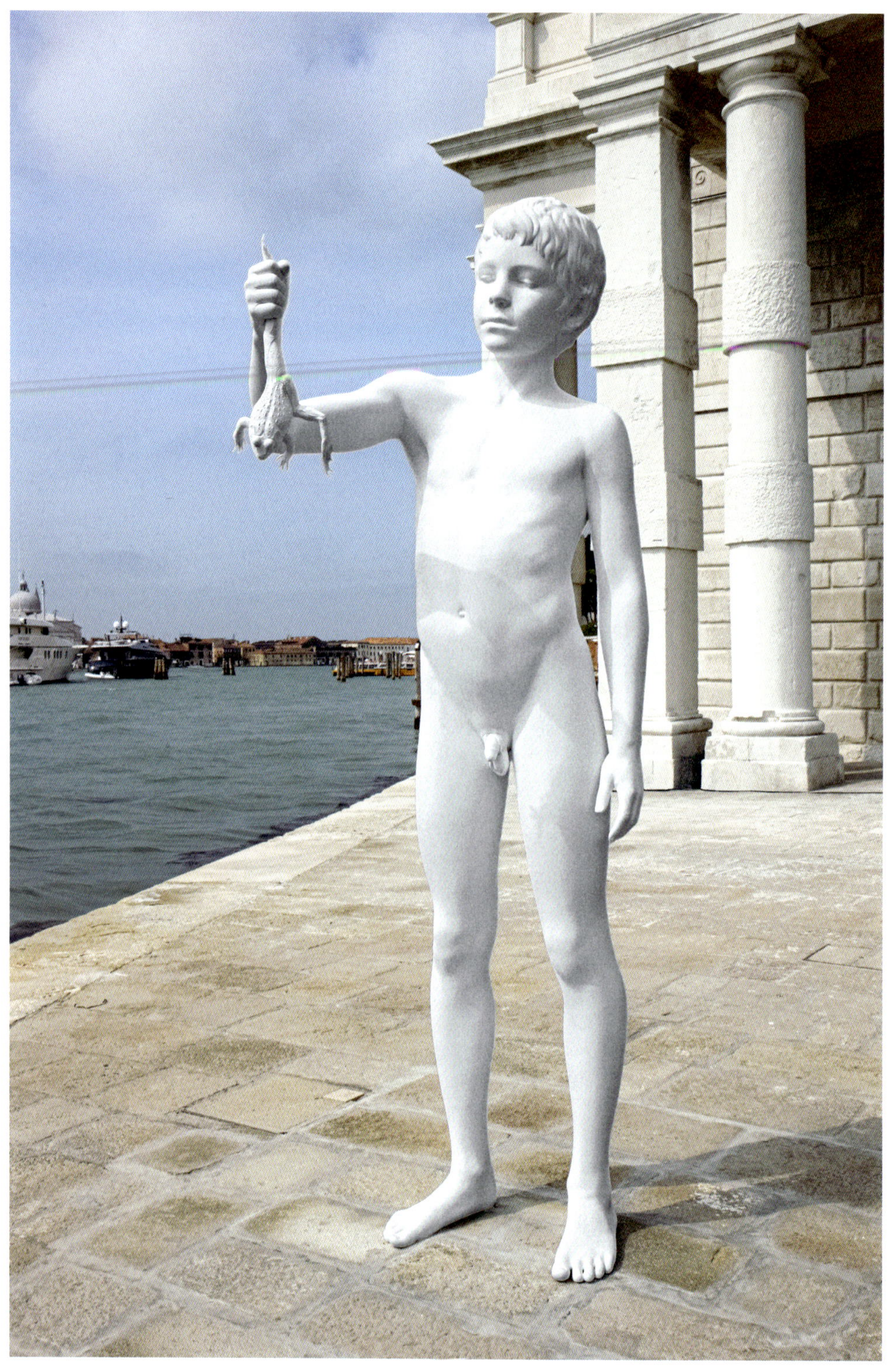

Pl. 9. *Boy with frog*, 2009

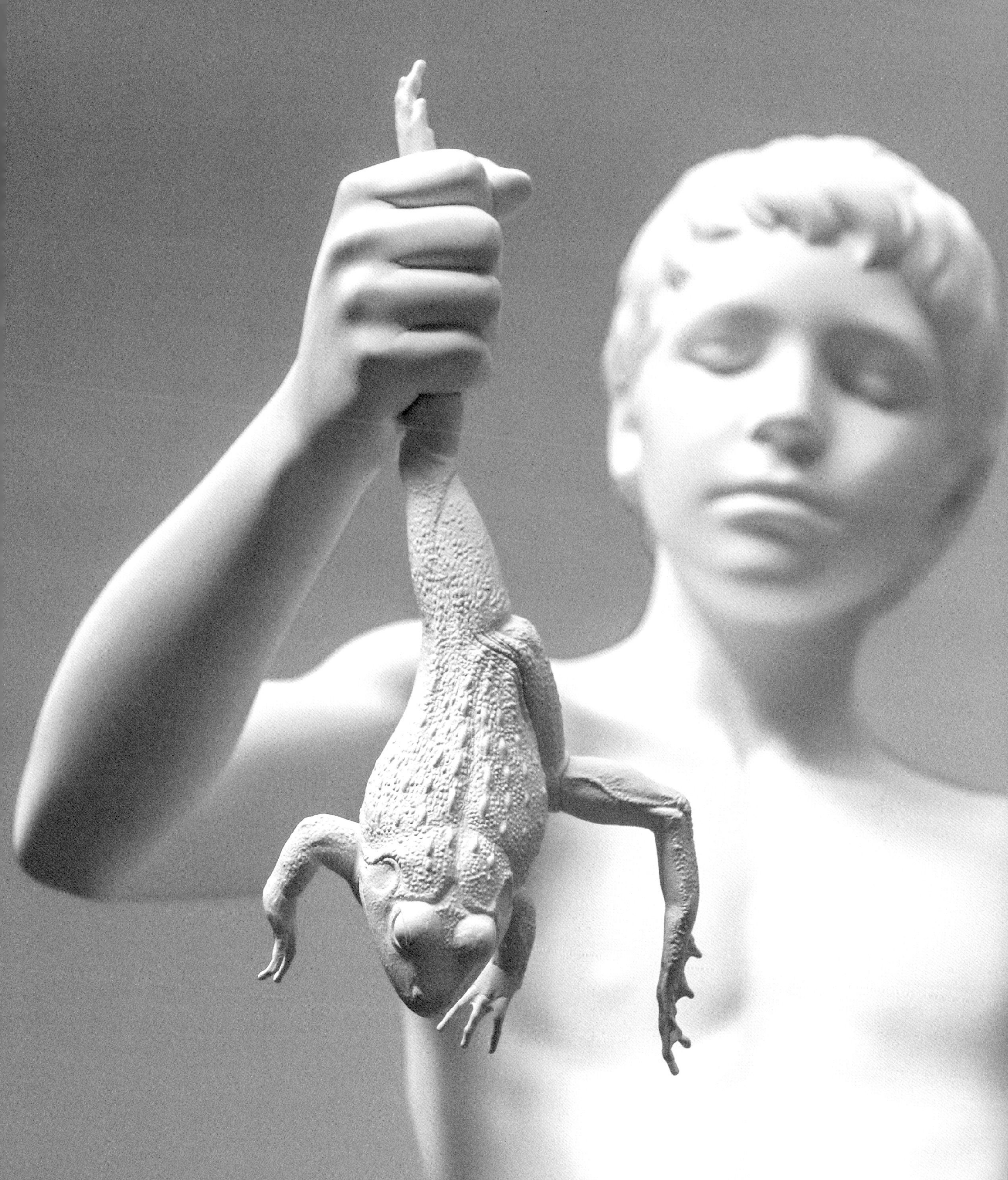

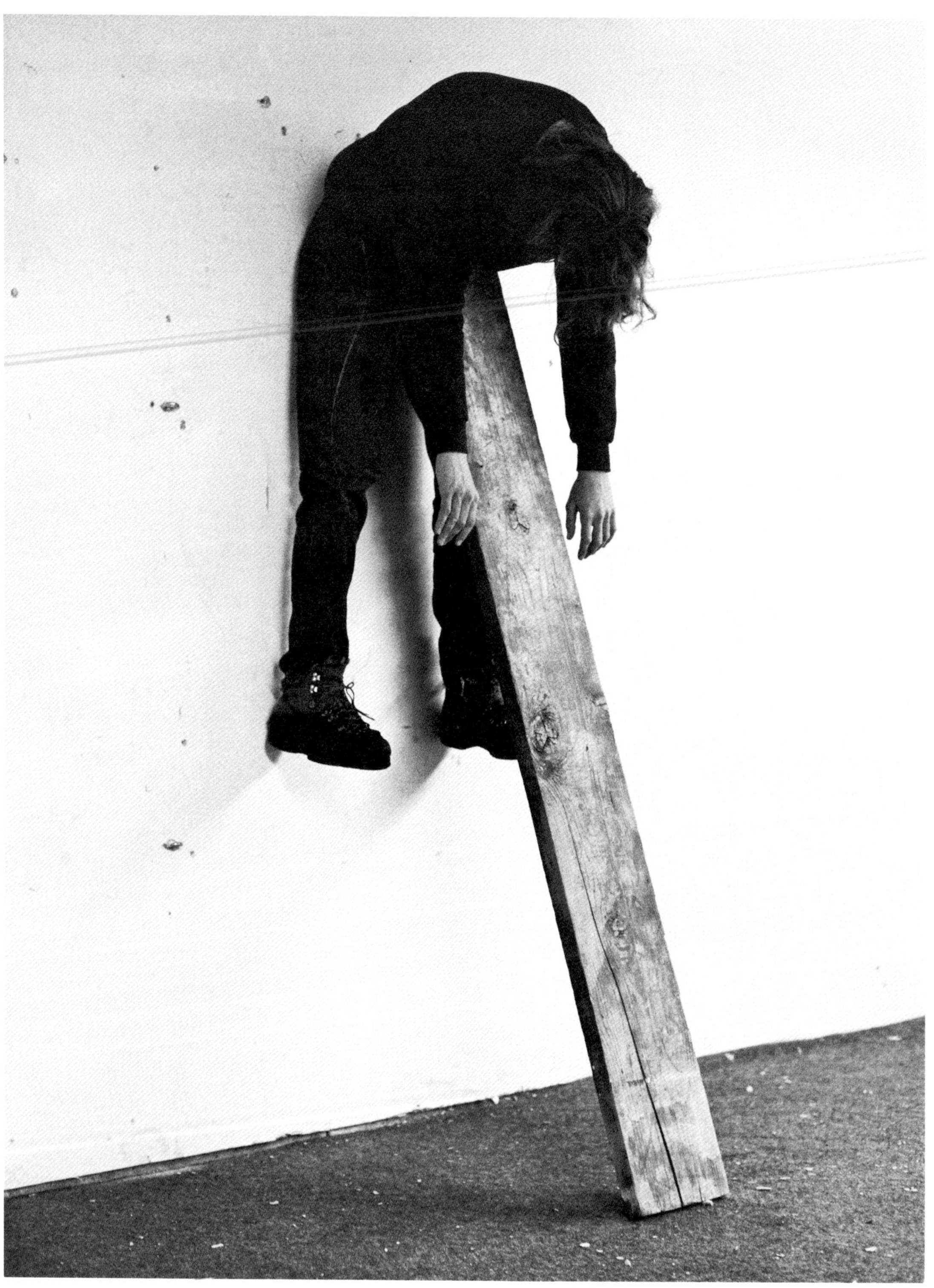

Pl. 10. *Plank piece I and II*, 1973

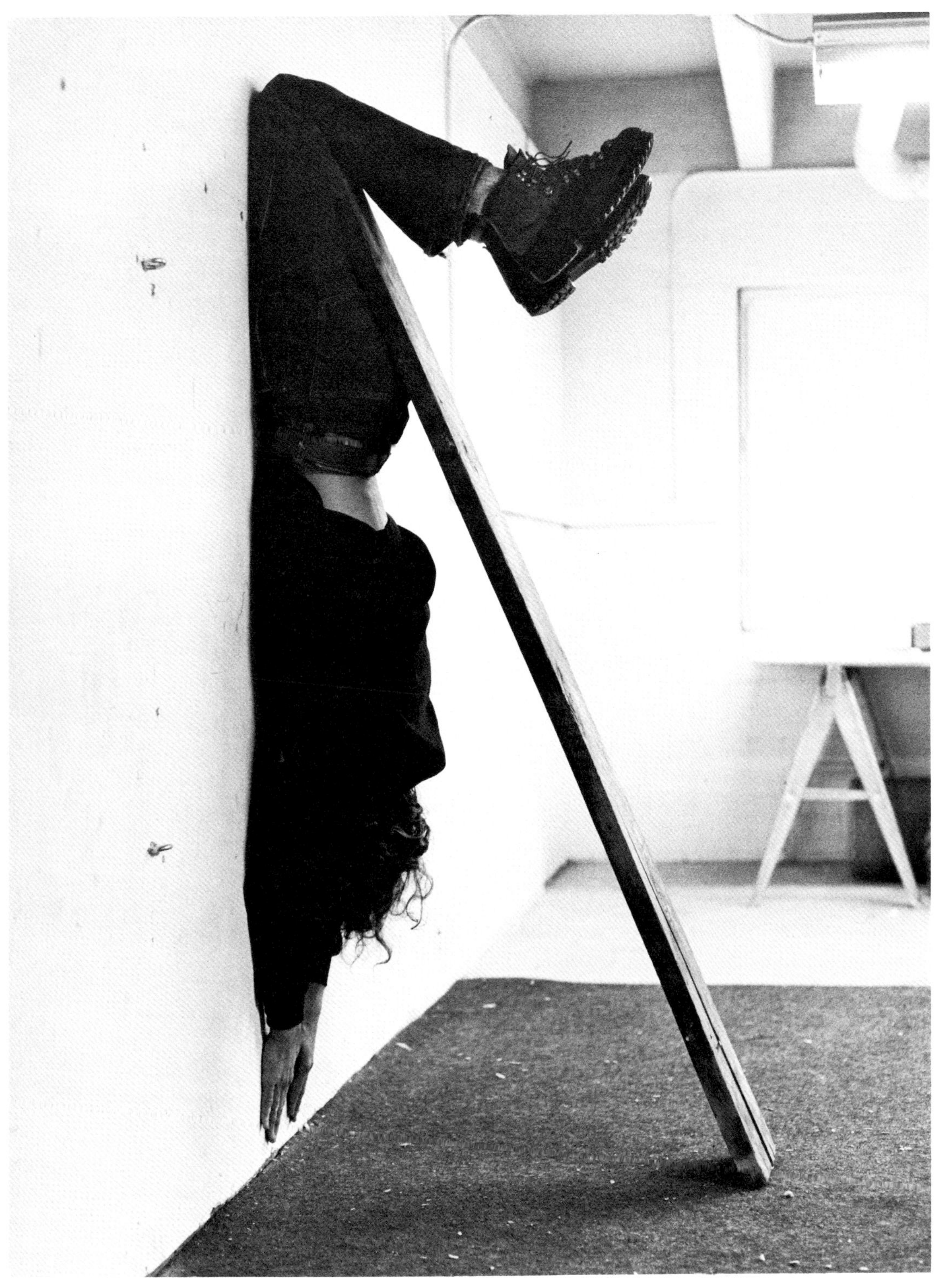

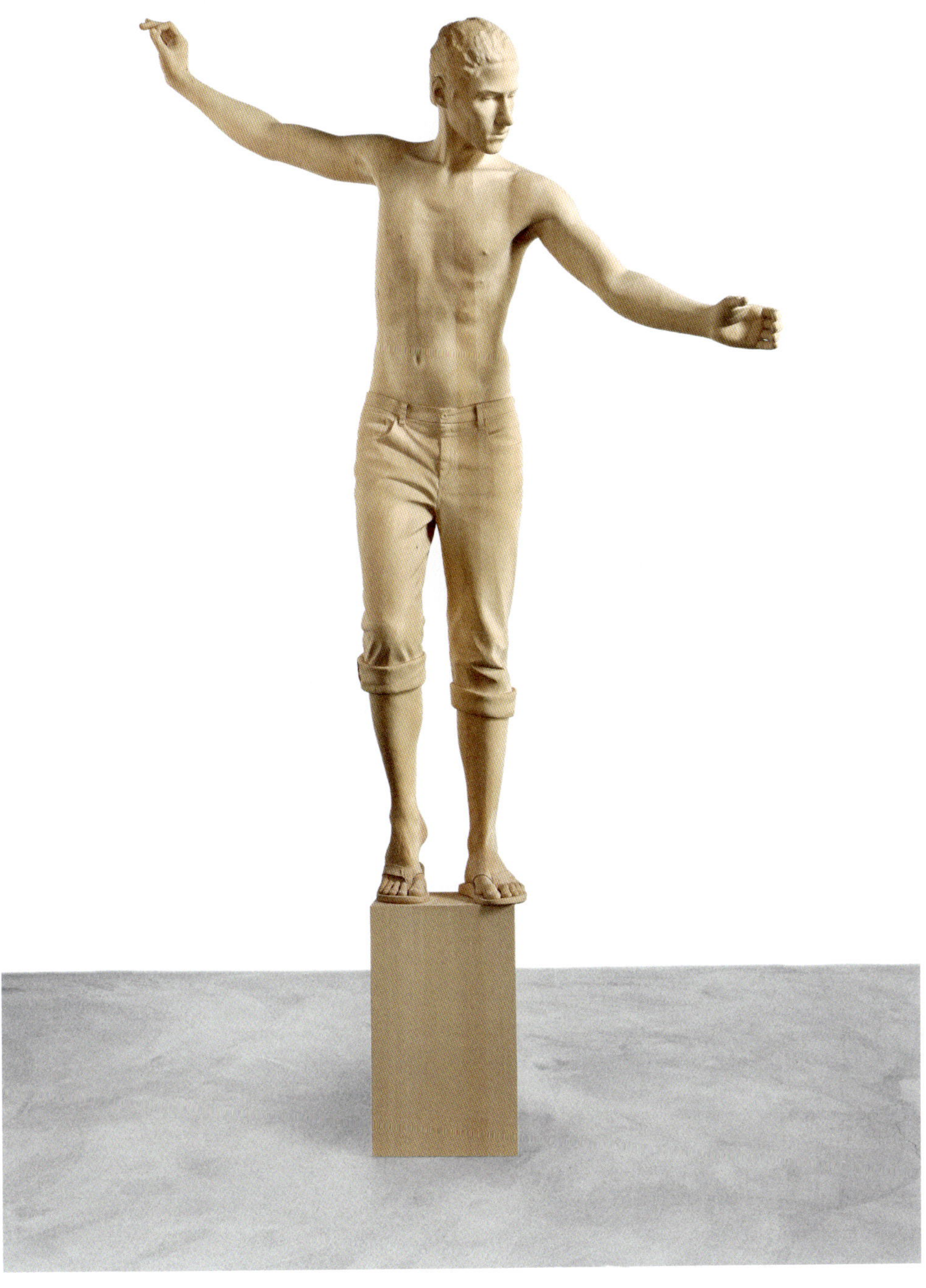

Pl. 11. *Archangel*, 2021

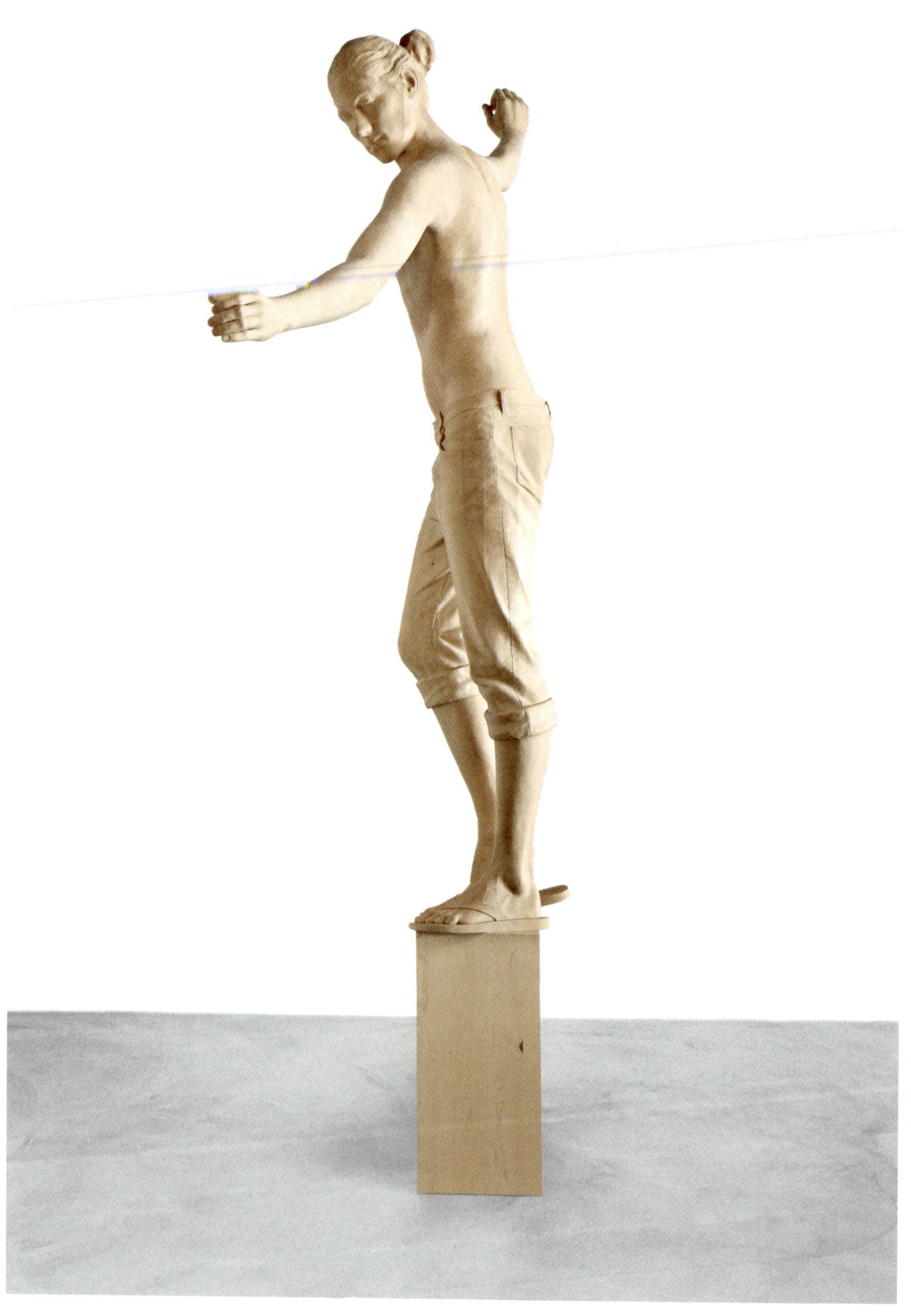

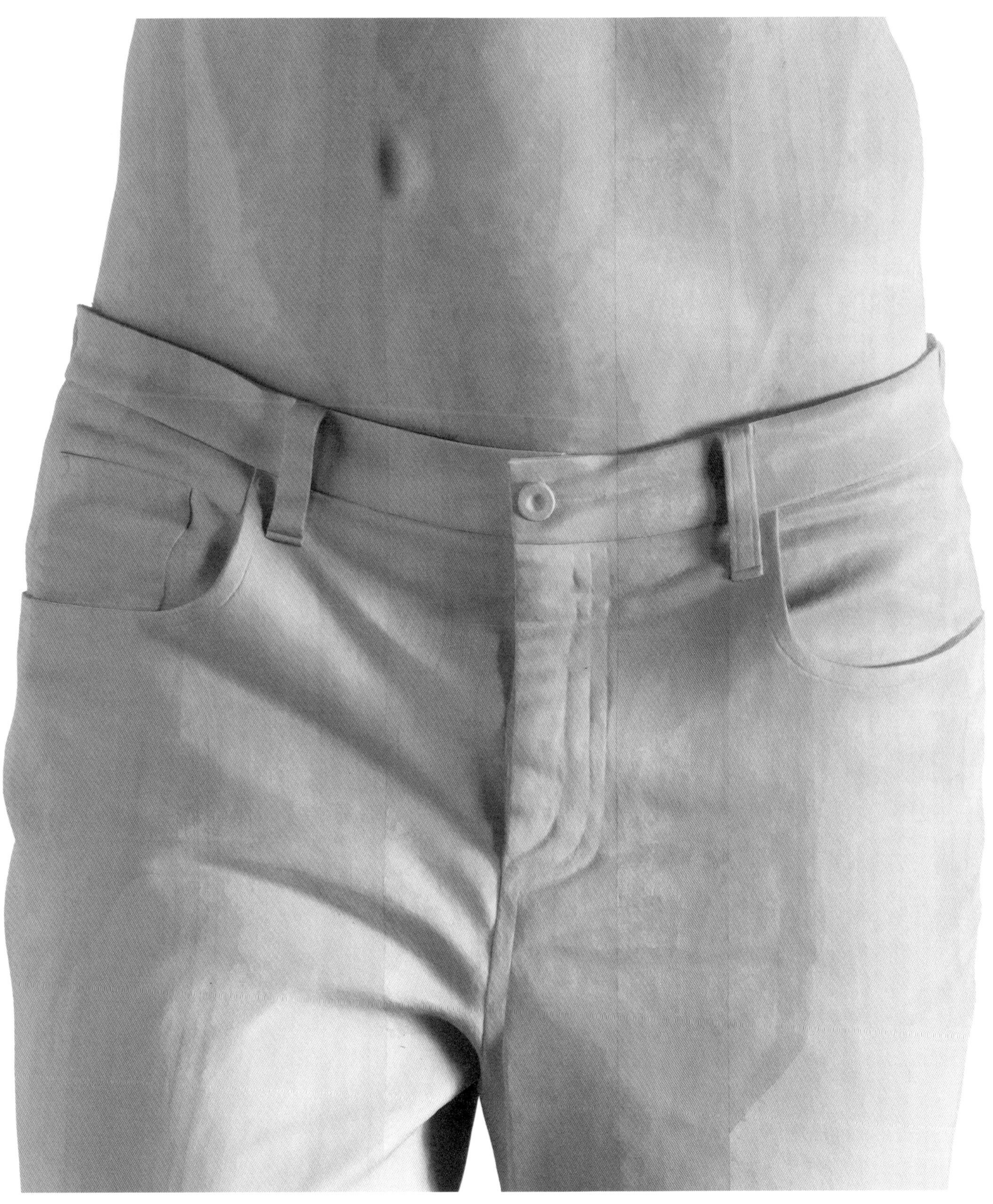

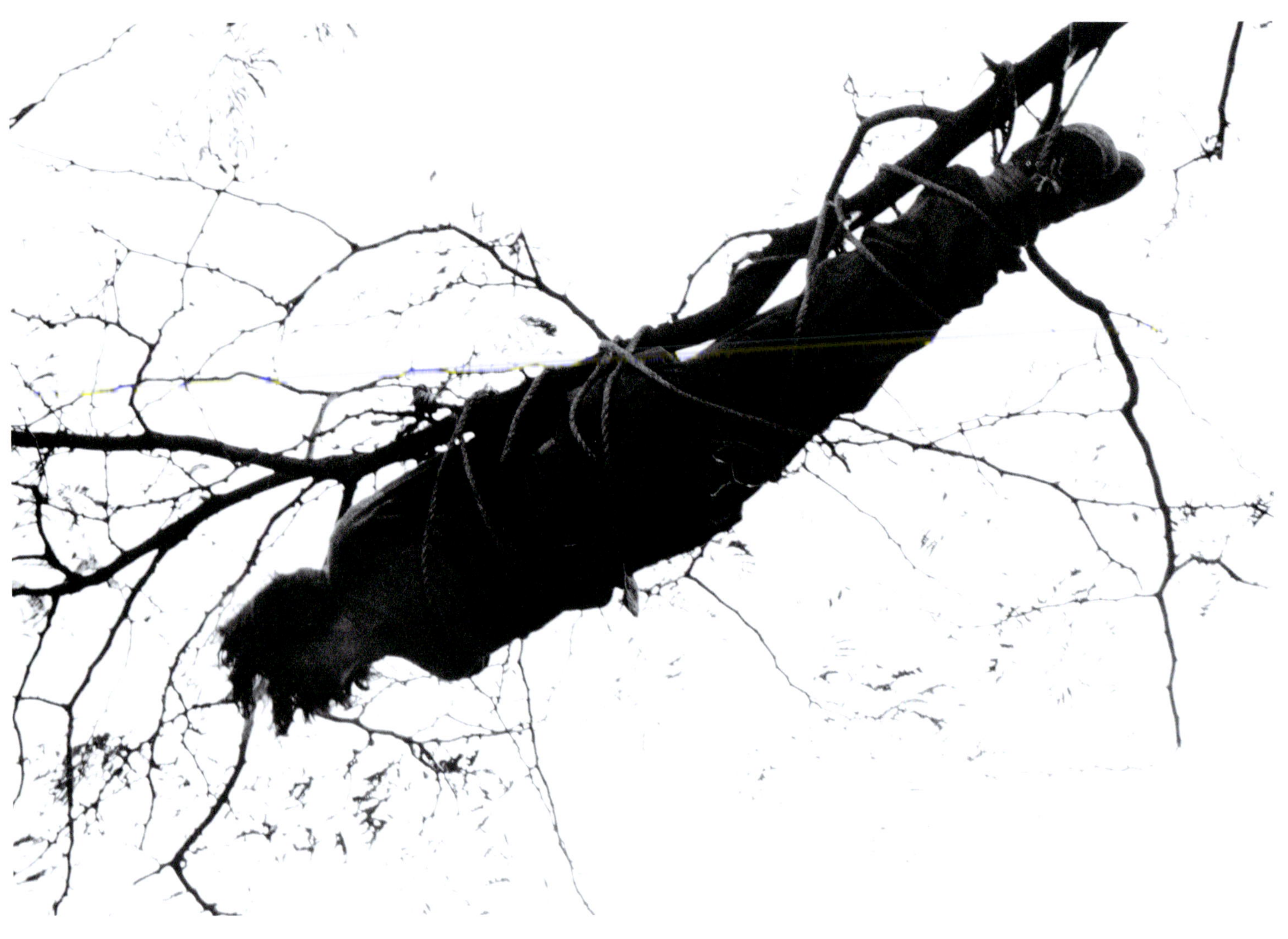

Pl. 12. *Untitled*, 1973

Pl. 13. *Rotating circle*, 1988

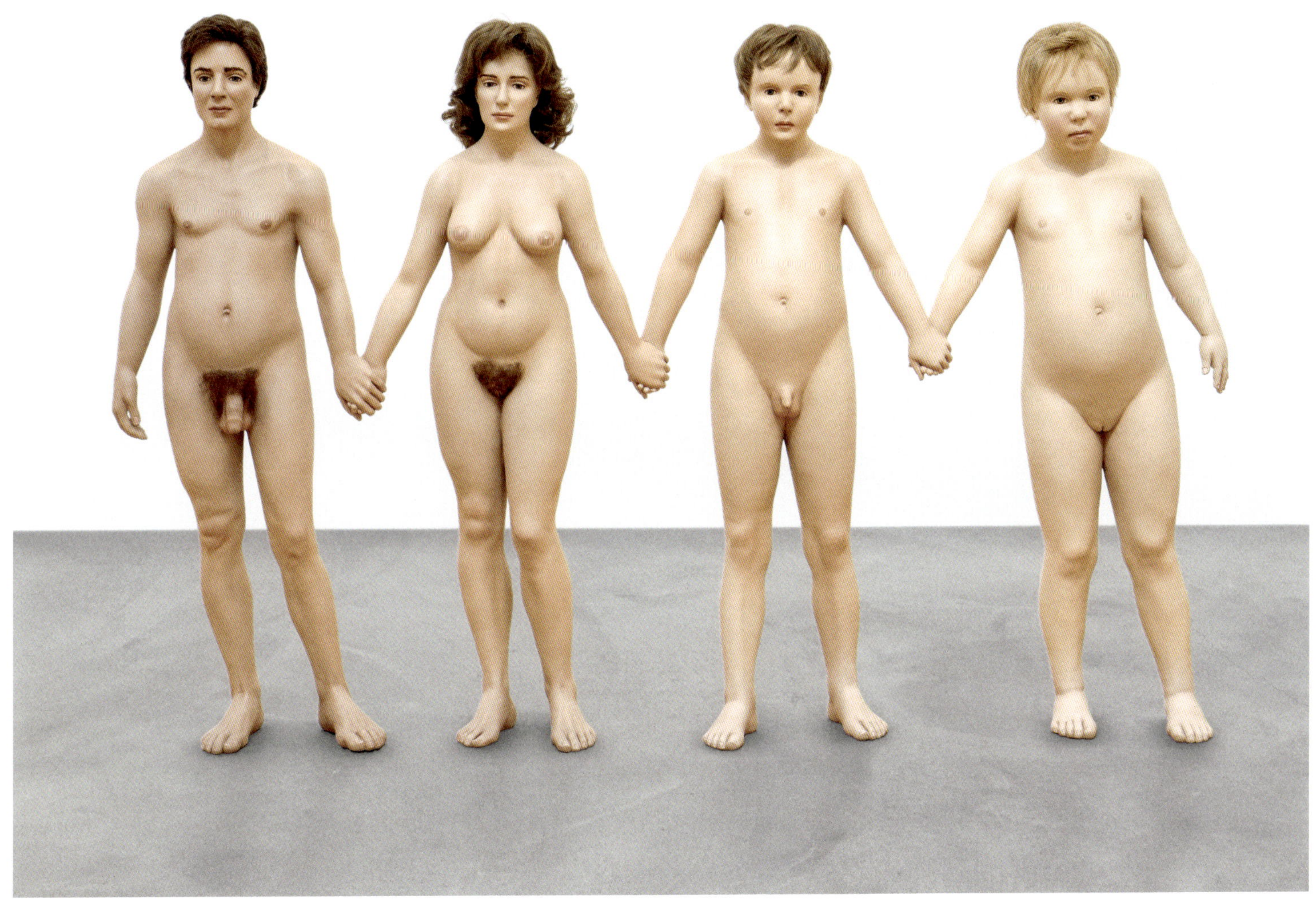

Pl. 14. *Family romance*, 1993

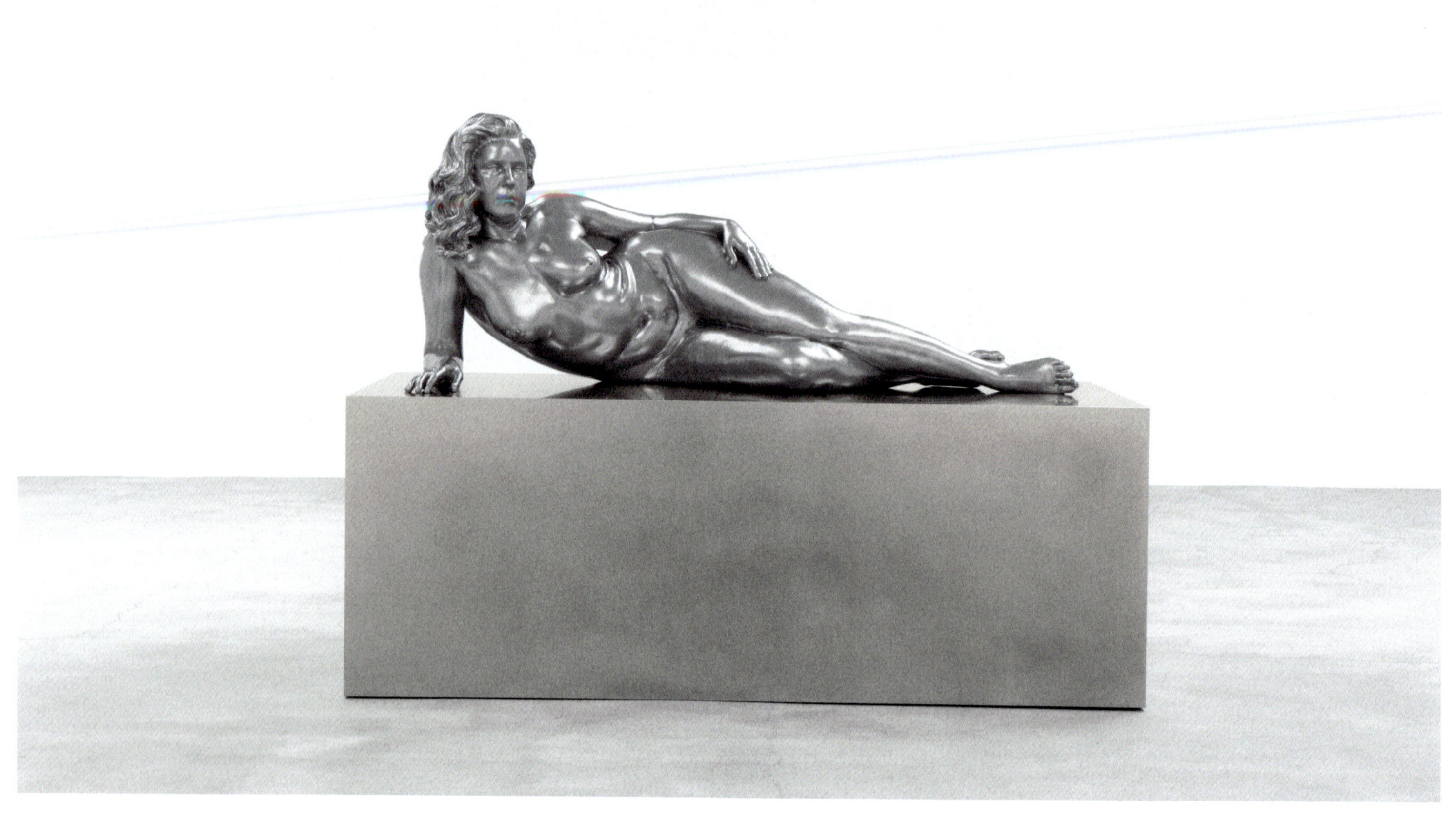

Pl. 15. *Reclining woman*, 2018

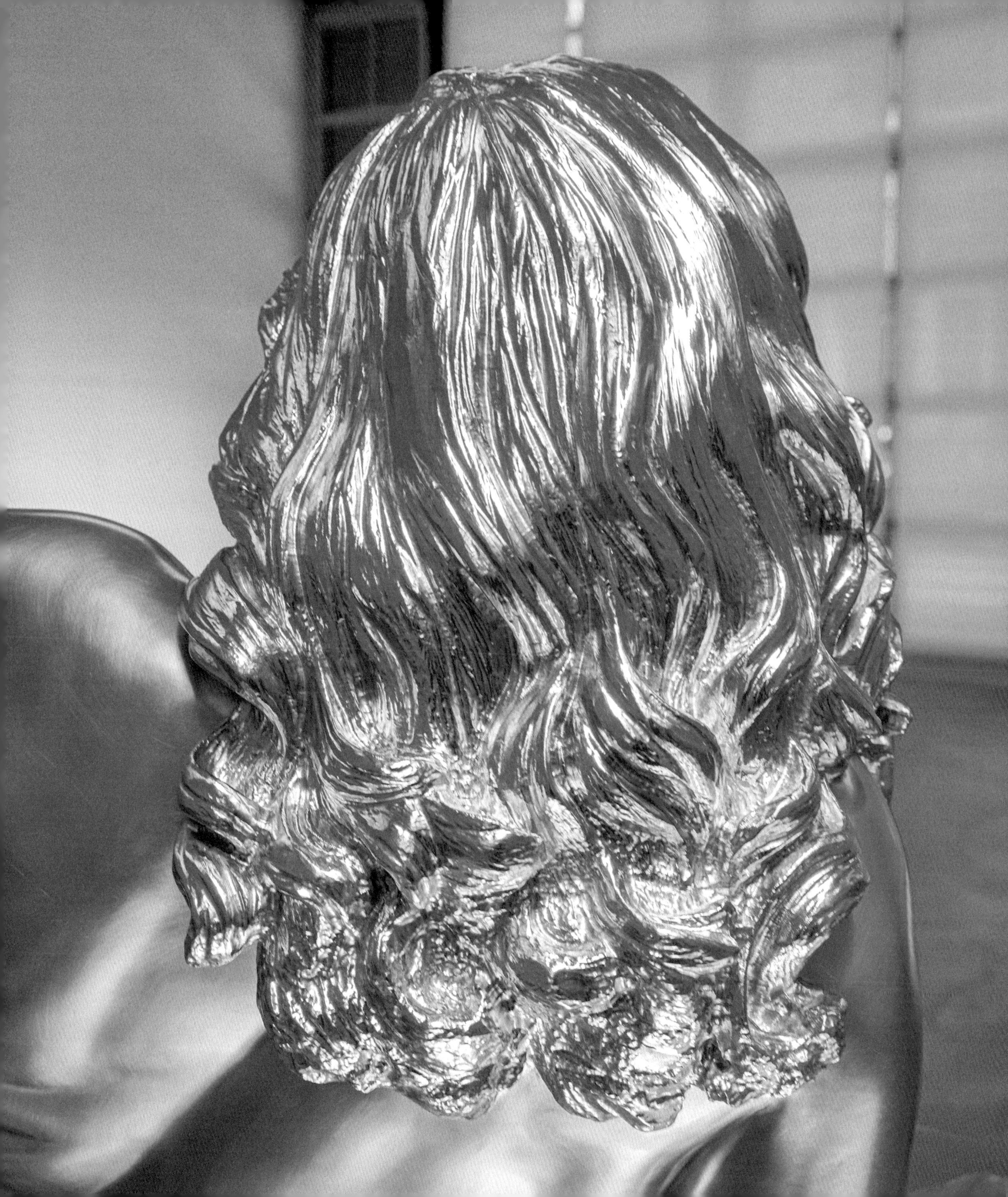

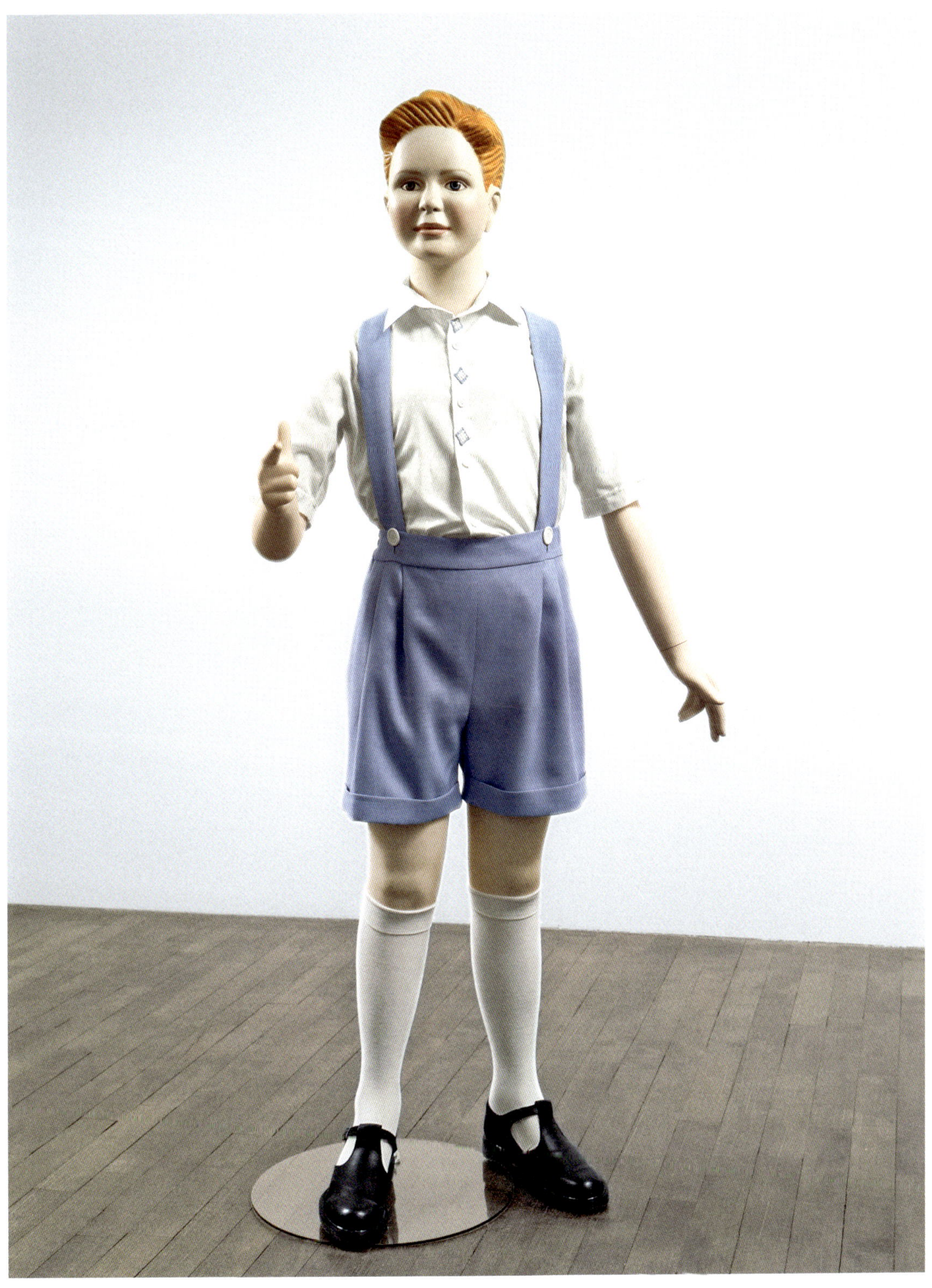

Pl. 16. *Boy*, 1992

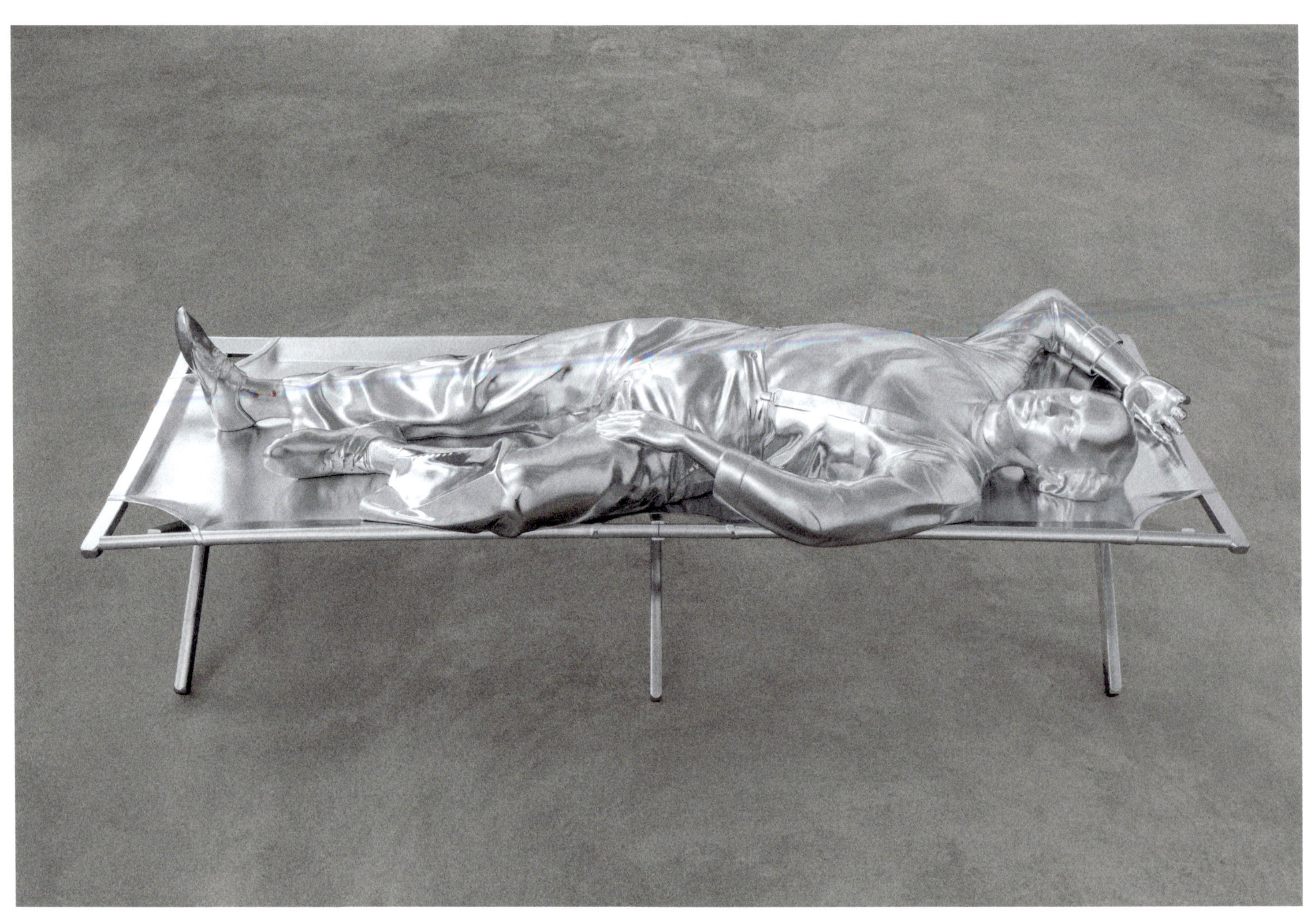

Pl. 17. *Mime*, 2014

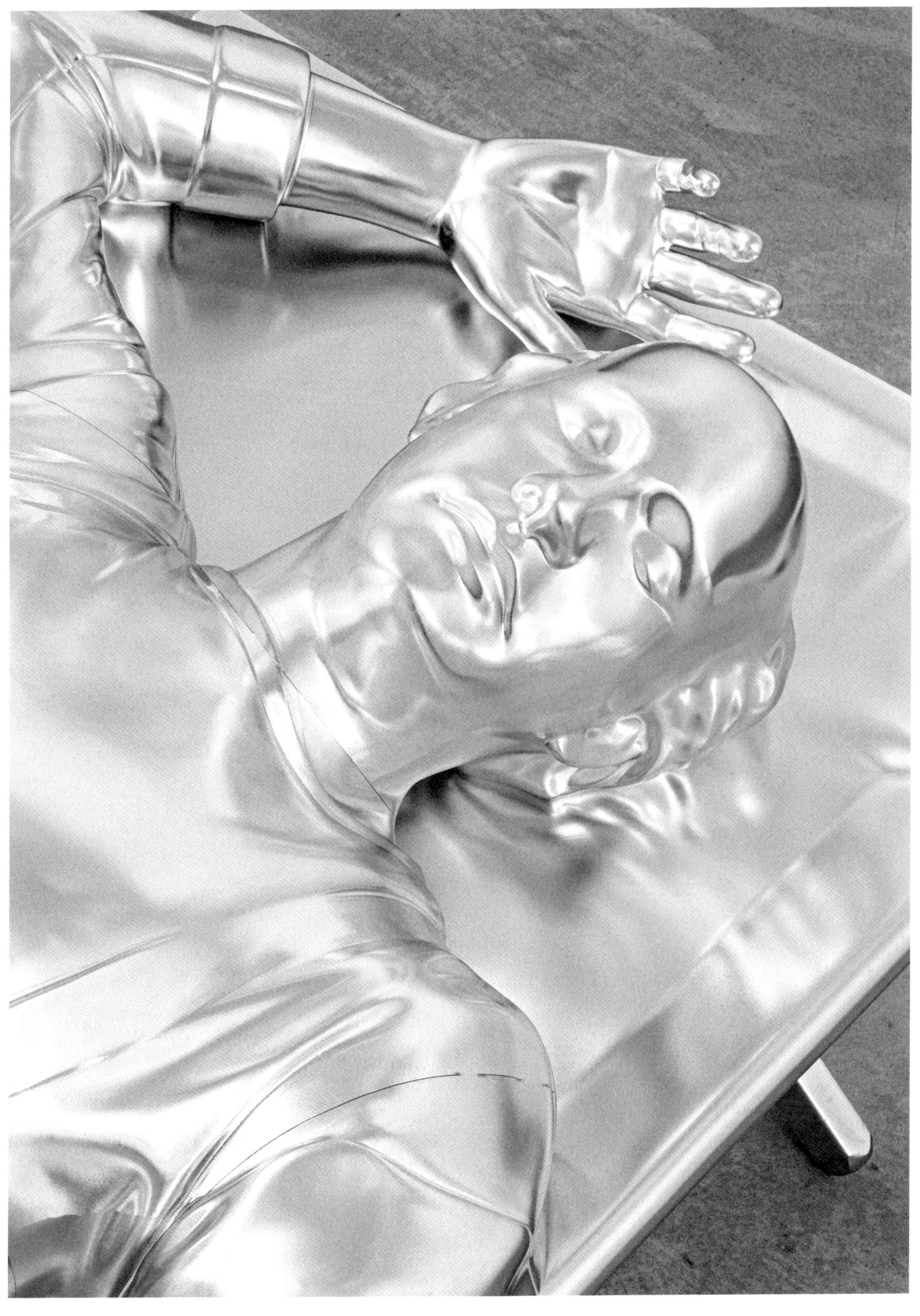

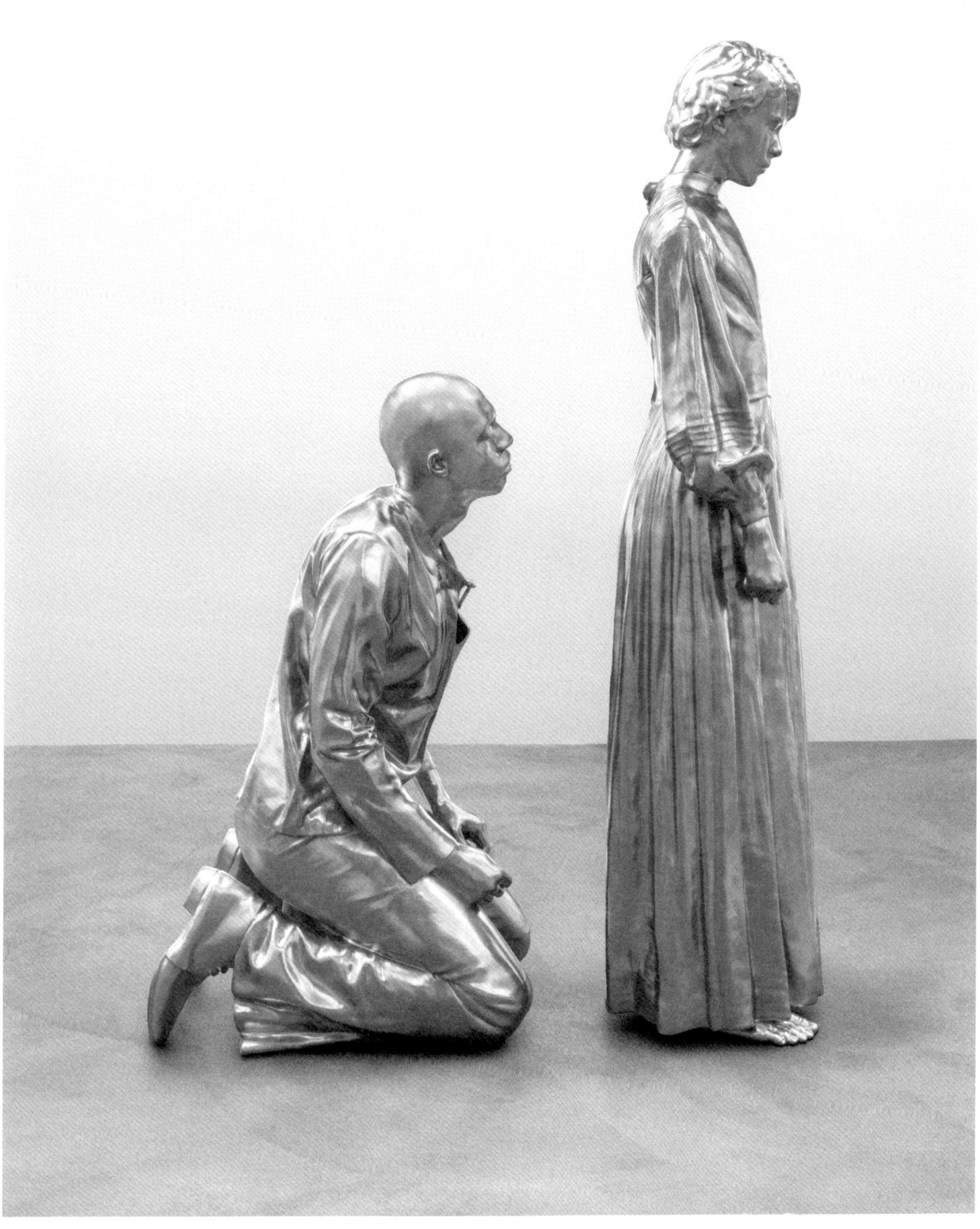

Pl. 18. *Sarah Williams*, 2021

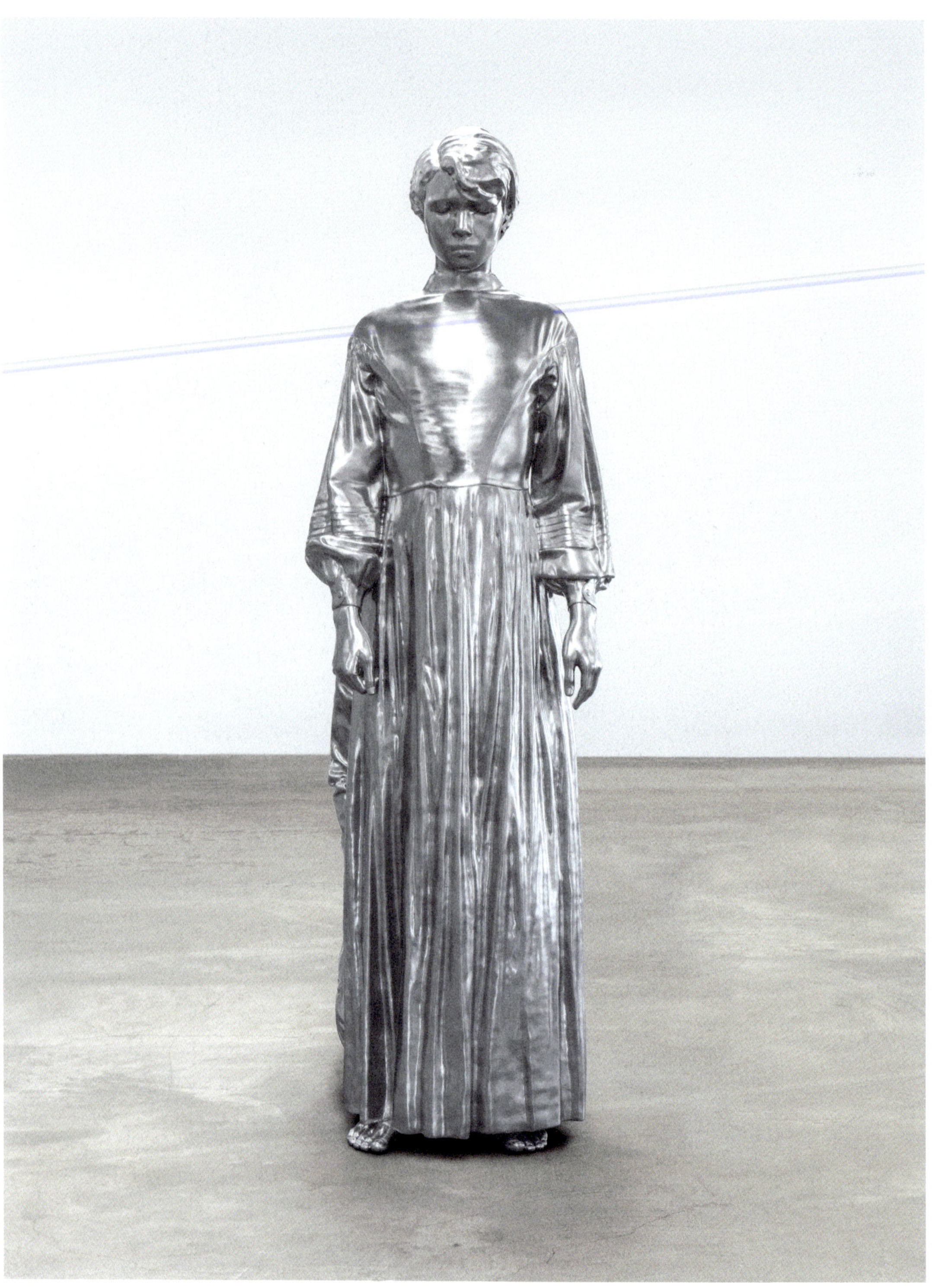

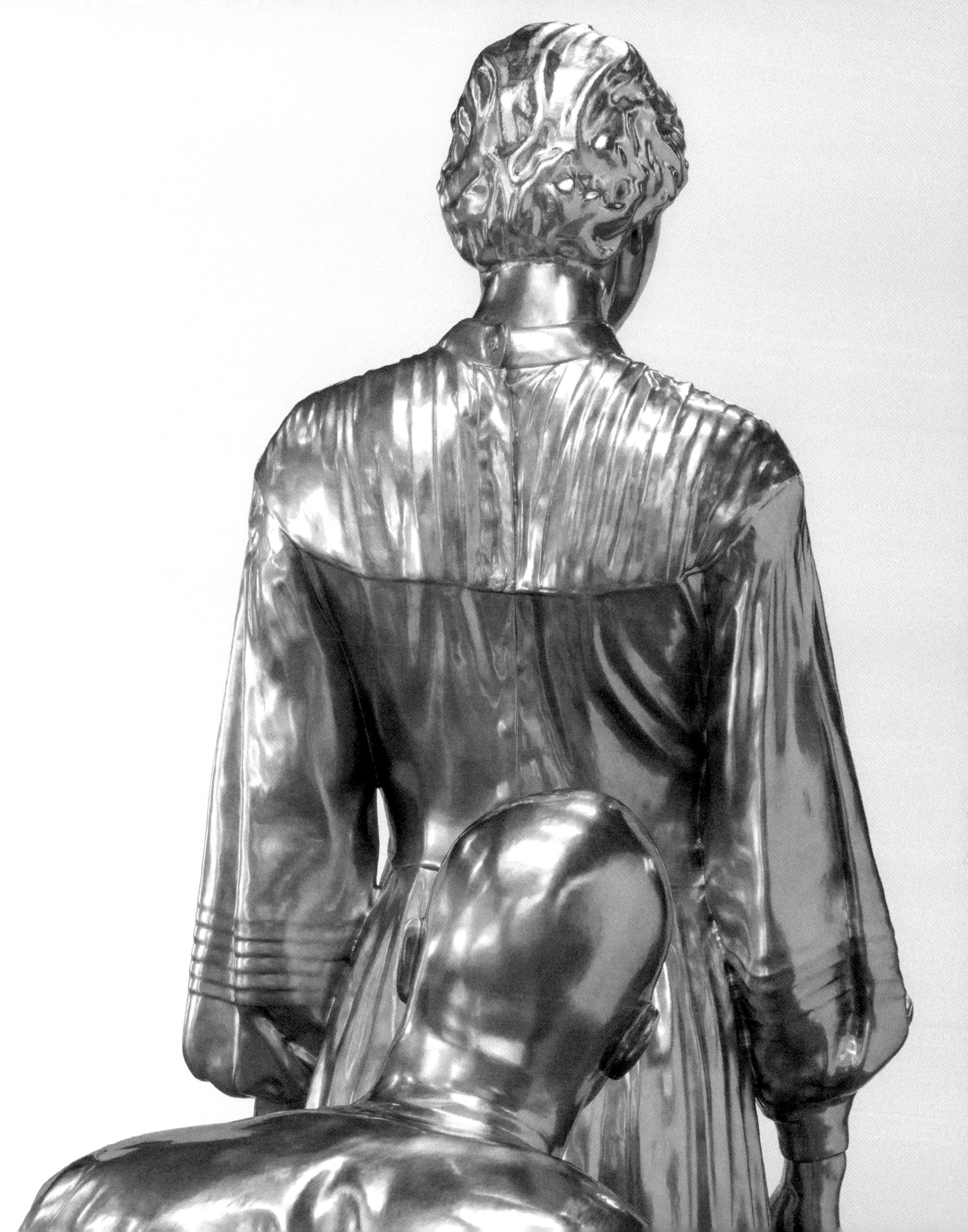

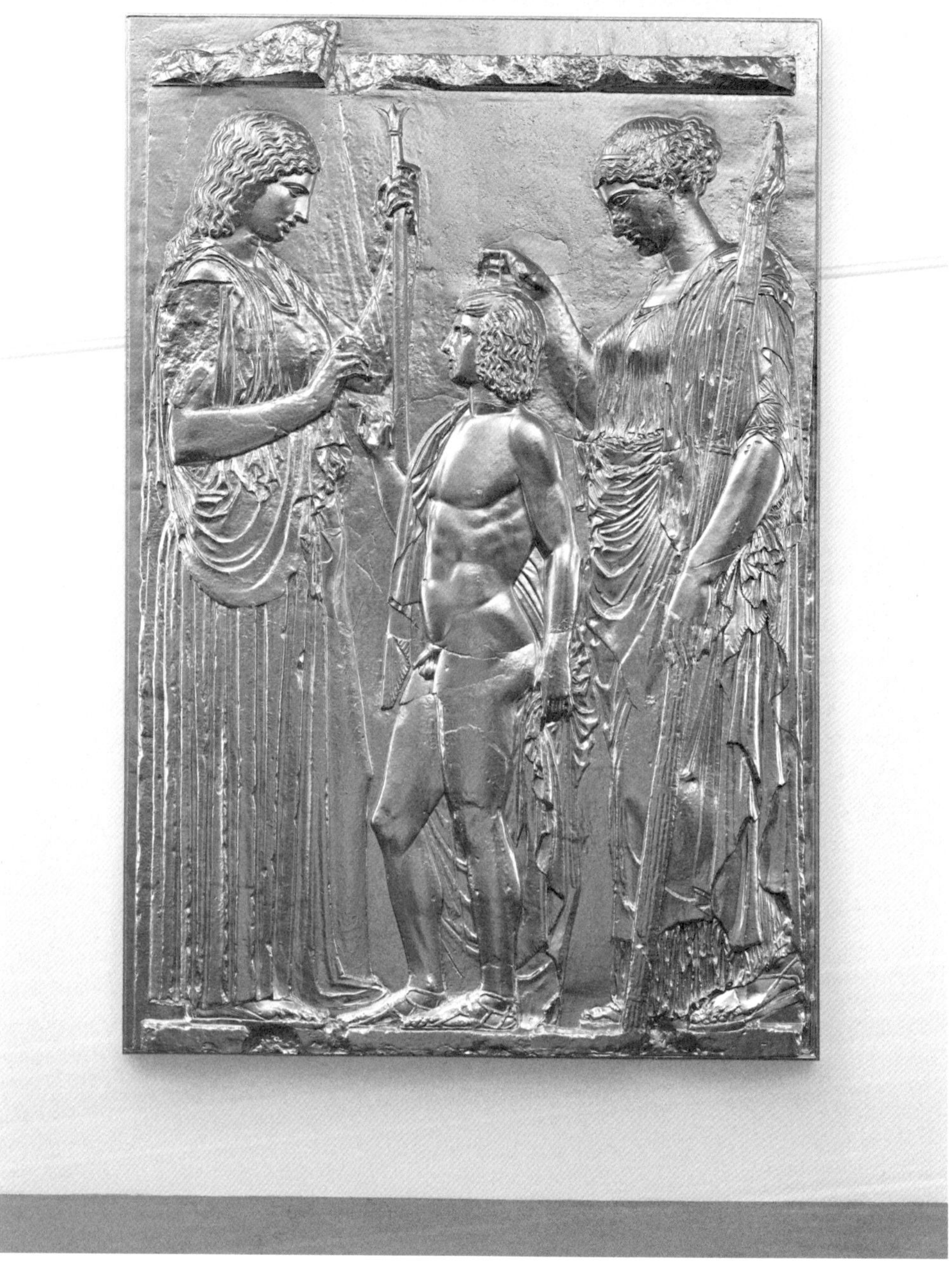

Pl. 19. *A copy of ten marble fragments of the Great Eleusinian Relief*, 2017

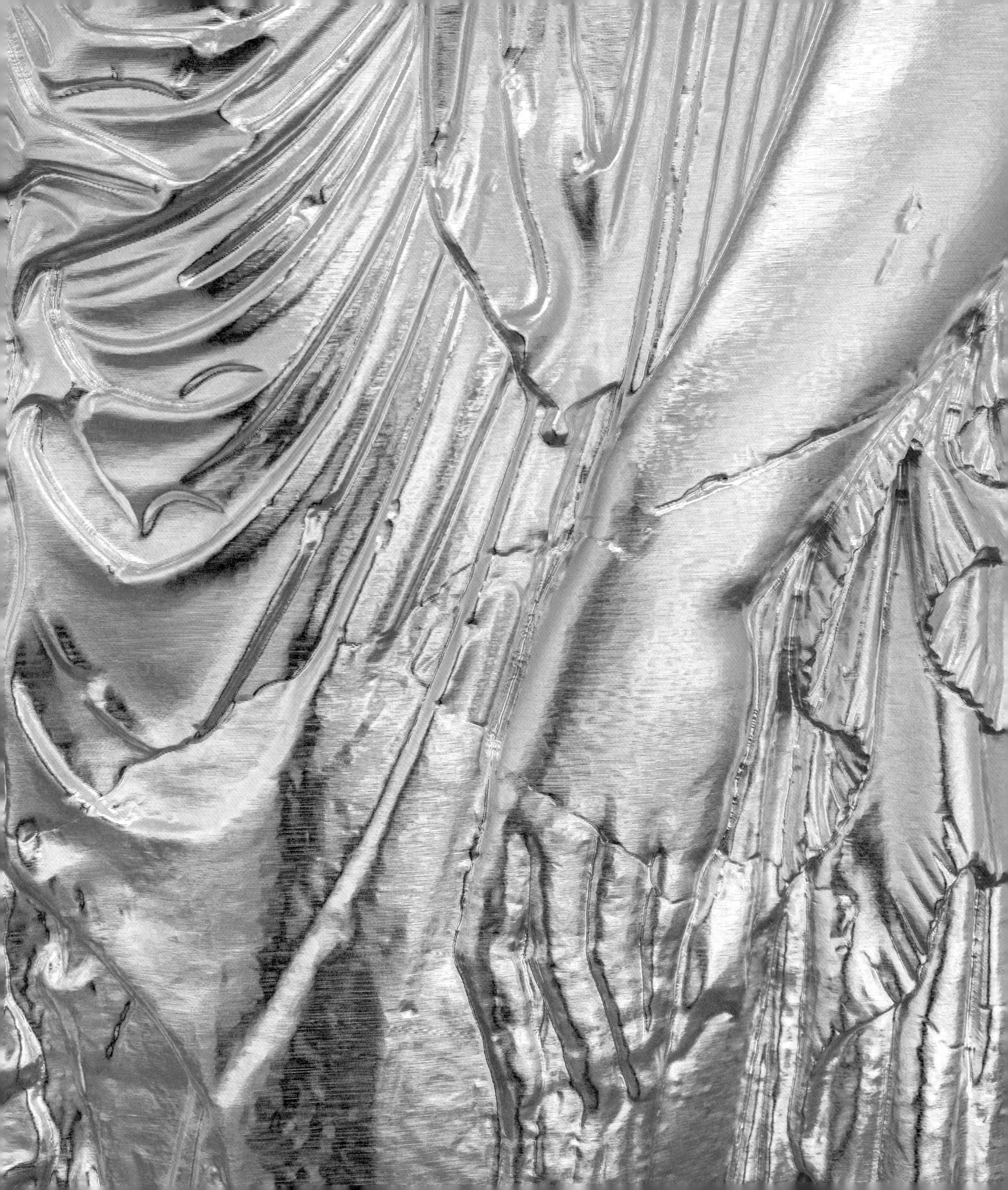

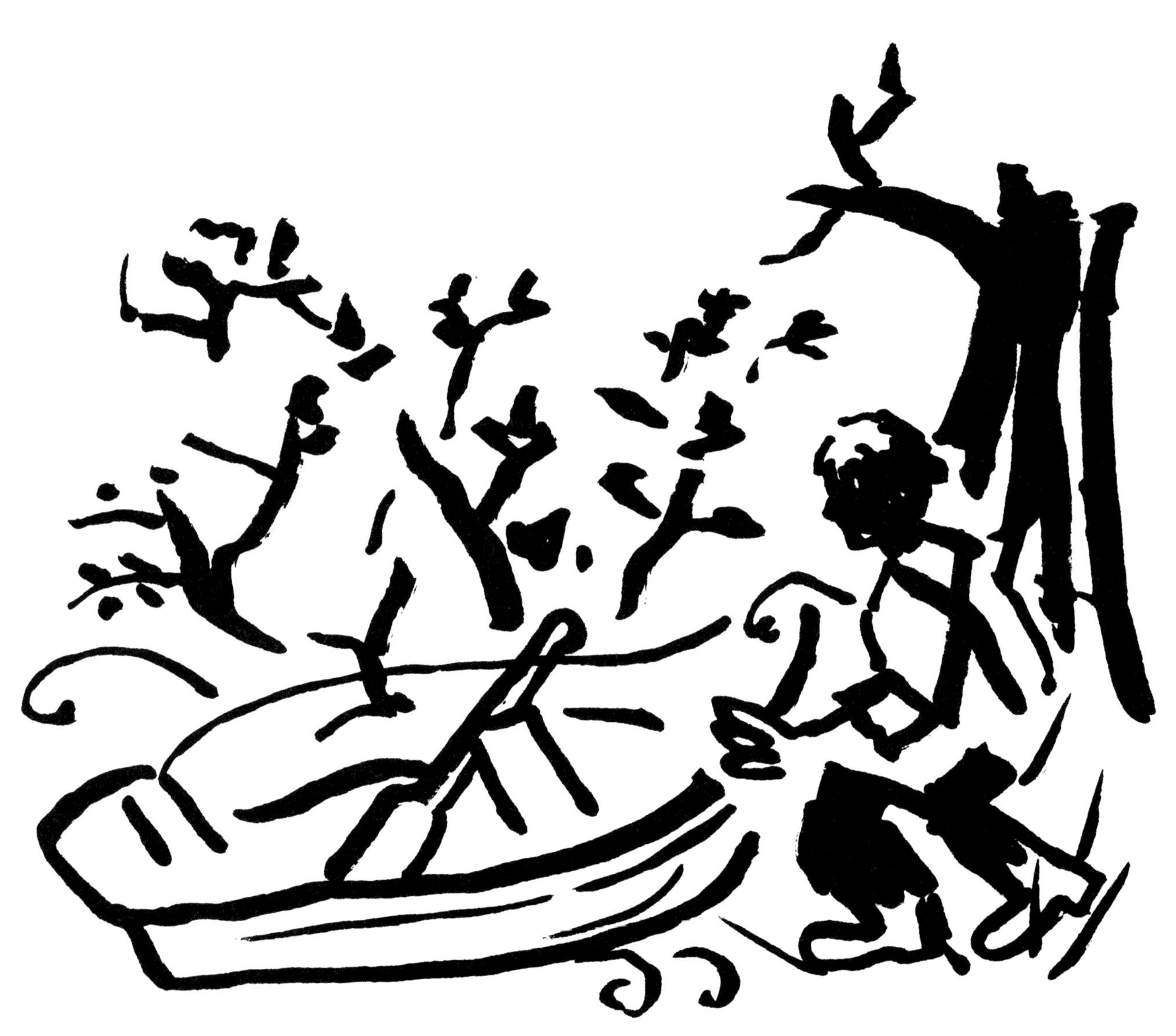

Floating through the Exhibition with Huck and Jim

Charles Ray

EXPLANATORY

In this book a number of dialects are used, to wit: the Missouri Negro dialect; the extremest form of the backwoods Southwestern dialect; the ordinary "Pike County" dialect; and four modified varieties of this last. The shadings have not been done in a haphazard fashion, or by guesswork; but painstakingly, and with the trustworthy guidance and support of personal familiarity with these several forms of speech.

I make this explanation for the reason that without it many readers would suppose that all these characters were trying to talk alike and not succeeding.

THE AUTHOR.

At the beginning of *Adventures of Huckleberry Finn*, the author Mark Twain makes clear that the various dialects used by characters in the novel are researched and purposeful. The accurate use of dialects brings a richness to the narrative and, as the river cuts through a landscape, the way people speak brings a political dimension equal to the snags and bars encountered in a current both geological and social. While drifting on a raft down the Mississippi with the runaway enslaved man Jim, Huck commented that they had no need for clothes no how.

Two or three sculptures in this exhibition broke from Twain's river, like oxbow lakes do when a river finds its shortest path through a bending curve. An oxbow lake is left behind—a

Fig. 44. Drawing by Charles Ray

feature in its own right. If *Huck and Jim* or *Sarah Williams* fell out of Twain's novel, they became features of my own sculptural landscape. Now, as David Smith would say, they are part of my own work stream. The various dialects or even genres encountered in this exhibition talk to you rather than each other.

Figure ground. *No*. The three eggs. *Boy with frog*. The sunken box. *Tractor*. *Huck and Jim*. *Table*. Plank one and two. The archangel. *Family romance*. *Rotating circle*. *Reclining woman*. *Boy*. Sleeping mime. *Untitled*. *Sarah Williams*. The Met relief. What do the works in this exhibition have in common? The subjects, while psychological and seemingly diverse, are in a certain sense materials of the exhibition, and in another sense simply unfathomable to me, the artist. My subjects come easy; their proper parts and the relationship between the parts are harder. The mereology of the sculpture itself, a relationship of details. Overall gestalt and the relationship to the viewer are much harder to bring into the world. *No* (pl. 1) is an infinite regress. The viewer moves through the genre of employee-of-the-month photography to a sculptural plastic rendition of the artist himself. As an ancient Greek philosopher commented, it's turtles all the way down. While this artwork is based on a philosophical structure, it is nevertheless a one-to-one depiction of what it feels like to be me, the subject of the portrait. You might turn the corner and see the eggs, *Chicken* (pl. 2), *Handheld bird* (pl. 3), and *Hand holding egg* (pl. 4), as a beginning, a beginning out of regress, but they also form a circle of space and a tactility that reaches deep into my soul and hopefully yours.

I made *Boy with frog* (pl. 9), which has roots in *Huckleberry Finn*, after an open-heart surgical operation to replace my aorta. It's hard to say what my relationship to my aorta and my heart and my heart-lung system really is. It seems to elude a sense of figure and ground. The idea for *Boy with frog* came quickly when François Pinault asked me to make a sculpture for the Punta della Dogana, the location of his new art museum in Venice. I instantly saw a boy holding a frog. The exact relationship to the ground was unclear, but perhaps everyone was given a frog to dissect in school, the first piece of biology we studied. A human life separate from our own transcending the reptilian. What one remembers is opening the external and looking into the internal.

The location of this sculpture, like the frog itself, was the skin (fig. 45). I had been to Venice several times but didn't understand the city. The figuration, the architecture, the squares, the line at Saint Mark's, the figuration on the Dogana itself and its relationship to the color of the water. Was this the ground for my figure? Or, like the frog, did it need to be opened up? I had no idea. I had no idea how to make my sculpture of a boy become a citizen of Venice—a public work that belonged at the entrance to the Grand Canal. I had no idea how to find a quality of civic-ness. What would the armature of the sculpture be? Would it be the trajectory of a gaze of a boy holding a frog by its leg? Could I

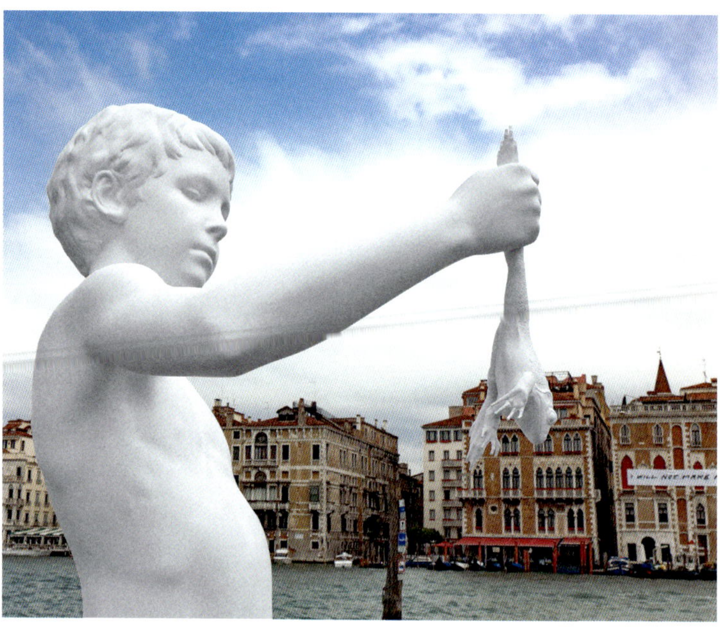

Fig. 45. *Boy with frog*, 2009 (pl. 9) installed in Venice, 2011

build a sculpture around a glance as if it were a wire armature to load clay upon? Or could the sculpture itself become an armature for contemporary Venice? What was this boy doing? Contemplating the other? Clarifying human curiosity? If the boy has a relationship to the frog, does the sculpture have a similar relationship to Venice? And what is our relationship to the sculpture and the sculpture's relationship to the statuary and the city? Can we find a bedrock to build the sculpture upon?

Both *Boy with frog* and *Huck and Jim* (pl. 7) were early statues to be toppled in this age of cultural reckoning. Several years after *Boy with frog* was made, an unstoppable Facebook campaign demanded that the nineteenth-century lamp it had replaced be returned to its rightful position. *Boy with frog* never became a citizen of Venice, but *Huck and Jim* was toppled before it was completed, the figures' nakedness and poses seen as potentially controversial. The Whitney Museum had asked me to make a fountain for its new building at the end of the High Line, a tourist destination. I thought for a very long time on what could fit both physically and culturally. It occurred to me that the full name of the museum was the Whitney Museum of American Art, and with that I had the realization that I needed to embrace not just what I could make, but what America could make and what America was. I returned to the river and to Twain and, most specifically, to chapter 19 of *Huckleberry Finn*.

Huck and Jim stand at the river's edge. While they are hiding, they look into the cosmos and have a debate. Were the stars made or were they always there? Jim believes that they were created—laid like eggs, by the moon—and Huck sees them as always there, always have been, and always will be. They just are. As for the sculpture, I saw the two figures as one beast—a forest of limbs. A chest full of joy in Huck, bending over, pulling out frog eggs from the river. And Jim standing hesitantly next to him, his gaze directed out at the voyage yet to be. Jim's hand hovers tentatively over Huck's back, an empty space between the two, a space that is simply a spacer for a world yet to come that perhaps never will (fig. 46). There are two gestures: joy and anxiety. Youth and early adulthood are contained in this sculpture. All of the details on and between Huck and Jim rain out of the novel, rain out of the two literary figures and their complex relationship. There is a gestalt of Huck and Jim that is primary to the sculpture. It is present before the details come into focus. Their nakedness is like the river water. The making of the sculpture is the river. And the sculpture itself is an oxbow lake fallen out of the novel.

Look now at *Plank piece I and II* (pl. 10), photographs from a much earlier time in my life—a documentation of two performed sculptures I made in one evening under fluorescent lights. My work and my sculptures at that time were behavior. I slid elements around the floor: chunks of steel beam, concrete blocks, ropes, and planks. This aesthetic was a formalism that came from my early understanding of modernist sculpture. But being in my own age in my own time, I saw the ability to enter and

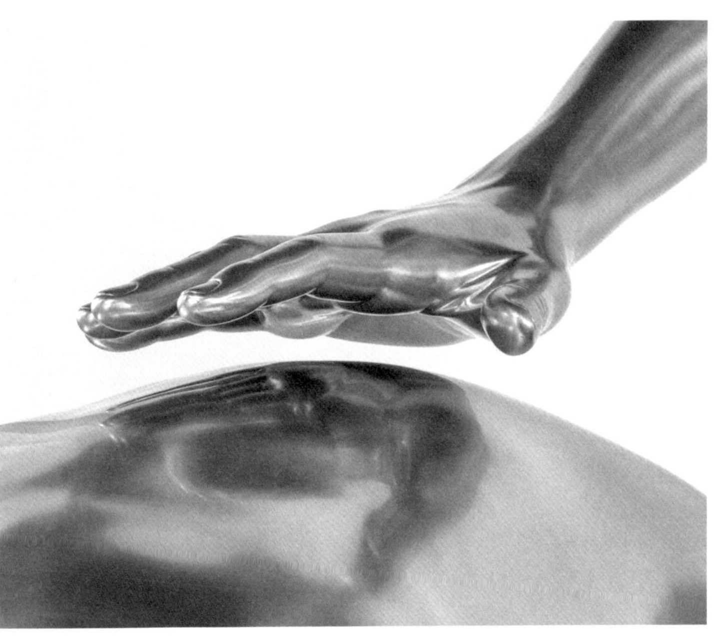

Fig. 46. *Huck and Jim*, 2014 (detail of pl. 7)

exit a sculpture with my own body. *Plank piece I* seemed to some like a humorous take on Richard Serra's *Prop* (1968; fig. 35), but I think together with *Plank piece II*, the initial joke dissolves into a felt-ness, into a relationship between the joints of the body, a plank, and a wall. As a young man I denied the empathy and saw only the structure and the weight and the gravity. And they're still out in this world working for me. A very fast moment long ago, its physicality today eludes me.

A number of years ago, *Plank piece I and II* were shown in London with *Table* (pl. 8), which is to your left. With objects set into its Plexiglas top, *Table* is topologically complete. It is open-ended. It is made of space. Space flows through it, under it, up through it. But the cotton jar rudely stops it and activates the space we're in. Additionally, I thought of the holes in the table and the bottom of the vessels as a way to ground the elements in a perfect still life, a way to keep the viewer's mind from moving a glass, a pitcher, or a jar. They would aesthetically lock the work together, thus bringing birth and vision to the space it's in.

Moving from one gallery into the next, another way to exist in space is before you. *Archangel* (pl. 11) was originally conceived as a third civic sculpture after *Boy with frog* and *Huck and Jim*. I was asked to make an exhibition at the Centre Pompidou in Paris shortly after the Charlie Hebdo massacre. How should I face this cultural moment? I considered a work for the sloping square in front of the museum that was once a marketplace, a favorite place for Parisians (fig. 47). I envisioned the archangel Gabriel descending into a city warm in our hearts, not dripping with blood. Our present-day conflicts are almost biblical, but the Muslim, Jewish, and Christian faiths all honor Gabriel.

I wanted to make it seem like Gabriel had just alighted upon the ground. To make him appear light on his feet and tentative in how he would land, I set my model on a tall box. While photographing him in the round, I banged on the box as hard as I could with a stick, making him constantly adjust his balance. When I finished the preliminary studies, I made a crude full-scale mock-up, in which the figure rested directly on the ground. But I missed the box, the narrow pedestal, and the point of view it enabled. Gabriel's feet are now at eye level and so present in our space and time (fig. 48). His modern flip-flops are certainly here and now. And as you travel up the sculpture, you notice that the button holding his jeans together is twisted from his belly (p. 73), and you finally come to his hair bun, which I wanted to be as remote from his feet as a moon of Pluto, if there is such a thing. A few years earlier, I had removed the sword from his hand. Excess baggage, I thought, leaving his outstretched hands empty, the line of his arms bisecting his body. But still I wondered what material he would finally be made in.

I decided to return to Japan, to a culture without a Gabriel, and have my friends who made *Hinoki* (2007; fig. 49) carve my sculpture from a pattern. The work is contingent on it being a single piece of material—the figure can't be removed from the base.

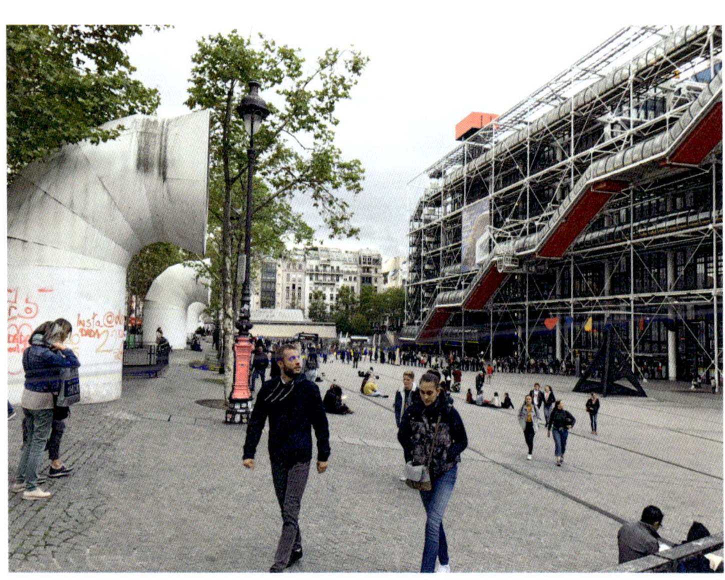

Fig. 47. Place Georges Pompidou, Paris

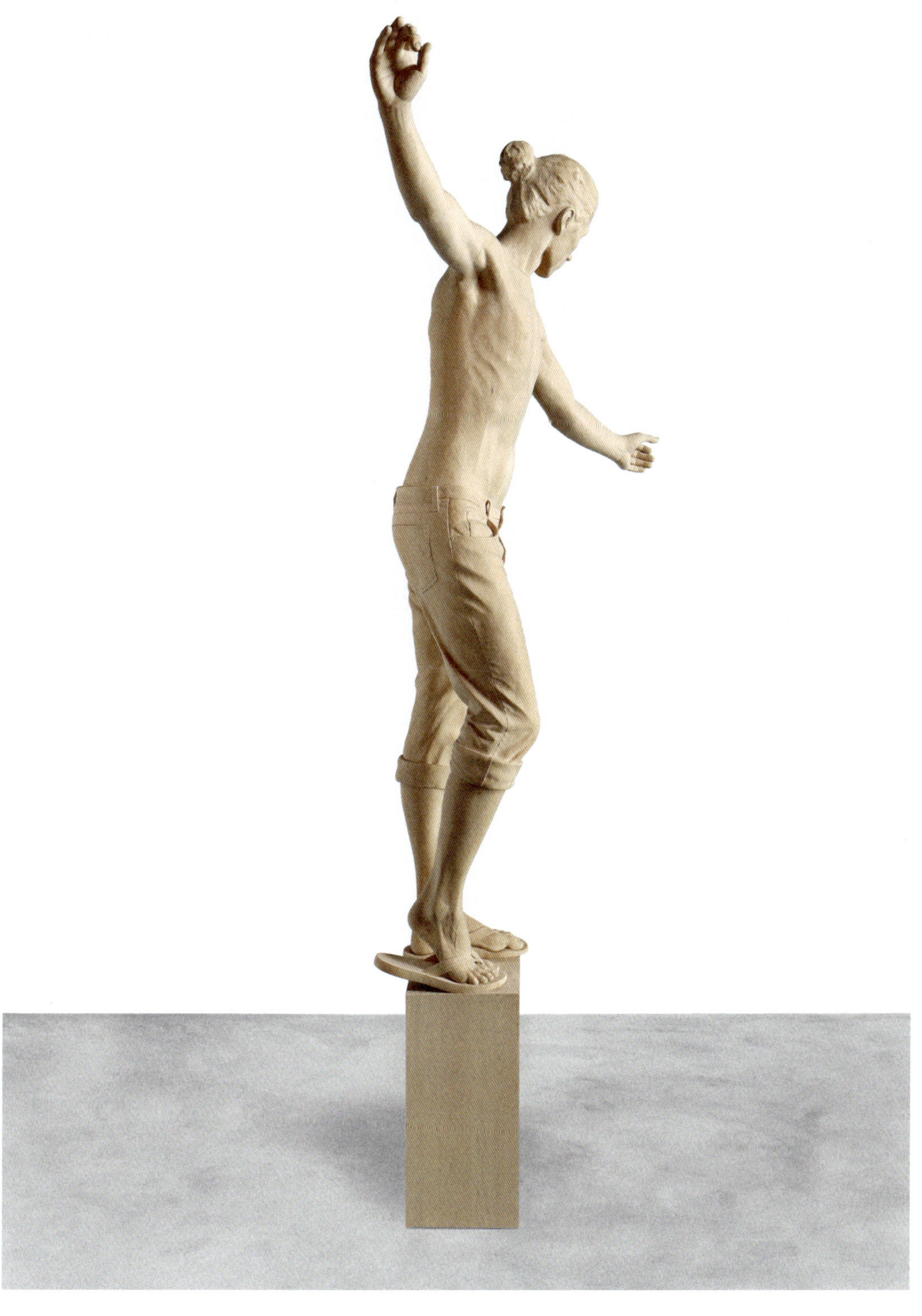

Fig. 48. *Archangel*, 2021 (pl. 11)

A central structural spine, a plank, runs up through the sculpture's laminations, from the bottom to the head. The sculpture slides into space rather than space sliding into the structure, as in *Table*. Anything that slips into space in such a way is sensual. Once I determined that the figure would be made of wood, I saw its relationship to a crucifix.

If you turn quickly to the right there's another photograph from when I was a young artist, *Untitled* (pl. 12). I am tied to a branch high in a tree that hung over a path at the University of Iowa. If you looked up you would see me. I thought of myself in a cocoon as a kind of caterpillar. But when I came down from the tree three hours later with the help of some friends and a ladder, I felt I hadn't metamorphosed; I was only tired and sore. My work didn't slip into the magic of the verb but stayed in the now as an image, and finally exists like *Plank piece I and II* as a photograph.

When you turn again, you might walk up to another figure, a sleeping mime. *Mime* (pl. 17), like all of us, is in this world tenuously. Like Gabriel on his box, the sleeping mime is on his cot. Does my mime sleep, or is he simply miming sleep, sleeping like I sleep? What state is my mime in? For years I looked upon my plaster model of the mime, the pattern, and I always saw it as an image, as something one experienced from the outside, with a line demarcating you and the sculpture. I wanted to shatter that window, to break down the barrier. I realized my method of construction—I used a robot to interpret a machine file of my pattern—was, in a sense, another hand, another aspect of what I was looking for to break down the distance or to bring the image back into the cultural realm. In metal the mime remains a figure, not an image. He is a figure because he is made, obviously so. Every line, every seam, how light is thrown around, the machined weight of the figure on the cot, your involvement with its surface rather than its image—all bring a figurativeness to the figure.

I like equations and run them in two directions. On either side of the equal sign, as we cancel out numbers, as we get simpler and simpler, attention builds. And as we factor down, that is how I sculpt. I sculpt the equation between you, the viewer, and the work. Perhaps it's more honest to say the equation is between me and the work. When you can't be removed, when the sculpture can't be removed from you or you from it, then I have found a completion. But perhaps we need to leave the math and walk across the room to *Reclining woman* (pl. 15). She's a figure, nearsighted, sculpted around the nerve connecting the squinting of her eyes to the involuntary movement of her toe. She finds her persona and we find her abstraction. Her nearsightedness allows you to look in without violation as she looks out at you. The base and the figure are one element, or should I say one sculpture made of two elements? Both are solid. Both are steel. The base is a brick held together by atoms and angles, while the reclining lady is organic and held together by molecules and biological functions. But they're not so different. One could say

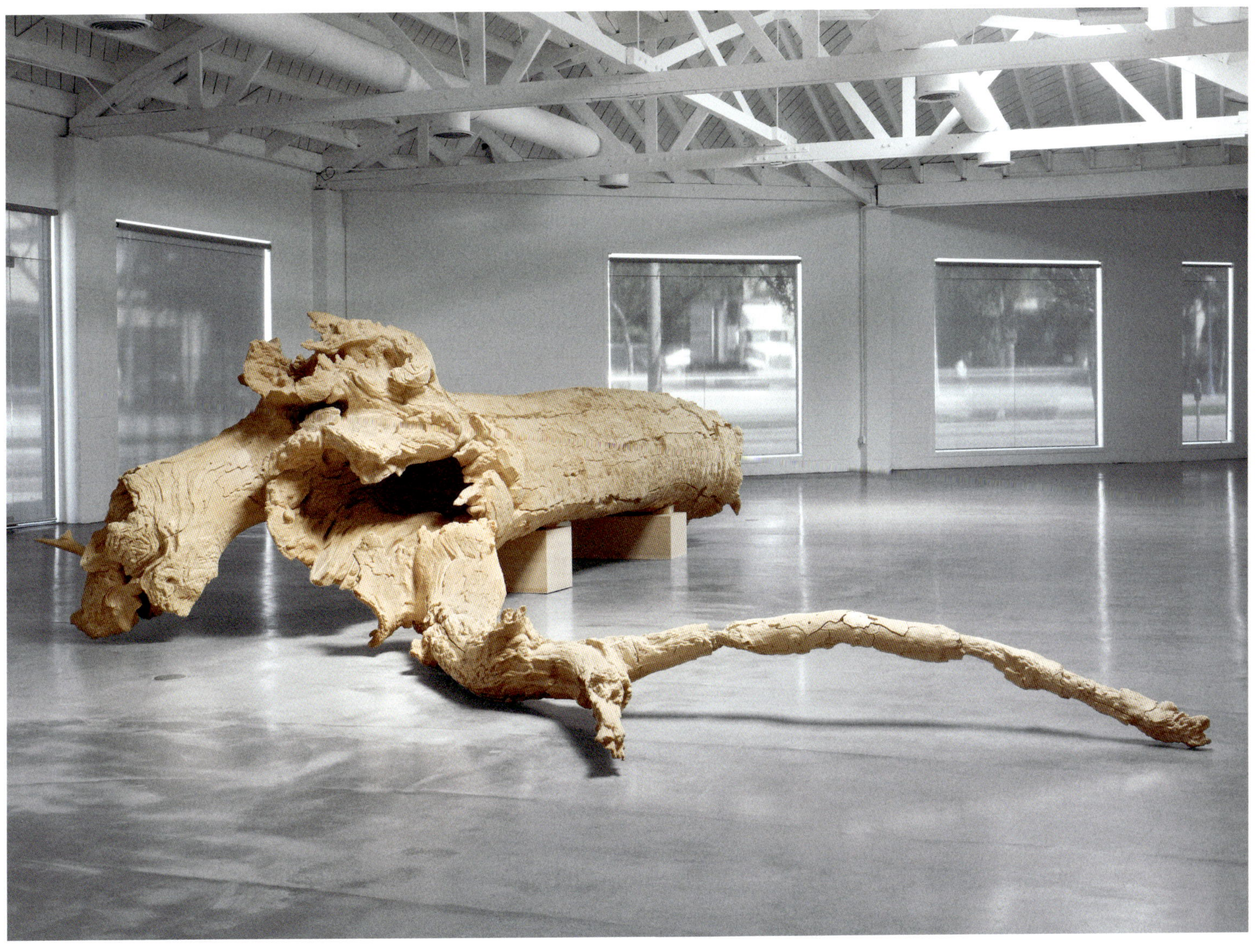

Fig. 49. Charles Ray. *Hinoki*, 2007. Cypress, 68 in. × 31 ft. 10 in. × 20 ft. (173 × 970 × 610 cm). The Art Institute of Chicago, Through prior gifts of Mary and Leigh Block, Mr. and Mrs. Joel Starrels, Mrs. Gilbert W. Chapman, and Mr. and Mrs. Roy J. Friedman; purchased with funds provided by Donna and Howard Stone (2007.771a–e)

there's a relationship between the two, the geometric and the organic. But this relationship perhaps isn't so true. They may be like the equation that runs in two directions simultaneously, one and the same.

Across from *Reclining woman* is *Rotating circle* (pl. 13). Early in my career I tried to pour all of my angst, all of my gestalt into one location, into one structure, and I made a work titled *Spinning spot* (1987), a disc in the floor the same color as the floor, spinning so fast it appeared stationary. Perhaps I misspoke. My angst was not to be poured into a location but simply to be manifested, to be squeezed out of my being. I wanted to make a sculpture that was so abstract it became real, or so real it became abstract. Later I took the structure, shrank it, and mounted it at head height in a wall like a portal or, possibly, like a self-portrait. A placid disk, a simple circle for a head, yet a crazy energy unseen like spinning thoughts in your lover's mind, unknown to you.

In front of this circle is *Family romance* (pl. 14). The title charts the relationship of an average American family. When I made this sculpture during the election cycle of 1992, all one heard from the political debates and advertisements was a discussion of family values—a candidate or candidates that would build a platform around the family, around the rules and religiosity of the family. The government would step away and let our family values bloom into a new American reality—a beautiful idea to remove the government from the authority of the father and the mother and the chronological order of the children. *Family romance* shifts that hierarchy. The children share equal scale with their parents, with every family member the same height. I have also always seen this sculpture as an abstraction of a relationship of parts, with the family members as placeholders for abstract elements. Meaning comes from the relationship of the joints. If it wasn't for the work's surreal Magritte-like frontal-ness, I would hail it as a masterpiece. When I turn away, I turn back toward my own frontal-ness.

Let's continue to think of figuration and what it is to sculpt a person. *Boy* (pl. 16) stands in the middle of the room, his finger like a clock hand that never points to any hour no matter where it is in front of the face. What is the function of a mannequin? What is the figuration? What is the abstraction? A mannequin can never smile. Its eyes are painted out, so it can never make eye contact either. Mannequins are just department store appliances, mirrors for you to see yourself or your children wearing the clothes they wear. *Boy* deals with scale, but unlike *Family romance*, the figure's childhood stature has been increased. He now looks at you squarely in the eye. And what was once a surface for projection and fantasy is finally a monster looking back at you. How do we come to terms with his sculpted hair, his shiny shoes and knee-high socks? Why is it that what we love turns around and becomes a horror? He's not a sculpture of a boy, he's a sculpture of a mannequin, and there the work finds its abstraction. But don't forget it needs its space. And if the civic-ness of

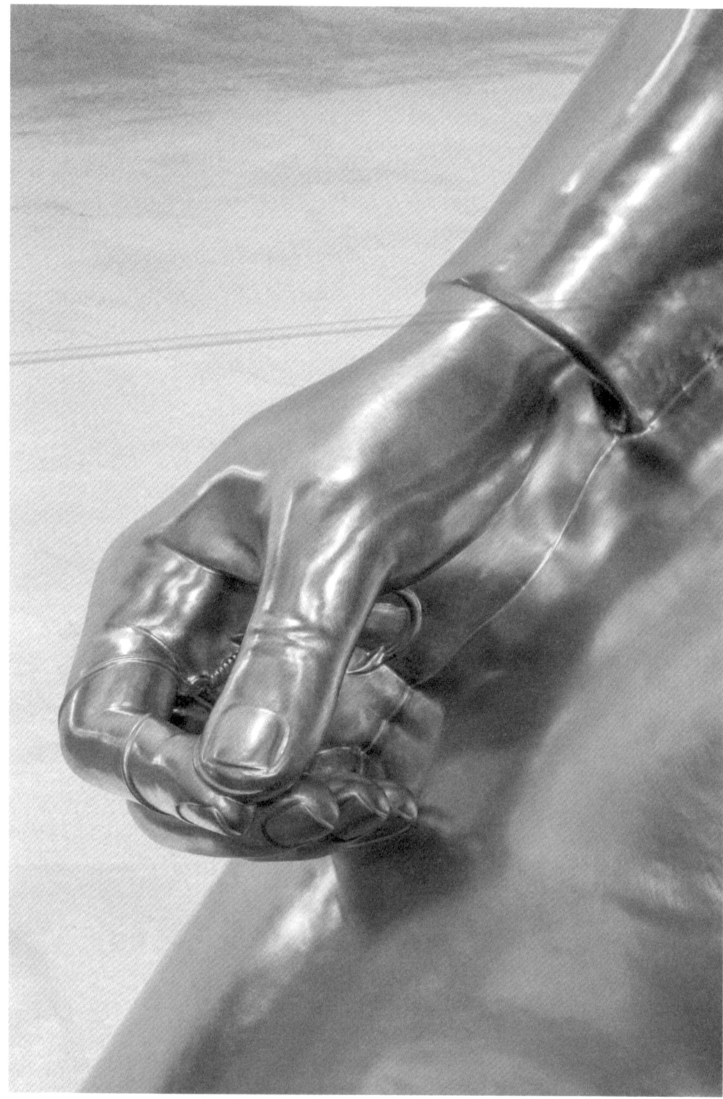

Fig. 50. *Sarah Williams*, 2021 (detail of pl. 18)

my toppled *Boy with frog* carries the whole Dogana into the exhibition, one sees we have entered a different age. The city square is no longer so civic.

And now, floating down and through this exhibition, we near the end, circling round both *Sarah Williams* (pl. 18) and *A copy of ten marble fragments of the Great Eleusinian Relief* (pl. 19), which are also snagged in figuration. Both are copies from the past—one from the meaning of my life and the other from the meaning of the work. In *Sarah Williams* Jim kneels behind Huck, hemming his dress so he can be sent into town to gather information about what folks think of their escape. The figures in *Huck and Jim* remain literary first and foremost. You read them as a scholar would—two characters from a great American novel, manifested in our present time, echoing back to the roots of many of our current conflicts. *Sarah Williams* is the opposite. Every detail, the fish hook in relief upon Jim's hand (fig. 50), the bellows-like folds of his trousers (fig. 51), his horseshoe heels, his gaze and eyes, the flesh on his head, the folds of the dress—all are details in an abstraction, with light bouncing gently between one quality and the other. Their presence reverberates out from the sculpture rather than being revealed immediately. And if the raft flows as you walk around it, stop and look at it.

You can think of *A copy of ten marble fragments of the Great Eleusinian Relief* as the first or last piece in the exhibition. Another figuration of great sexuality, the goddess Demeter's gift, the gift of seed. Track your eye through this piece. The time, the distance it takes to move from the boy's genitals up to the folds of the goddess's robes and back down to what he holds. But what is the deep meaning of this sculpture and why is it here? Its title is *A copy of ten marble fragments of the Great Eleusinian Relief* because it is a copy of a relief at The Met, which I had scanned and then machined out of aluminum. The Met's relief is itself a copy containing seven fragments from a Roman copy of an earlier Greek relief housed in Athens. These fragments are set into plaster molds taken from the original (fig. 42). Look closely at my copy and you can see the line of the broken fragments, but look closer and you can see two cultures, the Roman and the Greek. It is an interesting hybrid object, further hybridized by my idea of a Western hand, the hand of a robot. I walk away from this work and get swirled into an eddy, circling back around *Sarah Williams* and then spinning back out into the room. I won't bounce around the sculptures like a pinball in a machine. But perhaps as I circle around a few of my favorites, I will see the figure in me.

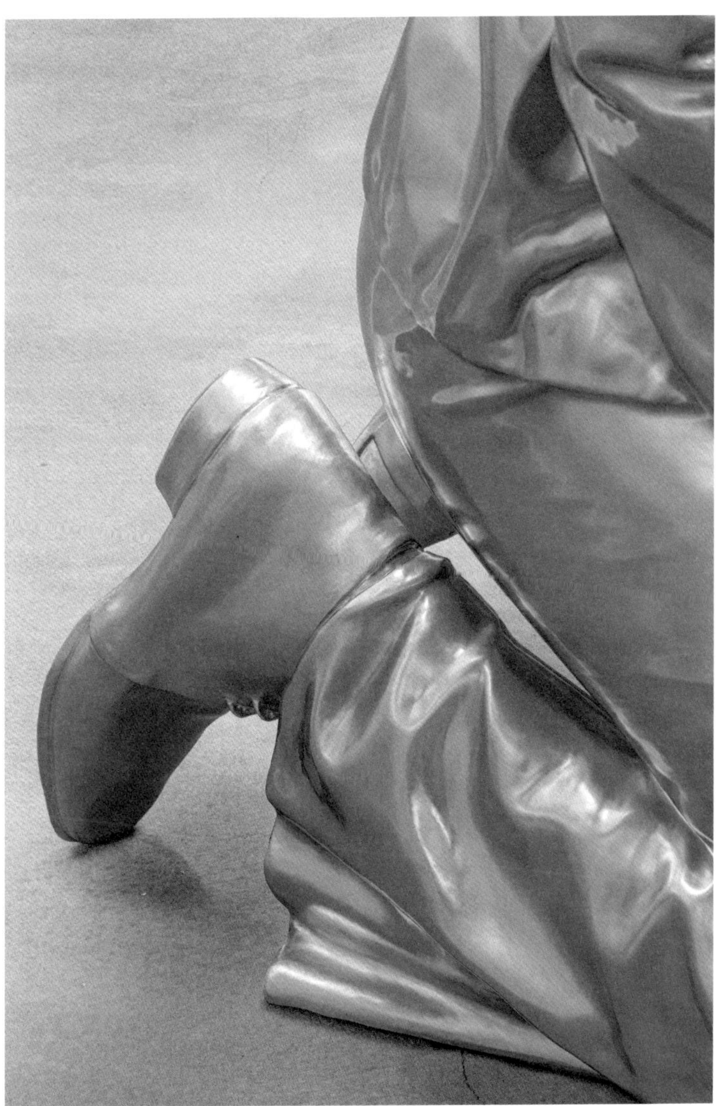

Fig. 51. *Sarah Williams*, 2021 (detail of pl. 18)

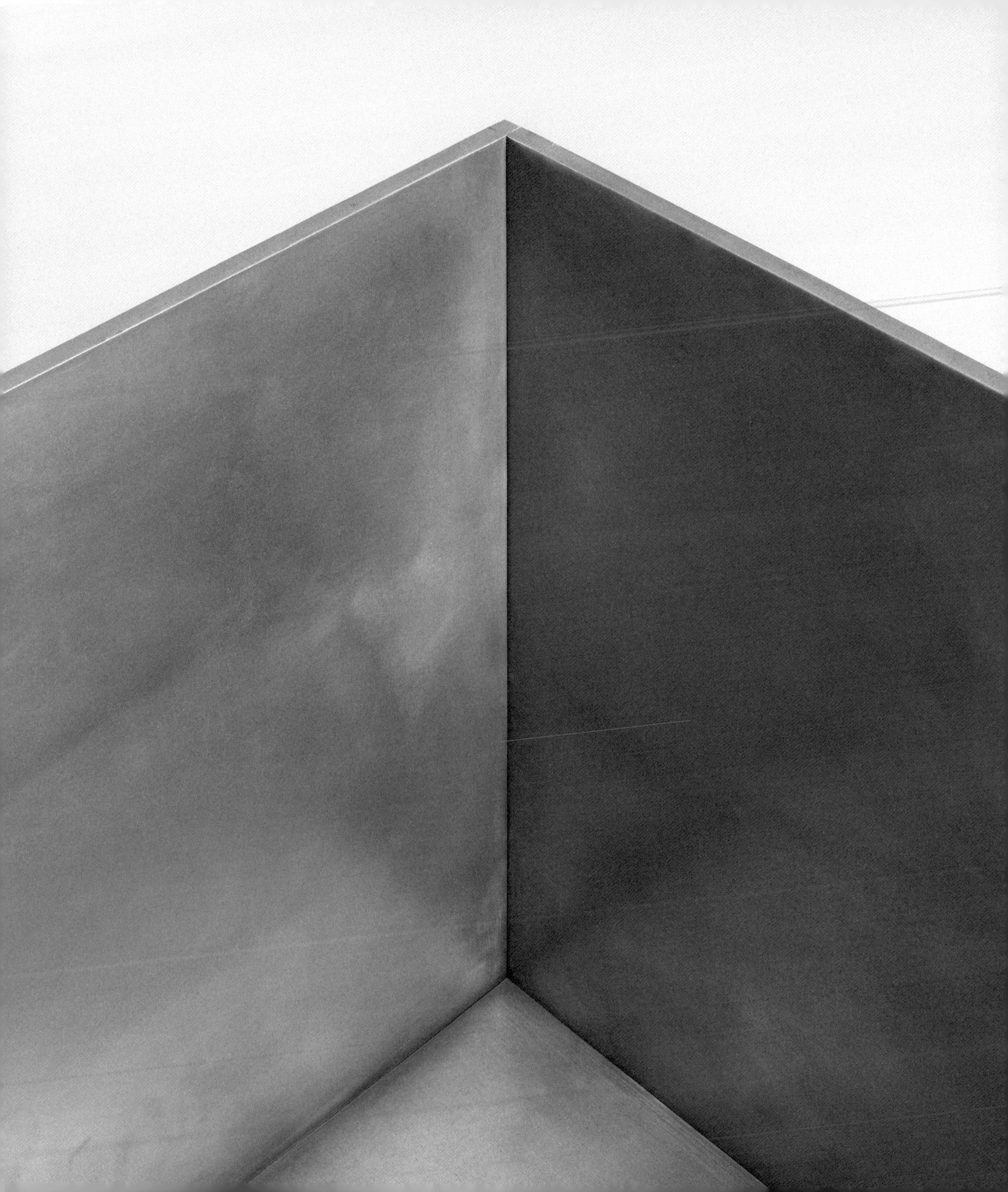

Notes

Patterns
Kelly Baum

1 For more on Ray's engagement with classical art, see Hal Foster, *Philosophical Objects: An Essay on the Sculpture of Charles Ray* (Los Angeles: Charles Ray Studio, 2019), pp. 19–27, and Richard Neer, "Tumbling into Time," in *Charles Ray: Sculpture, 1997–2014*, ed. Bernhard Mendes Bürgi and James Rondeau, exh. cat. (Ostfildern: Hatje Cantz Verlag, 2014), pp. 57–75. As Neer writes, "Ray's recent work is not classicizing or historicising in any familiar sense. . . . Anticipatory and retrospective in equal measure, these works might better be seen as rejoinders within a history that . . . affords particular 'limits and opportunities' in and through an ongoing process of revision and repetition. . . . For Ray . . . a relation to tradition is like a relation in space: fluid, plastic" (pp. 68–69).

2 Andrew Russeth, "Shoeless Ray: Charles Ray, Contemporary Art's Most Obsessive Perfectionist, Has a New Show at Matthew Marks," Arts, *New York Observer*, November 19, 2012, B10, as quoted in Neer, "Tumbling into Time," p. 68.

3 For more on the function of patterns in sculpture writ large, see Anne M. Wagner, "Pattern Languages," in *Carta(s): Thinking Is Three-Dimensional* (Madrid: Museo Nacional Centro de Arte Reina Sofía, 2019), pp. 25–33.

4 Charles Ray, in conversation with the author, September 8, 2020.

5 As Rosalind E. Krauss said in 1981, behind every so-called original lies not an origin, but a copy, what we might call a pattern. "The Originality of the Avant-Garde," in *The Originality of the Avant-Garde and Other Modernist Myths* (Cambridge, Mass.: The MIT Press, 1985 [first MIT Press paperback edition, 1986; ninth printing, 1994]), p. 162.

6 Charles Ray, email to the author and Brinda Kumar, April 13, 2021.

7 Charles Ray, ed., *a guide to Charles Ray Sleeping mime* (Los Angeles: Olympic Productions, 2017), pp. 13–35.

8 Ray, *a guide to Charles Ray Sleeping mime*, p. 17.

9 To make *Tractor*, Ray and his studio first disassembled the original tractor, which he had found in a backyard in the San Fernando Valley. Every part was then sculpted in clay by ten studio assistants, each with a particular style and approach, after which molds were taken and waxes created. From these, the parts were cast in aluminum and gradually assembled, working inside to outside. Asserting the status of *Tractor* as a representation was of utmost importance to Ray. This, along with the uniformity of material and color, foregrounds the sculpture's abstract qualities. See Charles Ray, "A Sculptural Differential: Charles Ray," interview by Zachary Cahill, *Mousse Magazine* 41 (December 2013–January 2014), p. 109; Charles Ray, "Tractor," in *Charles Ray* (New York: Matthew Marks Gallery, 2009), p. 30; and Charles Ray, "Tractor," in *Charles Ray: Sculpture, 1997–2014*, p. 110.

10 "Sculpture to sculpture, the first article sculpture was used as the basis for subsequent sculptures' evaluation so that they're not dissimilar from one another . . . there is uniformity . . . they're verging on identical from

individual part to individual part." Mark Rossi, "Visible Surfaces," in *A Guide to Charles Ray Sleeping Mime*, p. 31.

11 Ana Mendieta was a classmate of Ray's. He remembers taking some of Breder's courses with her and likewise attending many of the performances she staged while a student at Iowa. Ray, in conversation with the author, January 15, 2021.

12 For more on Ray's notion of civic space and civic art, see his discussion with Hal Foster in this volume.

13 Ray occupies a somewhat liminal art historical position. Born in 1953, he is a decade or two younger than the artists most closely associated with process-based sculpture and performance (some aligned more with conceptualism, others with postminimalism). Ray's work in this mode was contemporary with their own, but produced in the context of the university, and it tends not to appear in surveys such as *1965–1975: Reconsidering the Object of Art*, organized by the Museum of Contemporary Art, Los Angeles, in 1995–96, or *Out of Actions: Between Performance and the Object, 1949–1979*, organized by the Geffen Contemporary at the Museum of Contemporary Art, Los Angeles, in 1998.

14 For the most part, Ray's work in and with pictures, photographs specifically, has been considered separately from his work in and with sculpture, as in the case of the exhibition *The Last Picture Show: Artists Using Photography, 1960–1982*, organized by Douglas Fogle for the Walker Art Center, Minneapolis, in 2003.

15 According to Ray, *Plank piece I and II* derive from his work in process-based sculpture. "They were a superimposition of my working method onto my body, the studio and the plank itself." Charles Ray, "Charles Ray: A Geological Take on Time," interview by Massimiliano Gioni, *Artpress*, no. 458 (September 2018), p. 40.

16 For more on the work to which I refer above, *A copy of ten marble fragments of the Great Eleusinian Relief*—whose pattern is a work in The Met collection, Ten marble fragments of the Great Eleusinian Relief (ca. 27 B.C.–A.D. 14)—see Gavin Delahunty, "Toga in a Knot," in *Charles Ray*, exh. cat. (Athens, Greece: The George Economou Collection, 2017), pp. 46–48. See also Gioni, p. 41. As Ray says, *A copy of ten marble fragments of the Great Eleusinian Relief* is less a copy, despite its title, than a "hybrid object" made out of "another hybrid object," which is to say the relief in The Met collection, which is itself comprised of fragments of a Roman copy of an archaic original in which are mixed plaster versions of the missing parts, taken not from the Roman copy but from the original. As a result, Ray's work "zigzags across a cultural timeline" (Ray, "A Geological Take on Time," interview by Gioni, p. 41).

17 Charles Ray, "1000 Words: Charles Ray," interview by Rachel Kushner, *Artforum* 46, no. 1 (September 2007), https://www.artforum.com/print/200707/1000-words-charles-ray-15708. Ray also takes pains to prevent the reduction of his sculptures to the status of images by virtue of how and where they are installed in space. Of *Fall '91*, for instance, he said, "Without time and space for approach, the work becomes all image . . . an image but not a sculpture. How then to think of installing the works without creating trajectories of narration that will short-circuit sculptural language." Charles Ray, "How Many Sculptures Can You Fit in a Room," in *Charles Ray*, exh. cat. (Potomac, Md.: Glenstone Museum, 2018), p. 22.

18 Charles Ray, "Thinking Is Three-Dimensional," in *Carta(s): Thinking Is Three-Dimensional*, p. 6.

19 Ray, "Thinking Is Three-Dimensional," p. 13.

20 Hal Foster has consistently engaged with the notion of image in Ray's work, although for him "image" is generally equivalent to "subject matter." See the recording of Foster's conversation with Ray at the Hammer Museum in Los Angeles on March 6, 2019, https://hammer.ucla.edu/programs-events/2019/03/hal-foster-charles-ray. As Foster writes, "Ray places the image not only in tension with sculpture but almost in opposition to it. . . . Ray hesitates only when he comes to the 'richness' of the image, by which he means its associative power. Although this is difficult to do without, clearly part of Ray would like to be so 'free.' . . . With Ray, viewing [of the sculpture] does begin with the image and, unlike some of my colleagues, I think it is a mistake to bracket it" (*Philosophical Objects*, pp. 1–2).

21 Douglas Crimp, "Pictures," *October* 8 (Spring 1979) (Cambridge, Mass.: The MIT Press), p. 75.

22 An investment in images, pictures, and representations might also have been instilled in Ray via one of the teachers at Rutgers, Robert Watts, whose work straddles Pop and Fluxus. Because of Ray's reliance on the language of Pop art as well as minimalism, Hal Foster considers him both a late modernist and a postmodernist, more specifically, "a member of the Pictures generation" (*Philosophical Objects*, p. 11).

23 Krauss, "Sculpture in the Expanded Field," pp. 276–90.

24 For more on this body of work from the early 1970s, see Anne M. Wagner, "Life and Death in the Work of Charles Ray," in *Charles Ray: Sculpture, 1997–2014*, pp. 29–34.

25 Crimp, "Pictures," p. 87; Krauss, "Sculpture in the Expanded Field," p. 287.

26 Sculpture is "inherently multiple," Krauss writes ("The Originality of the Avant-Garde," p. 152). Wagner agrees. In an essay that accompanied an exhibition of Ray's work, Wagner wrote, "sculpture's unique quality is its replicability. Every sculpture is in essence the pattern of itself" ("Pattern Languages," p. 26).

27 Krauss, "The Originality of the Avant-Garde," p. 153.

28 Like much of Ray's work, *All my clothes* betrays a preference for the deadpan over the dramatic. For more on the pieces from the 1970s for which the artist's body serves as a supplement, see Wagner, "Life and Death in the Work

of Charles Ray," in *Charles Ray: Sculpture, 1997–2014*, pp. 32–33.

29 Ray, "A Geological Take on Time," interview by Gioni, p. 40.

30 In addition to creating unconventional self-portraits that insistently abstract and objectify the self, Ray traces many of his sculptures back to his own childhood memories, as in the case of *Tractor*.

31 The artist's interest in the mannequin derives equally from the places for which they're made. As a young man, Ray worked as a janitor at a department store. He later returned to department stores seeking objects for his still lifes, and took particular note of the sexual, democratic, and hallucinogenic qualities of their spaces, likewise the maze of reflections and reverberations they generate. Ray, in conversation with the author, January 15, 2021. For a short history of the mannequin in Western art, including Ray's own, see Brinda Kumar, "Proxy Figures," in *Like Life: Sculpture, Color, and the Body*, Luke Syson, Sheena Wagstaff, Emerson Bowyer, and Brinda Kumar, exh. cat. (New York: The Metropolitan Museum of Art, 2018), pp. 162–69.

32 Ray has described *No* as the "delusional" companion to the "hallucinatory" *Yes*. Quoted in Paul Schimmel, "Beside One's Self," in *Charles Ray*, ed. Paul Schimmel, exh. cat. (Los Angeles: The Museum of Contemporary Art, 1998), p. 85.

33 Ray, "Thinking Is Three-Dimensional," pp. 5–6. As he said of this work, "I brought the mannequin industry with me. I brought the mannequin techniques" (p. 6).

34 On the relationship of this work to its more general cultural pattern, which Ray calls a "civic model of sculpture," see "Thinking Is Three-Dimensional," p. 14. In addition to experimenting with a plastic toy of a horse and rider, Ray also made careful studies of Harry Jackson's sculpture of John Wayne, *The Horseman*. James Rondeau, "Alternative Americana: Two Public Sculptures by Charles Ray," in *Charles Ray: Sculpture, 1997–2014*, p. 93. Rondeau provides a rich, substantive reading of *Horse and rider*. See also Ray, "How Many Sculptures Can You Fit in a Room," p. 20.

35 Sigmund Freud, "Mourning and Melancholia," in *The Standard Edition of the Complete Psychological Works of Sigmund Freud, Vol. 14 (1914–1916): On the History of the Psycho-Analytic Movement, Papers on Metapsychology and Other Works*, trans. and ed. by James Strachey (London: The Hogarth Press and the Institute of Psycho-Analysis, 1957), p. 245. Ray himself has said of *Horse and rider* that it "brings out a great deal of anxiety that is embedded in both me and the horse" ("Thinking Is Three-Dimensional," p. 15).

36 Ray, "Thinking Is Three-Dimensional," p. 2. For a survey of Ray's sculptures of mannequins, see Wagner, "Life and Death in the Work of Charles Ray," pp. 34–37.

37 Ray, in conversation with the author, June 25, 2021.

38 Ray produced three slightly different sculptures with this title.

39 This illusion holds true only if no other objects are installed nearby, as they would allow viewers to judge the relative scale of the sculpture.

40 For Ray, it is this aspect of *Fall '91*, likewise its psychological charge, that generates meaning, less so the difference in scale between sculpture and viewer. Ray, "How Many Sculptures Can You Fit in a Room," p. 22.

41 Here Ray deftly exploits—we might say repurposes—the original "cultural function" of the mannequin, which is to stoke fantasies on the part of consumers. Put another way, it is the systematic evacuation of personality and singularity that allows mannequins in general and *Fall '91* in particular to function as vessels of desire. Ray, "Thinking Is Three-Dimensional," p. 2.

42 In both its content (White American boyhood, itself a convention or pattern) and its stylization, *Boy* anticipates a series of sculptures based on models of young White boys in stainless steel that Ray would make in the early twenty-first century. However, the schematization of these later works derives more from the idealism of the classical, not the abstraction of the mannequin. Importantly, Whiteness neither was nor is the primary, explicit subject of Ray's sculptures, but is instead a kind of secondary theme that results from his investigation of the mannequin as a cultural and sculptural trope. Because his "inspiration tumbled out of White culture," in other words, Whiteness inevitably comes into play. Whiteness is by no means incidental to his work, but (paradoxically) neither is it his primary thematic. "Race and politics were not my interests, but certainly part of the landscape I stood upon." Ray, in conversation with the author, June 25, 2021.

43 Ray, in conversation with the author, June 25, 2021.

44 For a fascinating reading of *Family romance* that takes Freud and the nuclear family as its point of departure, see Anne M. Wagner, *Mother Stone: The Vitality of Modern British Sculpture* (New Haven: Yale University Press, 2005), pp. 9–11.

45 Ray, "Thinking Is Three-Dimensional," p. 6.

46 On the work's relationship to Judd, see Ray, "Thinking Is Three-Dimensional," p. 7.

47 Ray's gesture is more artistic than political or critical, which distinguishes him from some of the artists in the Pictures generation. Since the late 1980s and early 1990s, scholars from a variety of disciplines have displaced gender, race, and even sex from the realm of the natural to the realm of the cultural, presenting them as social constructs, not biological facts or objective truths. At the same time, they recognize that gender, race, and sex wield considerable power, especially when yoked to gender, racial, and sexual prejudice. They might be ideas, but they are still *real*, holding actual sway over people's lives. On race, see Matthew Frye Jacobson, *Whiteness of a Different Color: European Immigrants and the Alchemy of Race* (Cambridge, Mass.: Harvard University Press, 1998) and

Nell Irvin Painter, *The History of White People* (New York: W. W. Norton & Company, 2010). On sex and gender, see Judith Butler, *Bodies That Matter: On the Discursive Limits of "Sex"* (New York: Routledge, 1993) and *Gender Trouble: Feminism and the Subversion of Identity* (New York: Routledge, 1999).

48 For more on mimesis and theatricality in Ray's work, especially as it relates to his reinvention of classical tropes and gestures, see Neer, "Tumbling into Time," p. 66.

49 Wagner offers an interpretation of Ray's career that proceeds along similar lines, although she does not come to exactly the same conclusion ("Life and Death in the Work of Charles Ray," pp. 25–55). For Wagner, Ray's work dramatizes a dialectical tension fundamental to sculpture itself (or, rather, to the illusion that sculpture sustains): between lifefulness and lifelessness, life and death.

50 Neer, "Tumbling into Time," pp. 63–65. Neer suggests not that *Mime* is miming these representations, but rather that Ray is borrowing from them.

51 Neer, "Tumbling into Time," p. 66. See also Wagner, "Life and Death in the Work of Charles Ray," p. 25.

52 For more on the concept of suspension in both mimes and *Mime*, see Michael Fried, "Charles Ray's Figurative Sculptures," in *Charles Ray: Sculpture, 1997–2014*, pp. 22–23; Ray, "Mime," in *Charles Ray: Sculpture, 1997–2014*, p. 136; and Ray, *A Guide to Charles Ray Sleeping Mime,* p. 9. For more on *Mime* in general, see Charles Ray, unpublished essay for Glenstone (version from October 2020) and *Three Christs, Sleeping Mime and the Last Supper*, Hill Art Foundation, New York, https://hillartfoundation.org/art/exhibitions/view/charles-ray-and-the-hill-collection/.

53 Along with *The new Beetle* (2006) and *School play* (2014), *Boy with frog* belongs to another trilogy focused on White American boyhood. This is part and parcel of Ray's interest in what Hal Foster calls "transitional moments," "moments of initiation, of formation" that are often traumatic. See the recording of Foster's conversation with Ray at the Hammer Museum on March 6, 2019, https://hammer.ucla.edu/programs-events/2019/03/hal-foster-charles-ray.

54 The relationship of boy and frog in *Boy with frog* also recalls the frontispiece of the first edition of the novel, in which a clothed Huck proudly holds aloft a rabbit he has killed.

55 Ray, in conversation with the author, June 25, 2021.

56 *Boy with frog* was installed at the Dogana between 2009 and 2013, until public pressure to restore the reproduction of a nineteenth-century lamppost it had replaced mounted. *Huck and Jim* never became part of the Whitney. For more on the debate in Venice, see Ray, "Thinking Is Three-Dimensional," pp. 9–11. For the debate over *Huck and Jim*, see Calvin Tomkins, "Meaning Machines: The Sculptures of Charles Ray," *The New Yorker*, May 11, 2015, pp. 54–63.

57 Ray, in conversation with the author, September 8, 2020. See also Rondeau, "Alternative Americana," p. 79. To Rondeau, Ray said that he saw Twain's "sense of space" as fundamentally American as well. For Ray, Twain retained the "newness," the unfamiliarity that accompanied Americans' experience of the natural world, even into the 1840s. Quoted in Rondeau, p. 79, p. 101 n. 9. Ray read *Huckleberry Finn* as a young boy, and it has remained a touchstone for him over the decades (Rondeau, p. 79).

58 T. S. Eliot, introduction to *Adventures of Huckleberry Finn* [1950], in *Adventures of Huckleberry Finn* by Mark Twain, ed. Thomas Cooley, Norton Critical Editions, 3rd ed. (New York: W. W. Norton & Co., 1999), p. 353.

59 In what follows, I provide my own reasons for considering Twain's novel distinctly American, and they are not necessarily Ray's.

60 My perspective is inspired in part by the 1619 Project, developed by Nikole Hannah-Jones and published in the *New York Times Magazine* on August 18, 2019, which set out "to reframe the country's history by placing the consequences of slavery and the contributions of black Americans at the very center of our national narrative" on the occasion of the four hundredth anniversary of the beginning of slavery in the United States. See https://www.nytimes.com/interactive/2019/08/14/magazine/1619-america-slavery.html. My perspective is equally indebted to the writing of Toni Morrison on American literature, Twain's book included. In describing the distinct characteristics of both American literature and the American nation as a whole, Morrison points to the centrality of what she calls the Africanist presence, especially as it's embodied by Black enslaved people. A "real or fabricated Africanist presence" has long been crucial to the construction, by White peoples, of both Whiteness and "Americanness." Toni Morrison, *Playing in the Dark: Whiteness and the Literary Imagination* (New York: Vintage Books, 1993), p. 6. See also p. 65.

61 For more on slavery in Twain's childhood, see Ron Powers, *Mark Twain: A Life* (New York: Free Press, 2005), pp. 11–13, 30. For more on the evolution of his position on race and racism, see Powers, pp. 35–37 and Carmen Subryan, "Mark Twain and the Black Challenge," in *Satire or Evasion? Black Perspectives on Huckleberry Finn*, ed. James S. Leonard, Thomas A. Tenny, and Thadious M. Davis (Durham: Duke University Press, 1992), pp. 91–102. For more on Twain's father-in-law, Jervis Langdon, whose home served as a stop on the Underground Railroad and who helped Frederick Douglass escape to freedom in 1838, see Powers, p. 243. Twain would meet Douglass, whom he admired, in 1869 (Powers, p. 278).

62 Insofar as it straddles the Civil War and the end of slavery, the novel essentially has two historical moments that are proximate but not identical. It also

comes at "the end" of two related events: slavery and Reconstruction, the conclusion of which essentially allowed slavery to return under a different guise. The gap between when the book is set and when it was written accounts for much of its complexity and ambivalence. On slavery's "return" after Reconstruction, see Saidiya V. Hartman, *Scenes of Subjection: Terror, Slavery, and Self-Making in Nineteenth-Century America* (Oxford: Oxford University Press, 1997).

63 See, for instance, Hartman, *Scenes of Subjection*, pp. 24–25.

64 See Twain, *Adventures of Huckleberry Finn*, pp. 220–27. Huck also considers turning Jim in and by extension returning him to slavery earlier in the novel, pp. 110–13.

65 Ray has spoken about the importance to him of this moment in the story. See "Thinking Is Three-Dimensional," pp. 15–16.

66 Ralph Ellison posits Huck's adolescence as a symbol for "a transitional period in American life," whose "artistic justification is that adolescence is the time of the 'great confusion' during which both individuals and nations flounder between accepting and rejecting the responsibilities of adulthood. . . . [Huck] embodies the two major conflicting drives operating in nineteenth-century America," humanism and individualism. By "allowing these two attitudes to argue dialectically in his work of art, [Twain] was as highly moral an artist as he was a believer in democracy." See "Twentieth Century Fiction and the Black Mask of Humanity," in *Shadow and Act* (New York: Vintage International, 1995), pp. 33–34.

67 These descriptors appear in Morrison's introduction to the 1996 Oxford University Press edition of the novel. Toni Morrison, "This Amazing, Troubling Book," in *Adventures of Huckleberry Finn* by Mark Twain, ed. Thomas Cooley, pp. 385–92.

68 Morrison, "This Amazing, Troubling Book," pp. 385, 392. Toni Morrison described Twain's characterization of Jim as an "over-the-top minstrelization." "Jim's portrait seems unaccountably excessive and glaring in its contradictions—like an ill-made clown suit that cannot hide the man within." Unlike the Black individuals described in Twain's nonfiction, Jim appears as "relentlessly idiotic." Morrison argues that Twain makes of Jim a "buffoon" in order to ease the pain of Huck's eventual separation from him ("This Amazing, Troubling Book," p. 388).

69 Morrison, "This Amazing, Troubling Book," p. 386. A few years earlier, Morrison argued for the importance of recognizing the novel's "contestatory, combative critique of antebellum America," avoiding "traditional [sentimentalized] readings too shy to linger over the implications of the Africanist presence at its center" (*Playing in the Dark*, p. 54).

70 Their quality of distraction and preoccupation is a trope that might have been inherited from the mannequins Ray sculpted in the 1990s.

71 In an earlier version of the sculpture, it was frog eggs that Huck collected. Ray chose to edit them out, however, thereby detaching the sculpture even further from the novel's narrative arc. For more on this work, see Brinda Kumar's essay in this volume.

72 Ray, "Huck and Jim," in *Charles Ray: Sculpture, 1997–2014*, p. 142.

73 As Ellison said of *Huckleberry Finn*, "Twain fitted Jim into the outlines of the minstrel tradition, and it is from behind this stereotype mask that we see Jim's dignity and human capacity—and Twain's complexity—emerge. Yet it is his source in this same tradition which creates that ambivalence between his identification as an adult and parent and his 'boyish' naïveté, and which by contrast makes Huck, with his street-sparrow sophistication, seem more adult. Certainly it upsets a Negro reader." For Ellison, Twain's reduction of Jim to the status of a boy, which makes his relationship with Huck come across oftentimes as that of "a boy for another boy rather than as the friendship of an adult for a junior," is the "lost fall in Twain's otherwise successful wrestle with the ambiguous figure in black face." "Change the Joke and Slip the Yoke [1958]," in *Shadow and Act*, pp. 50, 51.

74 Jim of *Huck and Jim* is Ray's first sculpture of a Black male nude.

75 Twain, *Adventures of Huckleberry Finn*, p. 136. Twain's narration implies they are without clothes during the debate referenced in chapter 19, which Ray has identified as the source of the sculpture.

76 The classical male nude is, of course, another of *Huck and Jim*'s patterns, one Ray revises and adapts. Leslie Fiedler broaches the subject of same-sex love in *Huckleberry Finn* in his irreverent, intriguing, and sometimes maddening "Come Back to the Raft Ag'in, Huck Honey!" from 1948 (in Leslie Fiedler, *A New Fiedler Reader* [Amherst, NY: Prometheus Books, 1999], pp. 3–12). In *Huckleberry Finn* and other American "boy" novels, Fiedler identifies the operations of an "archetype" or allegory, that of chaste love between White and Black males, which simultaneously reflects and conceals cultural anxieties on the part of Whites along with deep racial inequities.

77 Ray, email to the author and Brinda Kumar, November 5, 2020.

78 In the book, Huck also dons a bonnet, which Ray considered but ultimately decided against including, and spends much of the day practicing to walk like a girl.

79 In fact, it is not entirely clear if Jim is looking—or rather, if he is truly seeing—since Ray has not "nicked out" the pupils. For those figures rendered in stainless steel and aluminum in particular, it is almost impossible to tell if their eyes are open or closed. Indeed, depending on where the viewer stands in relation to the work, the same figure's eyes might appear open or closed.

80 Ray, in conversation with the author, June 25, 2021.

81 In a conversation on September 8, 2020, author and artist discussed the liquid quality of stainless steel, as applied to *Huck and Jim*, in relationship to the way Twain evokes the reflection of light on the water of the Mississippi River. In that same conversation, Ray called stainless steel "slippery, abstract."

82 Ray, "Huck and Jim," in *Charles Ray: Sculpture, 1997–2014*, p. 142.

83 Here, Ray is answering a question posed by Rondeau about the sculpture's homoeroticism (which Ray rephrased in terms of "desires fulfilled and unfulfilled"), but his comment applies to other aspects of the figures' relationship (and its Americanness) as well. Quoted in Rondeau, "Alternative Americana," p. 87. Morrison also recognized in Twain's dyad of Huck and Jim the absolute interdependence of Whiteness and Blackness, freedom and slavery, both in American literature and society at large. For her, the characters of Huck and Jim signal a distinctly parasitic form of interdependence insofar as Jim, an enslaved Black man, exists in the context of the novel mostly to enable the freedom of Huck, a White citizen (Morrison, *Playing in the Dark*, p. 57). She elaborates on this claim in her introduction to the novel ("This Amazing, Troubling Book," pp. 390–91).

84 Ray's attention to sculptural syntax, to the relationships among parts of a sculpture, derives in part from his careful study of Anthony Caro's work. For more, see Michael Fried, "Embedment: Charles Ray," in *Four Honest Outlaws: Sala, Ray, Marioni, Gordon* (New Haven: Yale University Press, 2011), pp. 67–120.

85 Ray, email to the author and Brinda Kumar, November 5, 2020.

86 Ray, email to the author and Brinda Kumar, November 5, 2020.

87 Ray, in conversation with the author, September 8, 2020. The disposition of limbs, the direction of eyes, the choreography of the work—all of this constitutes the sculpture's armature, a term Ray uses to describe that formal or structural aspect of a work from which its meaning derives. Foster has defined armature as "the structure produced with a sculpture, the syntax . . . that generates significance abstractly through an exact arrangement of formal elements" (*Philosophical Objects*, p. 9).

88 As Ray noted, the stainless-steel surfaces of these two works are not highly polished, which means they disperse light and abstract whatever reflections they capture. The artist sought a finish with luster but not a mirror quality. Ray, in conversation with the author and Brinda Kumar, January 28, 2021.

89 Borrowing from Roland Barthes's discussion of the photograph, we might say that Huck is the referent to Jim's picture (and vice versa). Accordingly, they are inextricably linked to one another. "The Photograph," Barthes wrote, "belongs to that class of laminated objects whose two leaves [the referent and the picture] cannot be separated without destroying them both: the windowpane and the landscape, and why not: Good and Evil, desire and its object: dualities we can conceive but not perceive." Roland Barthes, *Camera Lucida: Reflections on Photography*, trans. Richard Howard (New York: Hill and Wang, 1981), p. 6.

90 It is possible to read this gesture erotically as well.

91 Rondeau, "Alternative Americana," p. 81.

92 Then again, it might just be arrested, not unconsummated, in which case the gap between Jim's palm and Huck's skin becomes filled with possibility.

93 Morrison, "This Amazing, Troubling Book," p. 388.

94 Twain, *Adventures of Huckleberry Finn*, p. 4.

95 Ray, "Thinking Is Three-Dimensional," p. 14.

96 Ray, "How Many Sculptures Can You Fit in a Room," p. 22, and Calvin Tomkins, "Meaning Machines: The Sculptures of Charles Ray," *The New Yorker*, May 11, 2015, pp. 54–63. The artist has also called sculpture "a verb" (quoted in Lisa Phillips, "Charles Ray: Castaway," in *Charles Ray*, ed. Paul Schimmel, p. 98).

97 Ray, "A Sculptural Differential," interview by Cahill, p. 109.

98 Ray uses the term "philosopher's stone" to describe *Tractor*, but it applies to all of his work. Ray, "A Sculptural Differential," interview by Cahill, p. 109.

99 Ray, in conversation with the author, October 28, 2020.

Holding Space
Brinda Kumar

1 Charles Ray, *Charles Ray*, exh. cat. (New York: Matthew Marks Gallery, 2009), p. 26.

2 Charles Ray, in conversation with the author, May 14, 2021.

3 Ray, *Charles Ray*, Matthew Marks Gallery, p. 18.

4 On Bauhaus "hand sculptures," see László Moholy-Nagy, *The New Vision: Fundamentals of Design, Painting, Sculpture, Architecture* (London: Faber & Faber, 1939), p. 92.

5 "Your hand is a base, and you feel the detail as you see it." Charles Ray, interview by Hal Foster in this volume.

6 The conspicuously unnatural opening also signals that hatching, or the chicken-and-egg conundrum, is ultimately of little importance to the artist or to the work's origins, even though Ray did study the process extensively. For over five years he had an incubator in his studio, where he raised chickens. Matthew Marks Gallery, "Charles Ray," press release, November 2007, https://matthewmarks.com/exhibitions/charles-ray-11-2007.

7 "Its round aperture is paradoxically revealing and occluding, at once disclosing and activating the egg's obscurity. Like an eye—penetrating and penetrated—it looks back, drawing us into its fragile slip-cast

structure." John Kelsey, "Field and Factory," in *Charles Ray*, pp. 58–59.

8 In a full lecture on the subject, Ray, speaking of Henry Moore's sculptures, observed, "Philosophically, does anything happen when you move through the hole? Is space different on the other side? Or is it a way to make a passage, to flow through it? I guess I'm questioning: Is a hole a passage or, like I said before, is it a sculptural armature?" Charles Ray, "Sculpture with Holes: Lecture Number 1," in *Charles Ray: Three Lectures at the Menil Collection* (Los Angeles: Charles Ray Studio, 2018), p. 7.

9 Ray, *Charles Ray*, Matthew Marks Gallery, p. 12.

10 This reliance is even greater when the work is encountered in a gallery space, on a pedestal and possibly even in a vitrine (rather than held in one's hand).

11 "A mathematician sees an object with a hole through it as an object that cannot be shrunken to a point. This is a beautiful definition of a hole; it is also the idea of a primitive sculptural armature. Great sculptures have spatial armatures, they can't be shrunken to a point, nor can they be removed from the space they occupy. Space is not emptiness. Sculptures don't sit in space or fill space. They are made from it." Charles Ray, "The Space In Between: A Conversation with Charles Ray," interview by Joshua Reiman, *Sculpture*, July/August 2015, p. 43.

12 Charles Ray, audio on the subject of *Family romance*, published on the Museum of Modern Art website, last modified May 16, 2021, 1 min. 50 sec., https://www.moma.org/audio/playlist/1/197.

13 Charles Ray, quoted in Julie L. Belcove, "Charles Ray," *W Magazine*, November 1, 2007.

14 For Ray's recognition of tactility in Caro's work, see the discussion on *Table Piece XXII* (1967) in his conversation with Hal Foster in this volume. See also the discussion of Ray's relationship to Caro in Michael Fried, "Embedment: Charles Ray," in *Four Honest Outlaws: Sala, Ray, Marioni, Gordon* (New Haven: Yale University Press, 2011), pp. 78–79.

15 Ray himself acknowledged that three sculptures—*School play*, *The new Beetle*, *Boy with frog*—formed an "accidental trilogy," adding that "the sculptures were not conceived as a group, but they do chart a course through stages of this young boy's life." *Charles Ray: Sculpture, 1997–2014*, ed. Bernhard Mendes Bürgi and James Rondeau, exh. cat. (Ostfildern: Hatje Cantz Verlag, 2014), p. 138.

16 Charles Ray, "A Sculptural Differential: Charles Ray," interview by Zachary Cahill, *Mousse Magazine* 41 (December 2013–January 2014), p. 105.

17 "The abstract notion of an intrinsic space is what allows me to look at both ancient and contemporary sculpture as working on the same problem. . . . Like this Greek stela of a young girl you can see at the Met. She has a bird in her hand that she's about to kiss. I find it so touching, and so fundamentally sculptural—this bird and girl and kiss and breath. Everything is in relief, and the only space that flows through and around is between her mouth and the bird in her hand. The space is abstract—it's not our space—and yet it's so real. When I see things like that, how they've been able to take this narrative and produce such a fundamentally sculptural move that the meaning of the relief no longer matters, I worry less about abstraction. That relief in the Met was born alive. The breath is still there. It's so *modern*." Charles Ray, "1000 Words: Charles Ray," interview by Rachel Kushner, *Artforum* 46, no. 1 (September 2007), p. 439.

18 Paul Schimmel has described *Oh! Charley, Charley, Charley* . . . as a "public sculpture in the tradition of Auguste Rodin's *The Burghers of Calais* (1889)." Paul Schimmel, "Beside One's Self," in *Charles Ray*, ed. Paul Schimmel, exh. cat. (Los Angeles: The Museum of Contemporary Art, 1998), p. 87. Schimmel here seems to be drawing upon Ray's own account of the role of Rodin's *Burghers* in the genesis of his sculpture: "I was trying to make a figurative sculpture. I was interested in Rodin's *Burghers of Calais* but I couldn't do the L.A. City Council, it would have no contemporary foundation as a figurative sculpture. What would that be? My subject became the self as a projection of the other." Paul Dickerson, "Charles Ray," *BOMB*, Summer 1995, p. 46.

19 "There are these great gravitational pulls and pushes and abstractions between the figures. . . . You start moving in—none of these figures ever actually touch—you start moving in to the space of the figures and you just start going in and out of drapery and forces and pulls between them. And you start moving in and through and become totally involved in these kinds of abstract spaces and matrixes, and you try to go back to a face and an identity of a figure, but then you're just pulled right back into this matrix of internal spaces." Ray, "Matisse and Super Clay: Lecture Number 2," in *Charles Ray: Three Lectures*, pp. 14–15.

20 See the discussion of *Huck and Jim* and *Sarah Williams* in Kelly Baum's essay in this volume.

21 In chapter 19, as Huck and Jim float on a raft and look up at the night sky speculating about the origin of the stars, Jim suggests that the moon could have laid them, a suggestion that Huck found reasonable, "because I've seen a frog lay most as many, so of course it could be done." Mark Twain, *Adventures of Huckleberry Finn*, foreword by Shelley F. Fishkin, introduction by Toni Morrison, and afterword by Victor A. Doyno (New York: Oxford University Press, 1996), p. 159.

22 This is the case especially in museum contexts where visitors are explicitly directed not to touch the art. The presentation of *Handheld bird* in a vitrine renders it perennially beyond tangible access, contrary to what the artist intended.

23 Charles Ray, "Shoe Tie," in *Charles Ray: Sculpture, 1997–2014*, p. 134.

24 "Herder starts his treatment of the infinite sublime by identifying sculpture as that which does not have a

single point of orientation, rather it 'explores everything in the dark' (*im Dunkel*). Countering an aesthetics of light, an epistemology of illumination and an ontology of delimited singularity . . . there is the productive condition of the dark; of touching *im Dunkel*." Andrew Benjamin, "To Touch: Herder and Sculpture," in *Sculpture and Touch*, ed. Peter Dent (Farnham: Ashgate, 2014), p. 84.

25 James Rondeau writes, "He pantomimes holding a rein that—like the imaginary laces in *Shoe Tie*—is not furnished." "Alternative Americana: Two Public Sculptures by Charles Ray," in *Charles Ray: Sculpture, 1997–2014*, p. 97. Similarly, "The naked male figure of *Shoe Tie* is slim but no longer young, crouching—the lower knee doesn't rest on the ground—while he pantomimes tying the lace of a nonexistent shoe." Michael Fried, "Charles Ray," Reviews, *Artforum* 51, no. 6 (February 1, 2013), p. 248.

26 Quoted in Charles Ray, "The Space In Between," interview by Joshua Reiman, p. 42.

27 Charles Ray, "Notes on *Sleeping mime*," in *A Guide to Charles Ray Sleeping Mime*, ed. Charles Ray (Los Angeles: Olympic Productions, 2017), p. 5.

28 Lorin Eric Salm and Brooks Turner, "Interview," *A Guide to Charles Ray Sleeping Mime*, p. 9 (emphasis mine).

29 See discussion on the presentation of Constantin Brancusi's *Sculpture for the Blind* as *Sleeping Muse (Sculpture for the Blind)*. Sebastiano Barassi, "The Sculptor Is a Blind Man: Constantin Brancusi's *Sculpture for the Blind*," in *Sculpture and Touch*, p. 176.

30 Ray, email to the author and Kelly Baum, February 13, 2021.

31 Charles Ray, "Length, Weight, and Age of Aquarius," in *Charles Ray, volume 2*, exh. cat. (Potomac, Md.: Glenstone, 2021), p. 14.

32 Ray, "Matisse and Super Clay: Lecture Number 2," pp. 4–5.

33 "Here is the artist's brief remark: 'I am curious about seeing it [*Baled Truck*] with *Mime*. I feel these two sculptures would make an interesting exhibition titled *Two Carvings*.' Is Ray suggesting that *Baled Truck* was 'carved' by the irresistible force of a crusher? If so, then perhaps the idea is that the mime has 'carved' himself." Anne Wagner, "Life and Death in the Work of Charles Ray," in *Charles Ray: Sculpture, 1997–2014*, p. 50.

34 In describing the process of making *Mime* in aluminum, Ray's team noted that the left hand was produced at an initial stage as a sample, and a space was created between the hand and the pant leg where there had been none, an approach that remained in the finished sculpture. The sample also eventually became a standalone sculpture. Mark Rossi, "Aluminum Translation," in *A Guide to Charles Ray Sleeping Mime*, p. 28.

35 Ray, "Length, Weight, and Age of Aquarius," pp. 14–15.

Works in the Exhibition

Pl. 1
No, 1992
Chromogenic print in artist's frame
39 × 31 × 2 in. (99.1 × 78.7 × 5.1 cm)
The Museum of Contemporary Art, Los Angeles, Gift of Lannan Foundation (97.91)

Pl. 2
Chicken, 2007
Painted stainless steel, porcelain
1¾ × 2¼ × 1¾ in. (4.4 × 5.7 × 4.4 cm)
Glenstone Museum, Potomac, Md.

Pl. 3
Handheld bird, 2006
Painted stainless steel
2 × 4 × 3 in. (5.1 × 10.2 × 7.6 cm)
Matthew Marks Gallery

Pl. 4
Hand holding egg, 2007
Porcelain
3 × 8 × 3¾ in. (7.6 × 20.3 × 9.5 cm)
Matthew Marks Gallery

Pl. 5
81 × 83 × 85 = 86 × 83 × 85, 1989
Aluminum
Exterior: 31⅞ × 32 11/16 × 33 7/16 in. (81 × 83 × 85 cm); interior: 33⅞ × 32 11/16 × 33 7/16 in. (86 × 83 × 85 cm)
Pinault Collection

Pl. 6
Tractor, 2005
Aluminum
56⅝ in. × 10 ft. ½ in. × 61 in. (143.8 × 306.1 × 154.9 cm)
Glenstone Museum, Potomac, Md.

Pl. 7
Huck and Jim, 2014
Stainless steel
9 ft. 3½ in. × 54 in. × 53¾ in. (283.2 × 137.2 × 136.5 cm)
Collection of Lisa and Steven Tananbaum

Pl. 8
Table, 1990
Plexiglas, steel
35⅝ × 35⅜ × 52¾ in. (90.5 × 89.9 × 134 cm)
Collection of the artist, courtesy Matthew Marks Gallery

Pl. 9
Boy with frog, 2009
Painted stainless steel
96 × 29½ × 41¼ in. (243.8 × 74.9 × 104.7 cm)
Philadelphia Museum of Art, Promised gift of Keith L. and Katherine Sachs

Pl. 10
Plank piece I and II, 1973
Two gelatin silver prints
39½ × 27 in. (100.3 × 68.6 cm) each
Private collection

Pl. 11
Archangel, 2021
Cypress
13 ft. 5½ in. × 89½ in. × 45½ in. (410.2 × 227.3 × 115.6 cm)
Collection of the artist, courtesy Matthew Marks Gallery

Pl. 12
Untitled, 1973, printed 1989
Gelatin silver print
27 × 40 in. (68.6 × 101.6 cm)
The Metropolitan Museum of Art, New York, Purchase, Robert Shapazian Gift, Samuel J. Wagstaff Jr. Bequest, The Horace W. Goldsmith Foundation Gift through Joyce and Robert Menschel, and Harriette and Noël Levino Gift, 1995 (1995.474)

Pl. 13
Rotating circle, 1988
Electric motor, disc
Diam. 9 in. (22.9 cm)
The Museum of Contemporary Art, Los Angeles, Gift of Lannan Foundation (97.86)

Pl. 14
Family romance, 1993
Painted fiberglass, hair
53 × 85 × 11 in. (134.6 × 215.9 × 27.9 cm)
The Museum of Modern Art, New York, Gift of the Peter Norton Family Foundation, 1993 (281.1993)

Pl. 15
Reclining woman, 2018
Stainless steel
59¾ × 83 × 44 in. (151.8 × 210.8 × 111.8 cm)
Collection Glenn and Amanda Fuhrman NY, Courtesy the FLAG Art Foundation

Pl. 16
Boy, 1992
Painted fiberglass, steel, fabric, glass
71½ × 39¼ × 20½ in. (181.6 × 99.7 × 52.1 cm)
Whitney Museum of American Art, New York, Purchase, with funds from Jeffrey Deitch, Bernardo Nadal-Ginard, and Penny and Mike Winton (92.131a–h)

Pl. 17
Mime, 2014
Aluminum
25½ × 77¼ × 29 in. (64.8 × 196.2 × 73.7 cm)
Hill Charitable Collection

Pl. 18
Sarah Williams, 2021
Stainless steel
94⅛ × 31 × 68¼ in. (239.1 × 78.7 × 173.4 cm)
Collection of the artist, courtesy Matthew Marks Gallery

Pl. 19
A copy of ten marble fragments of the Great Eleusinian Relief, 2017
Aluminum
91½ × 63¼ × 4¾ in. (232.4 × 160.7 × 12.1 cm)
Collection of Joshua and Filipa Fink, New York

Index

Page references in *italics* refer to illustrations.

This catalogue is published in conjunction with *Charles Ray: Figure Ground*, on view at The Metropolitan Museum of Art, New York, from January 31 through June 5, 2022.

The exhibition is made possible by the Barrie A. and Deedee Wigmore Foundation.

Additional support is provided by the Jane and Robert Carroll Fund, the Diane W. and James E. Burke Fund, the Gail and Parker Gilbert Fund, Lisa and Steven Tananbaum, and The Andy Warhol Foundation for the Visual Arts.

This publication is made possible by Lannan Foundation and The Sachs Charitable Foundation.

Published by The Metropolitan Museum of Art, New York
Mark Polizzotti, Publisher and Editor in Chief
Peter Antony, Associate Publisher for Production
Michael Sittenfeld, Associate Publisher for Editorial

Edited by Briana Parker
Designed by Jon Key, Morcos Key
Production by Paul Booth
Bibliographic editing by Alicia Badea
Image acquisitions and permissions by Jenn Sherman

Typeset in Studio Pro Neretto by Carol Liebowitz
Printed on 150 gsm Arctic Volume White
Separations, printing, and binding by Trifolio S.r.l., Verona, Italy

Cover illustrations: front, *Untitled*, 1973 (pl. 12); back, *Sarah Williams*, 2021 (pl. 18)
Page 2: *Boy with frog*, 2009 (detail of pl. 9); page 4: *Rotating circle*, 1988 (pl. 13); page 6: *A copy of ten marble fragments of the Great Eleusinian Relief*, 2017 (detail of pl. 19); page 100: *32 x 33 x 35 = 34 x 33 x 35*, 1989

First printing

The Metropolitan Museum of Art
1000 Fifth Avenue
New York, New York 10028
metmuseum.org

Distributed by
Yale University Press, New Haven and London
yalebooks.com/art
yalebooks.co.uk

Cataloguing-in-Publication Data is available from the Library of Congress.
ISBN 978-1-58839-742-3